The World of
George Orwell

Edited by Miriam Gross

Simon and Schuster
New York

George Orwell and Burma by Maung Htin Aung
was an address delivered to the Royal Central Asian Society in 1969

First U.S. printing
SBN 671-21124-2
Library of Congress Catalog Card Number: 73-164705
Designed by John Wallis
Manufactured in Great Britain

Contents

List of Illustrations

Foreword

This collection of essays is an attempt to see George Orwell both in terms of what he means today and as a man whose achievement very much needs to be set in the context of his own period. Since his death more than twenty years ago, his reputation has not undergone the customary period of decline, partly, perhaps, because the political controversy which his work has continued to arouse has made it relatively immune from the shifts of literary fashion, and partly because the directness and vigour of his writing still give it an almost deceptively contemporary feel. But though he remains an influential writer, and though much has been written about him, there are still many gaps in the picture, while misconceptions inevitably arise as the period and the issues about which he wrote begin to slip away into history.

Though Orwell himself did not want his biography to be written, his own autobiographical writings reveal a great deal about him in his middle years. The personal reminiscences in this collection deal with the periods which are less familiar. Apart from his grim prep-school memoir 'Such Such Were the Joys', little beyond the bare facts is known about his childhood and early family life, and Jacintha Buddicom, a close friend at that time, discloses an unexpectedly confident and outgoing side of the young Eric Blair. Other friends recall him in the Nineteen-forties, a period for which he left no account of himself comparable with *Down and Out in Paris and London* and the other works of reportage of the Thirties. William Empson and T. R. Fyvel provide first-hand sketches of him in his two main war-time jobs, at the BBC and on the staff of *Tribune*; Michael Meyer, who also knew him well in these years, describes him in more unprofessional settings; Malcolm Muggeridge's essay is both a personal memoir and a general assessment of what he stood for in the eyes of a contemporary.

Much of the social world which Orwell knew is, of course, still part of the present – more so perhaps than is sometimes admitted, as with the snobberies and built-in assumptions about class discussed here in the essay on his school-days. In many respects, however, conditions have been completely transformed. Dr Htin Aung, who met Orwell during his time as Imperial policeman, describes a Burma already seething with political unrest, but one in which the British still regarded their rule as an unalterable fact of life. Orwell's Paris is in its own way almost equally remote: the account of it here particularly brings out how much it was still the city of the Twenties expatriates. And the atmosphere in the industrial North of the Depression was arguably closer to the nineteenth century than to the present. Ian Hamilton, retracing Orwell's footsteps on the road to Wigan Pier, considers his reactions to the working class and records some of their reactions to him.

A third group of essays is devoted to his more immediately political positions. Edward Crankshaw re-examines the whole development of his attitude to Communism and relates it to the intellectual climate of his time, underlining the qualities which set him apart from his contemporaries. Other contributors analyse his response to Imperialism, one of the areas where his views have been most often misrepresented, and unravel the tangled political background of his involvement in the Spanish Civil War. As these essays show, Orwell has stood up remarkably well against critics of the old fellow-travelling type, but this is not the only position from which he can be quarrelled with: D. A. N. Jones highlights some of his inconsistencies and shows that not all the arguments surrounding his work are likely to be decided in his favour.

For all the intensity of his political convictions, it is as a creative writer rather than as as a political commentator that he would have wanted to be judged. As he himself said in 'Why I Write', he 'could not do the work of writing a book, or even a long magazine article, if it were not also an aesthetic experience'. Among the contributors who stress the more literary aspects of his work, John Wain shows how his ambitions to be a novelist were modified without being extinguished by the tensions of the Thirties. His pioneer studies of popular culture are also looked at afresh, as are the attitudes behind his self-exposure to extreme poverty, while Matthew Hodgart relates *Animal Farm* and *Nineteen Eighty-Four*, works too often discussed in exclusively political terms, to the whole tradition of utopian satire. Finally, David Pryce-Jones traces the vicissitudes of Orwell's reputation, both literary and political, over the past forty years.

I would like to thank Mrs. Sonia Orwell and Mr. Ian Angus for their help and advice.

MIRIAM GROSS

Jacintha Buddicom
THE YOUNG ERIC

WE were playing French cricket in the roughish field-part of the garden, by the clump of elm trees. The occasion is well remembered, but the date is long forgotten. It was probably in the spring or summer of 1915: at Shiplake-on-Thames in Oxfordshire.

In the farmer's adjoining field, on the other side of the wire boundary fence, a boy, rather bigger than my brother Prosper, was standing on his head. This was a feat we had never observed before, and we found it intriguing; so one of us, polite but curious, asked him 'Why are you standing on your head?'

To which he replied: 'You are noticed more if you stand on your head than if you are right way up.'

This appeared an obvious invitation for attention, so we asked him to come over and play with us. He said his name was Eric Blair and that he lived at Roselawn in the Station Road. He was a year older than Prosper, and his sister Avril, five years his junior, was a year younger than our sister Guinever.

From that sunny afternoon, we three Buddicom children and the two younger Blairs were very close friends indeed. The elder Blair girl, Marjorie, five years senior to Eric, was virtually 'grown-up' when we first met them. She had her own activities, and we seldom saw her.

The two little girls, Guiny and Avril, were the right age to be companions. Prosper, Guiny and I had different interests, but Eric shared them equally and impartially. Everyone used to play croquet, and cards, and paper-games together; but at other times we were allied separately.

With Prosper and Guiny he played tennis and went shooting, fishing, and birds' nesting. They were all very keen on sporting pursuits, but I thought that shooting and fishing were cruel and that eggs should be left in the nests of the birds that laid them. When Prosper and Eric killed a beautiful hedgehog and baked it in clay as they had heard the gipsies did, I would not speak to them for a week. Our cook was not best pleased when she found this already-sepulchred corpse in the oven; but when, a few days later, they set up an amateur 'whisky-still' on top of the kitchen stove while she was having her afternoon rest, and the whole contraption blew up, she gave notice.

With me, Eric *talked*. We both had independent minds and many ideas in common, and we shared a love of books. We were inveterate readers, and Eric had a vast vocabulary (our collective term) of volumes. He was always giving me books, lending me books, exchanging books with me. He said that reading was good preparation for writing ... *any* book could teach you something, if only how not to write one. Of course Eric was always going to write: not just as an author, always a FAMOUS AUTHOR, in capitals. His tastes in literature

2

covered a wide range, but our chief preference was for ghost-stories. It is surprising he did not write a collection of them.

We had in our house a copy of Wells' *Modern Utopia*, which was so greatly fancied by Eric that it was eventually given to him. He said he might write that kind of book himself. Broadly, *Nineteen Eighty-Four* is classifiable as 'that kind of book'. And the genealogical tree of *Animal Farm* has its roots in *Pigling Bland* by Beatrix Potter. *Pigling Bland* was Guiny's book: Eric and I were far too old for it, but we adored it all the same. I remember him reading it through to me from beginning to end, to cheer me up one time when I had a cold. The heroic Pigling Bland was a white pig, and in *Animal Farm* the white pigs Major and Snowball are the *good* pigs. But it is a sorry metamorphosis for the delicious black Berkshire Pig-wig to be displaced by the dreadful black Berkshire Napoleon. Mr Pilkington is a relative of Mr Piperson, I think.

On his list* of 'best' short stories, I recognize his old favourites Poe's *Premature Burial*, Kipling's *Baa Baa Black Sheep*, Wells's *Slip Under the Microscope*. Eric gave as rules 'If it is possible to cut a word out, cut it out', and 'Never use jargon' ... splendid aphorisms which he got straight from M.R. James, who became Provost of Eton in 1918, and to whom much of his style is undoubtedly owed.

Eric's father was secretary of the Golf Club at Harpsden, and from Roselawn the Blairs moved to a house in St Mark's Road, Henley. This was less than two miles away and we all had bicycles, so we still met almost daily. We Buddicom children spent weeks at a time with my grandfather in Shropshire, and Eric usually went with us. There was proper shooting and fishing there.

Sometimes schoolfriends of Prosper's, or one of mine, came to stay with us, and we in turn with them. But I don't remember any friend of Eric's staying with the Blairs, or even that he had any friends in Henley. Prosper once went to Cornwall with the Blairs, and Eric once accompanied Prosper and Guiny to a friend of Prosper's in Bournemouth.

As time went on, Eric was not able to allot so much of it to mere amusement: often when the rest of us wanted to go on playing, he had to go back home to 'swot'. He had holiday tasks, preparing for the scholarships and exams that seemed such child's-play to him. Having achieved a scholarship to Eton so early that he had to wait for a place, he got another to Wellington where he spent the intervening period. The two boys were at different schools: Prosper went to Harrow.

When the Blairs moved again, to a rather small and inconvenient flat at Notting Hill Gate, it was arranged that Eric should spend a good part of his

---

* *New Statesman*, 25 January 1941, quoted by John Atkins in *George Orwell*.

holidays with us. So we saw more of him than ever. In the summer of 1921 we shared a house at Rickmansworth: my mother and stepfather with us three, and Mrs Blair with Eric and Avril. I do not remember Mr Blair ever being there, but Marjorie came down sometimes from London. It was a gloriously, unforgettably hot summer. 'I'm forever blowing bubbles' and 'The Chinese wedding procession' hogged the gramophone from my favourite 'Chaconne' by Durand. A lot of tennis was played, and fishing was rented at the local reservoir. At the end of a long day, packing up to go home, Eric shouted across from his side of the reservoir to Prosper on the other, 'I haven't caught anything, have you?' To which Prosper shouted back, 'Not actually, but I've had one good bite.' The pleasure of fishing seemed to lie in the fishing itself, and not in any by-product such as fish.

At this Rickmansworth house was a collection of *Greyfriars Annuals*, on which we fell with hilarity, competing as to who could find the page with most 'Urghs' and 'Groans' on it. *Greyfriars* was new to me then: I never remember Prosper and Eric reading the *Gem* or the *Magnet*. Their periodicals were such magazines as the *Strand* and *Windsor*, and when in Shropshire they browsed happily through the back numbers of my grandfather's *Fishing Gazette* which had accumulated since their last visit.

During the Rickmansworth holiday there were interminable conversations between my mother and Mrs Blair, united in deploring old Mr Blair's obstinate attitude with regard to Eric's future. Old Mr Blair had been 'Indian Civil', and Indian Civil was the only career he would tolerate for his son. It was the last thing Eric wanted, but the tramlines were laid down. Eric – a born scholar – a boy who lived for books, had his heart set on going to Oxford.

There seemed a whole generation between the vivacious, spirited Mrs Blair (who was rather pretty, with curly hair) and her dour, discouraging husband whom we classed a contemporary with our grandfather. Mrs Blair, I suppose, was rather left-wing: she had Fabian connections (lucky Eric had actually visited E. Nesbit) and she and her feminine relatives had been fairly militant suffragettes. My mother (who did a bit of historical biography herself) was a firm Conservative. But both agreed that a university education was the 'proper thing' for a boy. My mother was very fond of Eric, and I know she had some correspondence with Mr Blair, backing Eric and his mother up. But old Mr Blair was adamant. Nothing could alter his determination.

Eric was not a jealous or envious boy, but he had a strong sense of justice and of what was fair. It seemed rather unfair that Prosper, who was not at all academically-minded, should 'at whatever sacrifice' by my mother, be assured of a place at Oxford; whereas Eric himself, who would have so appreciated the opportunity and would have worked so hard to gain an almost-certain scholarship, was forbidden it by his father.

And Eric was exiled to the Burmese Police.

He wrote me three letters from Burma. The first was a long one, very disconsolate but unspecific, in the strain 'You could never understand how awful it is if you hadn't been here', but he didn't explain. I replied that if it was as awful as all that, hadn't he better leave and come home. He answered briefly that he *couldn't* leave; and afterwards he wrote at greater length but guardedly. I got the impression that correspondence might be looked at. I did not reply to these two letters, for which I am very sorry indeed.

On his return to England in 1927, he stayed with my aunt in Shropshire (my grandfather was dead) to see Prosper and Guiny who were there; but circumstances prevented me from joining the party. Guiny says that he had 'altered'. And my aunt wrote to me at the time that he was 'very different'.

After that he completely disappeared. We did not know that he had changed his name, and he never contacted any of us.

Guiny and I can remember the first day we met him. Shiplake was such a small village then that a strange indigenous child was as rare as a winged dragon. But neither of us can remember the last time we saw him before he left for Burma. His family had moved by then to Southwold, and Suffolk was out of our orbit. There was no farewell party at the docks to which we were invited, or anything of that sort.

I never saw him again, though we had some correspondence in 1949 when I discovered he was now George Orwell, author of the unparalleled *Animal Farm*. Given a hundred books and told that one of them was the work of Eric Blair, I should not have hesitated to choose *Animal Farm*. It is so exactly like him, so exactly the book he might have been expected to write, so exactly the book he would have loved to read if someone else had written it when he was a boy.

Reading his books, it must be difficult for people who didn't know him to realize what he was like as a boy. He certainly didn't care for his prep-school, but lots of boys don't care for their prep-schools and it didn't seem to worry him unduly in the holidays. From his accounts to me he quite enjoyed Eton, where he had a good deal of freedom, and the desirable privilege of breakfasting with his literary hero M. R. James. Certainly he would have realized that *some* other boys had parents more affluent and influential than his own, but the young Eric was too intelligent, too independent, above all far too philosophical, to be affected by mundane circumstance. He disliked the name Eric because it reminded him of *Eric or Little by Little*, the Victorian boys'-school story of which he took a particularly dim view.

His parents' finances were doubtless straitened when Mr Blair retired and Marjorie's school fees had to be found as well as Eric's; but when we knew the family they did not seem drastically impoverished. The children had the usual little treats that we had, and Eric had enough pocket-money to buy quantities of books for me as well as himself. He had a gun, a fishing-rod, a bicycle, like Prosper and his contemporaries, and the Blairs went for seaside holidays, more than once to Polperro. There was no harping on inferiority and poverty by Eric *then*. In any contest with Prosper and his friends, Eric gave as good as he got: usually better, because he had more brains. The picture painted of a wretched little neurotic, snivelling miserably before a swarm of swanking bullies, suspecting that he 'smelt', just was not Eric at all.

I knew the boy Eric very well indeed for about seven years. We were constant companions during the holidays, and when he was at Eton and I was at the Oxford High School, we wrote to each other nearly every week. I knew plenty of boys to compare him with, and in such a comparison Eric would rate a very high score. He may not have been quite so good-looking as the handsomest, or have achieved a place in a cricket XI or rowing crew; but among all the boys we knew, Eric was one of the most interesting, the best informed, the kindest, the *nicest*.

He was a particularly considerate and thoughtful boy. One Christmas he gave me *Dracula*, which he had just discovered with great excitement. Carefully packed separately in the same parcel were a crucifix (he knew I would not be likely to have one) and a clove of garlic, difficult to obtain in Henley. These proven safeguards against vampires were to reassure me, so that I should have the pleasure of the book without being so scared by it as he had been. On the several occasions when I went to tea with him in St Mark's Road that December and January, Eric escorted me all the way home, although we went by train, so that I should not have to walk by myself up the long dark lane from Shiplake Station to Quarry House, with every bush a bear and the Count hanging bat-like from any passing tree.

We had so many happy times during all the holidays together. The young Buddicoms were in general happy children: and the young Blairs, I truly believe, were happy with us. It is strange that in his writing Eric seems to have omitted this period altogether. After the 'awfulness' of Burma and his untoward descent into the underworld, was it deliberately blotted out because it *was* happy? This is a sad thought. Reading over again Eric's old letters to me, I can picture us 50 years ago at Quarry House, playing those many different

Childhood

1   Ida Mabel Blair with baby Eric.

2 Ida Mabel Blair in 1937.

3 (*Below left*) Richard Walmsley
Blair, Orwell's father.
4 (*Below right*) Orwell's maternal
grandfather, Frank Limouzin.

5 Eric Blair aged fourteen.

6 Eric Blair with Guinever and Prosper Buddicom.

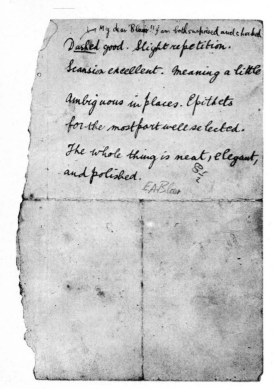

7 and 8 Cyril Connolly's school exercise
poem 'Kitchener' written at St. Cyprian's
in 1916 with Eric Blair's criticism appended.

9 Eton in the early years of the century:
Fourth of June celebrations.

10 (*Far left*) M. R. James, Provost of Eton 1918–36.
11 (*Left below*) Etonians gambolling on the beach near Athens, summer vacation 1919. Eric Blair far right.
12 (*Left*) On his way back from Athens.

13 (*Above*) The Eton Wall Game team of 1921: Eric Blair back row extreme right.

E·A· Blair K·S·

Bought this Book

much against his will

For the study

of Milton

a poet

for whom

he had

no

love;

but

he was

compelled

to study

him or abandon

English Extra Studies

which not being

commendable to him

he was compelled to

Squander three & sixpence

On this nasty little book.

14 (*Above left*) Eric Blair's view of Milton at the age of eighteen – an inscription in a book given to Guinever Buddicom, August 1921.

15 (*Above right*) The Blairs' flat in Notting Hill Gate where the family lived from 1918 to 1921.

16 (*Right*) Eric Blair, 1921.

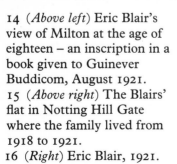

word and paper games which were an endless source of pleasure to us both. 'Set-piece' poetry was our favourite, but of the dozens of verses which resulted none, alas, now remain. Reflecting on those days, it seems to me appropriate to recall the kinds of poems we used to exchange and in doing so, perhaps, to commemorate our friendship.

Ave Atque Vale
George Orwell

25 June 1903 – 23 January 1950 – 1984

Hail and Farewell
To youth and lost companion.
His funeral knell
Woke Freedom long ago:
No force can quell
The Ultimate Britannian
Though winds of Hell
Through other deserts blow.
But how can brave young hopes such wastes foretell
Until
The shadows chill?
Hail and Farewell.

Farewell. And Hail
To those who walk hereafter
His blazing trail
The rock-firm path he trod.
Of what avail
Is life bereft of laughter
O Infidel?
The Innocence of God
Beset – betrayed – bedevilled – does not fail:
Man still
Has heart and will.
Farewell – and Hail.

The Envoy
Ex Memoriam

So rhymes and runes are cast once more.
Reflecting through the written page
We trace beyond death's distant door
The dreamdays of our golden age.
Some foreprint of a masterplan
With children other children share –
The child IS father to the man –
George Orwell once was Eric Blair.

Remembering the young Eric, who disapproved as 'far too cynical' *The Pilgrim of a Smile* by Norman Davey with which I had been greatly impressed, the novels of George Orwell baffle me. Occasionally a person one might like to meet may flitter across a page, but the main characters are so unmercifully fated to frustration: they only escape their stars to be defeated by themselves.

It is as though the dial counted only shadowed hours, where sunny hours could have no rightful place: it is as though simple enduring happiness was something he had been brought to consider as not only impossible but also in some way wrong.

And that is the saddest thing of all.

Francis Hope
SCHOOLDAYS

To begin with the sadly obvious: as Orwell knew, one cannot discuss England without discussing education, and one cannot discuss English education without discussing class. There are many snobbish countries in the world, and many varieties of snobbery in each. But England is perhaps the only one where the first testing question, whether from prospective employer or potential mother-in-law, is more likely to be 'Where did he go to school?' than 'Where does he come from?' or 'What did his father do?'

We are speaking, of course, of the world of Orwell's youth: roughly the second decade of this century. To ask whether the same is true today would be rudely polemical, although Orwell himself once wrote in a book review: 'It is hard to disentangle admiration from dismay when one learns that Eton in 1948 is almost exactly what it was in 1918.' [*Observer*, 1 August 1948.] In those days, then, Englishmen of a certain class progressed along a well marked path – even today I have heard it described as the *cursus honorum* – which was both entrance ticket and apprenticeship for a small sector of the adult world. Orwell entered on that path in September 1911, when he went to St Cyprian's preparatory school, near Eastbourne. He stayed there just over five years, winning one scholarship to Wellington and another to Eton. He left at Christmas 1916, spent the Lent Term of 1917 at Wellington, and then moved to Eton as soon as a vacancy came up for his relatively low place on the scholarship roll. At Christmas 1921 he left Eton to join the Burma Police.

By the standards of those institutions, it was not a brilliant career: no prizes, no university entrance, no prospects of passing top into the Civil Service, no first foot on a ladder leading to Ministry, Embassy, Fellowship, or Knighthood. At the same time, it clearly left Orwell in a state of social unease, consciously cut off from most other Englishmen. To his credit, he did not rail at this; also to his credit, he certainly felt it. The English class system is so subtle an instrument of discomfort that its victims can suffer pains quite imperceptible to those on the receiving end of a sharper divisiveness. Orwell was a connoisseur of social shame both upwards and downwards: a poor boy at Eton, an Etonian among the poor. Those at either extreme might sometimes have asked what the fuss was about. That would be a mistake, although the general principle that one shouldn't fuss about such things is both admirable and Orwellian. In the long run, his education did not matter very much. Perhaps that is the most one can ask of any education. Certainly to make it true of an English private education at the beginning of this century is a powerful negative achievement.

Suppose Max Beerbohm had drawn an 'Old Self and Young Self' of Orwell, how could he have set about it? The visual side is easy enough. The young

Blair could appear as he does in a contemporary photograph of the Eton and Harrow Match: walking with a gilded exquisite, but himself ferociously untidy, in old-fashioned, ill-fitting and well-worn Eton clothes, with unbrushed hair and a disorderly grin.* The old Orwell, moustached and crooked-toothed, would have exchanged tail-coat and waistcoat for tweed jacket and pullover; a forbidden cigarette might lie in one hand; doubtless the adult's face would be more ravaged by the world's cares than the schoolboy's. But the caption? It is hard to imagine anything beyond the conventional note of wry surprise: 'So you made it as a writer, after all.' Beerbohm's series depended on a chasm across the years. But Orwell's old self was still young. (According to Julian Symons, 'Orwell always wrote from the point of view of a child'. [*London Magazine*, September 1963]) It also seems true that Orwell's young self was already old. His 'eyes of a child', even when literally a child's, saw further than other children's. This is a great help in resisting the influence of school.

Maturity is not to be confused with precociousness, which schools can easily harness. Cyril Connolly has written a famous account of his schooldays, overlapping with Orwell's both at St Cyprian's and at Eton, which perfectly bears out the distinction. Connolly was precocious; Orwell was mature. They were both bookish, of course; both scholarship-fodder at St Cyprian's, both 'advanced' in their choice of reading (apart from the bogus incentive of a prize awarded for the 'best' list of books taken from the school library during the term). 'I think I was ten or eleven,' wrote Orwell to Julian Symons [May 1948] 'when Cyril Connolly and I got hold of a copy of Wells's *The Country of the Blind* (short stories) and were so fascinated by it that we kept stealing it from one another. I can still remember at 4 o'clock on a midsummer morning, with the school fast asleep, and the sun slanting through the window, creeping down a passage to Connolly's dormitory where I knew the book would be beside his bed. We also got into severe trouble (and I think a caning – I forget) for having a copy of Compton Mackenzie's *Sinister Street*.'

All good clean fun, even the caning; quite publishable in the old school magazine. Not all of Orwell's memories would be. Mr Connolly also remembers him saying of the First World War 'Of course, you realize, Connolly, that whoever wins this war, we shall emerge as a second-rate nation'. [*Enemies of Promise*.] No doubt he was quoting something he had read. But, as Christopher Hollis says, to dredge that out of one's reading was a remarkable feat for a schoolboy in the smash-the-Huns atmosphere of the time. Orwell's sister also

* Mr Christopher Hollis recalls an Eton beating at which he noticed that Orwell's trousers were particularly shiny: a notable extension of Trollope's comment on a master who beat him so often that he may have been unable to recognize him by his face.

recalls him, at the outbreak of the war, discussing it 'in a very grown up way' with their mother. [Avril Dunn, *Twentieth Century*, March 1961.] But as she was several years younger than him, he may have seemed 'very grown up' whatever he did.

Orwell's real offence against St Cyprian's was the publication of his bitter essay 'Such, Such Were the Joys' – so bitter, in fact, that it was not published in this country for a long time because of fears of libel. Many people have suffered at many such second-rate institutions, and much of what Orwell describes – the beatings, the poor food, the cramming, the prevailing mindlessness – could be matched elsewhere. What is unusual is Orwell's insight into the snobberies of the school: the absurd little boys' showing-off about their homes, and the more important endorsement of such standards by the staff. Schoolmasters are often the keenest supporters of school snobbery, not least when they are putting their own children through expensive schools either with scholarships or at trade rates. The headmaster of St Cyprian's, according to Orwell, went into ecstasies over Eton because they gave the boys (including his own son) fried fish for supper. Fried fish! Orwell comments: the weekly luxury of the working class. To be grateful for such largesse is either pathetic or foolish.

The point about these memories is that they are very unusual ones for a child. Some critics have accused Orwell of retrospective hindsight, or of unnatural self-pity. As Mr Hollis points out, most schoolboys are too ignorant to be genuinely snobbish. Their own school comes top in the social world, their sporting rivals next, and then a dim penumbra of oiks and factories. (At what age does the average privately educated child realize how small a minority he has joined?) Within the school, one or two sets of parents may be even more shaming than the rest, and such anomalies as a birthday cake without icing or a grey overcoat instead of a black one may lend the schoolboy's pathological hatred of nonconformity an extra edge of social scorn. But none of this goes very deep, because it is not related to any coherent idea of the world.

But Orwell was not so simple. He may have been 'unduly' sensitive about money, though the adverb usually comes from those who are not short of it. There is some evidence, both in *Down and Out in Paris and London* and in *Keep the Aspidistra Flying*, of the frantic bourgeois refusal to admit poverty, which comes oddly from somebody determined to write with utter frankness about it. It is possible that nobody picked on him for being poor, although Mr Hollis's argument that nobody was nasty to *him* in similar circumstances at a different school is not exactly the disproof direct.* Perhaps Orwell exagger-

* All accounts of someone else's schooldays become an excuse to recall one's own. For my twopenny-worth, I would offer the fact that my preparatory school was an excellent one, where I was much better

ated, when he said, in *Keep the Aspidistra Flying*, that to send a child to school among children richer than itself was the greatest cruelty one could inflict on it. But he saw something – and he must at least have glimpsed it at the time – which most private schoolboys do not see, and which is true: the unacknowledged role of money in their lives.

Preparatory schools exist in a curious atmosphere of insecurity. The clever boys may not get scholarships, and will then – horror of horrors – sink into the state system if they cannot afford a public school's full fees. The stupid boys may fail the 'Common Entrance' to the public school of their choice, thereby setting their rich and powerful parents against the school. Not one boy in a hundred realizes this, but that is part of the school's power. Orwell was different. It is admirable rather than pitiable that he should write so little about the personal relations and common-room politics which others can fluently recall, and so much, though so harshly, about the staff. Not for the first time, he had grasped a point which eluded his contemporaries.

In any case, he got his Eton scholarship, thereby discharging whatever debt he may have owed St Cyprian's. Once again, he was put among richer boys. Most Eton Collegers would have gone to Eton without a scholarship, or to another large public school with one, if they had failed the exam. They begin in the middle of the upper-middle class, whereas Orwell, with scrupulous accuracy, described himself as *lower* upper-middle class. A very successful Colleger might not notice such a thing for a moment. But Orwell was not very successful, which set him apart again. In college at Eton, to excel is to conform. He entered twelfth in an 'election' (annual intake or 'class' in the American sense) of eighteen boys, and sank rather than rose in subsequent exam-based pecking orders. He was a science specialist, which was not a great catch in those days. He played for college at the Wall Game, but since only Collegers are expected to take that miserable mudlark seriously, there was not much athletic glory in that. Most of the time, he preferred to 'take exercise' by games of fives, the traditional refuge of the unskilled. One contemporary kindly recalls him as 'a not very distinguished member of a brilliant election'. Another simply says that he was the dimmest of the lot then, just as he is the most famous now. The same source did not learn until Orwell's last years that the distinguished author of those much discussed books was the Blair whom he had known at school.

taught than at Eton. But in that fatal fifth summer, as the scholarship season came round, every stick was used to beat us over the stile, not least the crudest threat of social disgrace. I remember being told – in 1952, by an otherwise civilized teacher of the classics – that 'there's many a man sleeping on the Embankment tonight because he forgot his tenses'.

And always, incidentally, known as 'Blair'. Perhaps his Christian name was not classy enough. ('People always grow up like their names', he wrote to Rayner Heppenstall [April 1940]. 'It took me nearly thirty years to work off the effects of being called Eric.') Perhaps he simply rejected intimacy. Etonians are dreadful little clubmen, and many memorable school careers are based on conversation and charm rather than membership of the Sixth Form or the First Eleven. Not Orwell's. The socially ambitious Colleger quickly cultivates a grander circle of friends among the Oppidans, or non-scholarship boys. Orwell never did. Within college, he was not so much unpopular as aloof. He was known as 'the election atheist', and was a useful spokesman when the whole group was summoned for a real or imaginary offence. (The 'election' above was very large, and therefore contained some members of lower than usual intellectual calibre and correspondingly higher than average authoritarian ways. Hence the incident, reported in *Enemies of Promise*, when Orwell and another boy were beaten by those barely senior to them for being late for prayers.) He was a welcome companion on the long Sunday walks which Etonians sometimes take in winter to the Copper Horse in Windsor Great Park: a fund, apparently, of strongly held original opinions. He was known as 'Cynicus' in the appallingly self-conscious diary kept by Mr Connolly's junior, Le Strange. Mr Hollis recalls him taking a poll of new boys' religions, and when one replied 'Christian' saying: 'We haven't had one of those yet.' It is a slender score for so self-conscious an institution, with all its apparatus of debating societies and *Vale* books, college records and mutual memoirs. Orwell seems to have passed through it like some unclassifiable particle through a recording chamber: a dog that significantly didn't bark.

Some contemporaries remember him as an entirely unliterary figure; others describe his contributions to a hand-written newspaper called the *Election Times* and his editorship of another, grander ephemeral magazine. Neither Eton College nor the Orwell archives at University College, London can offer any help. Doubtless their silence is what Orwell would have wished.

Independents like Orwell are happier in college at Eton, no doubt, than they would be at an Eton house, or at a smaller and more Spartan public school. Defenders of the system can, if they wish, note Orwell's remarks in a letter to Cyril Connolly [14 December 1938]: 'I've always held that the public schools aren't so bad, but people are wrecked by those filthy private schools long before they get to public school age.' In *The Lion and the Unicorn* Orwell recommended flooding the public schools with state-aided pupils, but wanted the private schools abolished altogether.

As for the 10,000 'private' schools that England possesses, the vast majority of them deserve nothing except suppression. They are simply commercial undertakings, and in many cases their educational level is actually lower than that of the elementary schools. They merely exist because of a widespread idea that there is something disgraceful in being educated by the public authorities.

When he came to choose a school for his adopted son Richard, Orwell stuck to the same principles.

I am not going to let him go to a boarding school before he is ten, and I would like him to start off at the elementary school. If one could find a good one. It's a difficult question. Obviously it is democratic for everyone to go to the same school, or at least start off there but when you see what the elementary schools are like and the results, you feel that any child that has the chance should be rescued from them. [To Julian Symons, October 1948.]

Later, like many other liberal parents in the same dilemma, he was thinking of sending Richard to Westminster. 'They have abandoned their top-hats, I learn.' [To Julian Symons, June 1949.] But he always put a democratic educational system high on the list of necessary English reforms. Doubtless his own experience played some part here.

Educationally, the residue is very slight. Orwell uses a Latin tag rather more often than one might expect – particularly in his reviews. But most of the formal erudition displayed in his work, particularly in history, appears to be the product of his own adult reading. (His French was good, which is hardly surprising from a man with French relatives who lived for some time in France.) When John Strachey announced that he had put a son down for Eton because 'given our existing society it was the best education', Orwell's comment is scrupulously fair: 'Actually I doubt whether it is the best, but in principle I don't feel sure that he was wrong.' [To Julian Symons, October 1948.] In 'Shooting an Elephant' he describes himself as 'poorly educated'. I remember an Eton master (himself an old Colleger) reading this essay aloud, and breaking off with an ironical smile at this phrase. 'He'd only been in College at Eton.' If one sees what Orwell meant, one may also see why the master couldn't see it.

The experience of being a fish out of water may have marked Orwell; but tracing the influence is apt to lead either to useless speculation (*if* he had been more successful and gone to university, would his work have been less pessimistic?) or to ignoble reductionism (all he *really* criticized was his own childhood). It is probably a good thing that he stood aloof from the English professional literary class, by whatever route he reached that aloofness. His perpetual sense of social embarrassment, taking in everything from smell to cash, may have been sharpened by his education. 'Going slumming' is a useful weapon against the assured moneyed beasts of Eton and Cambridge, and one that comes readily to an un-moneyed beast from Eton alone. Orwell's defensiveness about his own middle-class origins, as expressed in the muddled third part of *The Road to Wigan Pier*, probably gained an extra edge from his education. (*If he had gone to a local school . . .*) But it will not do to dismiss his keen sense of England's class-ridden society as a 'mere' product of St Cyprian's and Eton.

Nor will it do to make him a 'typical' Etonian in his untypicalness – an inverted tribute which that particular school is particularly fond of. As his fellow-Etonian Christopher Hollis puts it: 'He wrote little about College at Eton because he was little interfered with there. But it does not follow from that that Eton had little influence on him.' It does not follow, but I believe it to be true. Why should we doubt Orwell's own words, in answer to an American questionnaire? (Collected Essays, Journalism and Letters, vol. 2 p. 23.) 'I was educated at Eton, 1917-21, as I had been lucky enough to win a scholarship, but I did no work there and learned very little, and I don't feel that Eton has been much of a formative influence in my life.' Later critics have read heroic or shameful efforts at self-denial into this phrase. It is simpler to take it at face value. It is not the education which turns the mind, but the praise, the successes, the glittering prizes. Orwell had none of these, except that initial scholarship, and did not miss them. The most infuriating thing about the English public schools is neither cruelty nor stupidity, but a doglike desire for gratitude. Against it, indifference is the best and cruellest weapon. The best thing most English writers can do with their schooldays is to forget them.*

It is not always as easy as Orwell found it. 'Alexander at the head of the world never tasted the true pleasure that boys of his own age have enjoyed at the head of a school', wrote Horace Walpole in 1736. Nearly two hundred years later Cyril Connolly, after a triumphant visit to St Cyprian's, pondered on the emptiness ahead. The headmaster, who could hardly find much reflected glory in Orwell's obscure course, was hugely proud of Mr Connolly. 'A Balliol scholar has the ball at his feet.' Mr Connolly was less enthusiastic. 'Already I felt embarrassed to know what to do with it.' What was Balliol, after all, with its hearty dons and its 'blokey armchair' to a sunny room on Sixth Form Passage, redolent of white roses and clove carnation soap? Only the wistful consolations of literature remained, with Mr Connolly quoting Mallarmé: '*La chair est triste, hélas, et j'ai lu tous les livres.*' After Eton, all was decline.

* Mr Hollis is on firmer though more cynical ground when he suggests that it did Orwell's literary career no harm to have two such old schoolfellows as Cyril Connolly and Sir Richard Rees.

16

Orwell's views on this can be found in *Inside the Whale*. He quotes (or slightly misquotes) a famous passage from *Enemies of Promise*: 'Were I to deduce anything from my feelings on leaving Eton, it might be called The Theory of Permanent Adolescence. It is the theory that the experiences undergone by boys at the great public schools are so intense as to dominate their lives and to arrest their development.' On which Orwell comments:

When you read the second sentence in this passage, your natural impulse is to look for the misprint. Presumably there is a 'not' left out, or something. But no, not a bit of it! He means it! And what is more, he is merely speaking the truth, in an inverted fashion. 'Cultured' middle-class life has reached a depth of softness at which a public-school education – five years in a lukewarm bath of snobbery – can actually be looked upon as an eventful period.

It would be a mistake to read this as a gladiatorial contest. Orwell rightly admired Connolly's remarkable testament. When critics of *Nineteen Eighty-Four* objected that its torture scenes were reminiscent of school bullies, Orwell smiled. 'He was convinced that for people who had grown up among the safe conventions of democratic England – and the intelligentsia above all – the only English parallel for the nightmare of totalitarianism was the experience of a misfit boy in an English boarding school.' [T. R. Fyvel, *Encounter*, July 1959.] But there is an important temperamental difference – to use Mr Connolly's own terms – between the school-minded and the school-proof. 'Permanent adolescence' might also be christened 'premature maturity' – according to Professor Kaldor, the English economic disease. If Orwell avoided it, it must have been through some genuine stubborn maturity of his own.

No doubt Orwell himself would find all this too glib. It is typical – and rather public school – that he should object to middle-class life on the grounds of softness. Elsewhere he wrote [*Observer*, 1 August 1948] that one of Eton's few virtues was that it 'partly escaped the reform of the public schools set on foot by Dr Arnold and retained certain characteristics belonging to the eighteenth century and even to the Middle Ages'. These characteristics would probably no more stand close inspection than the traditions of the Navy survived Churchill's tongue ('rum, sodomy and the lash'). But it is an old radical strategy to attack the Right for its lack of *true* conservatism. Orwell hated the Empire-baiters of London drawing-rooms, and could see the virtues of public-school stoicism just as he could see the virtues of imperial stiff upper lips, particularly in unfashionably tight spots. Of John Cornford's death in Spain he wrote ['My Country Right or Left']: 'The Young Communist who died heroically in the International Brigade was public school to the core.'

Cornford's poem before the storming of Huesca is not unlike Orwell's first published work (in the *Henley and South Oxfordshire Standard* of 2 October 1914)

> Awake! oh you young men of England,
>   For if, when your country's in need
> You do not enlist by the thousand,
>   You truly are cowards indeed.

This is a useful exhibit for two reasons. First, it can prove that the public schools 'really' have something which comes in handy at a pinch; second, it can show that Orwell was 'really' an old-fashioned patriot, a product of his class, and the rest. The record seems to point the other way. Wherever Orwell learnt to appreciate the virtues which English schools have falsely claimed as their prerogative, it was not at English schools. There is no reason why Orwell should have been grateful to Eton, nor for commentators on his work to give the old place a passing tribute. Its failure to influence him was not the product of large-minded liberalism on the school's part, but a proof of his obstinate and early independence. The one thing that academies of 'character' can neither spoil nor stand is a genuinely strong character. The young Blair must have been one of the strongest.

Maung Htin Aung
GEORGE ORWELL
AND BURMA

IN the long history of Anglo-Burmese relations, which began in 1752 with the first British envoy from the East India Company kneeling stiffly in his uniform before the Burmese king, and ended in 1948 with the last British Governor of Burma waving farewell from a warship as it steamed slowly out of Rangoon harbour, the darkest period (excepting, of course, the years of actual war, namely, 1824–6, 1852 and 1885) was from 1919, when the Government of India Act was passed, to 1930, when a peasants' rebellion broke out against the whole might of British rule. Before 1919, the English and the Burmese were friends, and after 1930 they were merely political opponents; but during that dark period between 1919 and 1930 they were bitter enemies, each despising the other. George Orwell, still known then as Eric Arthur Blair, lived and worked in Burma during that critical period, and his *Burmese Days*, first published in 1934, was a valuable historical document, although in the guise of a novel, for it recorded vividly the tensions that prevailed in Burma, and the mutual suspicion, despair and disgust that crept into Anglo-Burmese relations as the direct result of the Government of India Act leaving out Burma from the course of its reforms. Orwell himself considered the book to be a documentary, as can be seen from a letter he wrote in 1946 to F. Tennyson Jesse, a sentimental novelist of the Burmese scene:

In your book you said nothing about our economic exploitation of the country . . . and though you did mention it, you soft-pedalled the social misbehaviour of the British and the friction to which it has led over a long period . . . We have treated Burma better than we have treated some countries, but on the whole it is a sordid story . . . Did you ever read my novel about Burma (*Burmese Days*)? I dare say it's unfair in some ways and inaccurate in some details, but much of it is simply reporting of what I have seen.

Eric Arthur Blair was a very young man when he reported for duty with the Indian Imperial Police at Rangoon on 27 November 1922, for he was then only nineteen years old. The Indian Imperial Police was next in rank and status only to the Indian Civil Service, and for Blair to get into the Indian Civil Service he would have had to spend three years at Cambridge reading for a degree and then wait another year, preparing to take the competitive examination. Like an ICS probationer, an Imperial Police probationer had the privilege of choosing the particular province of India in which he would serve, and Blair chose Burma, in those days a province of the Indian empire, doubtless because, as he said in a second letter to Miss Tennyson Jesse, 'I have family connections with the country over three generations. My grandmother lived forty years in Burma.'

When he landed in Rangoon, Blair must have dreamed of becoming an empire-builder and looked forward to years of endeavour among the 'simple and charming Burmese people in the beautiful land of Burma'. Doubtless, he remembered Kipling's 'Mandalay', especially the following lines:

> By the old Moulmein Pagoda, lookin' eastward to the sea,
> There's a Burma girl a-settin', and I know she thinks o' me;
> For the wind is in the palm-trees, and the temple-bells they say:
> 'Come you back, you British soldier; come you back to Mandalay!'

But when, after being posted to the police training school at Mandalay, he proceeded to the Golden City, he found the temples dark and silent and the city tense, because only in the previous month an Imperial Policeman had had his nose cut off in a riot by a knife-wielding monk. What had happened to the gentle and pious monks about whom he had read so much? For that matter, where were the lovely Burmese girls? They were in the markets and in the streets, shouting slogans against the British Government and were throwing away their tortoiseshell combs with contemptuous gestures, for the Burmese word for 'tortoise' was similar to the Burmese word for 'English'. Like the prince in the Burmese folk-tale who suddenly found that the lovely maiden in his arms was really an ogress in disguise, Blair must have recoiled from Burma and the Burmese in horror and disgust. He must have felt angry with himself, with the books on Burma that he had read, and also with the Burmese people. So, in his novel *Burmese Days*, he set out to destroy the conventional picture of Burma as a green and pleasant land, and the Burmese as a charming, carefree and childlike people. The key to the mood of the novel was to be found in the quotation from *As You Like It*, given on the title page:

> . . . this desert inaccessible,
> Under the shade of melancholy boughs.

Throughout the novel, Orwell brought out the ugliness of the Burmese country-side, the physical repulsiveness of Burmese men and women, and the meanness of their characters. To take but one example, in describing the Burmese dance which had been acclaimed by English writers and artists as graceful and exquisite, Orwell deliberately emphasized its grotesque elements. In spite of himself, however, he still loved the Burmese countryside and he made a desperate struggle to escape from the witch's coils. Thus in *The Road to Wigan Pier* he confessed: 'I find that anything outrageously strange generally ends by fascinating me even when I abominate it. The landscapes of Burma, which, when I was among them, so appalled me as to assume the qualities of nightmare, afterwards stayed so hauntingly in my mind that I was obliged to write a novel about them to get rid of them.' In the same book he also admitted that he was attracted to the Burmese people, by the gracefulness of their bodies and their easy, friendly manners. So, in later life, Orwell recognized that it was a fault of the English to take a romantic view of Burma and the Burmese people, and this was why he disagreed so vehemently with sentimental novelists like Tennyson Jesse. Nonetheless, in the earlier years of his service as an English official in Burma, he shared the attitudes and anti-Burmese prejudices of his contemporaries, and only towards the end did he become conscious of the aspirations of the Burmese nationalists and begin to hate his position 'as a cog in the machine of imperialism', finally resigning from the service in 1927.

As Orwell noted in *Burmese Days*, there existed in his time there a wall of racial prejudice, harder than granite, dividing the English officials from the Burmese. But the wall was of recent origin and not many months old when young Blair found it. There can be no doubt that in the beginning the Burmese, while resenting English rule, liked the English officials as individuals, and the English on their part found the country and the people attractive; Kipling was merely voicing the opinion of his contemporaries in 'Mandalay'. After living in the thickly populated and arid regions of India, they found Burma to be a 'greener and a fresher land', and after observing the caste restrictions and religious restraints of Indian society, Hindu and Muslim, the open and almost classless nature of Burmese society, with its centuries-old emphasis on the dignity of the individual and equality of all men and women, surprised and delighted the English officials. Even that proud conqueror of Ava, Lord Dufferin, although he was received with dark looks by the Burmese during his state visit to Mandalay early in 1886, wrote back to a friend in England, extolling the grace, charm and freedom of Burmese women. Those early English officials mixed freely with the Burmese as social equals, and learned to speak and read the Burmese language, and soon came to understand and appreciate Burmese customs, manners and attitudes. There were even some marriages between English officials and Burmese women. By Blair's time, however, such fraternization had ceased, no decent Burmese woman would become friendly with any English official, and the English officials on their part no longer cared to become friendly with any Burmese, man or woman. Thus only sordid affairs were possible, like the one in *Burmese Days* between the hero and his servant-mistress.

The reason for the change of attitude towards the Burmese people on the part of the English officials was their annoyance that such charming and simple people should dare to dream of political freedom. Young Blair in 1922 very likely acquiesced with this view, but not the Orwell who in *Burmese Days* wrote of the District Commissioner as follows: 'Mr Macgregor stiffened at the

Burma

17 Catching wild
elephants in
Burma.

19 Moulmein, Burma.

18 Officers of the Indian Imperial Police in
Burma. Eric Blair back row, third from left.

word "nigger", which is discountenanced in India. He had no prejudice against Orientals; indeed, he was deeply fond of them. Provided they were given no freedom he thought them the most charming people alive.'

When in 1885, as a result of the third Anglo-Burmese war, the whole of Burma fell under British rule, the Burmese, although reeling under the blow, dared to expect that their country would be turned into a protectorate or a separate colony, with an identity of its own. They were therefore shocked and humiliated when the British turned Burma into a mere province of India. In many of the remoter villages the simple peasants rose in rebellion, although, being armed only with swords and sticks, they were easily caught and hanged. But in the towns the people were prepared to give English education and English liberalism a trial, and sent their sons and daughters to the government schools, then to Rangoon College and finally to the Inns of Court. These young barristers came back to Burma with an admiration for the British democratic institutions. While remaining loyal to Britain, they hoped to work to regain at least some measure of political freedom. But when the Montagu-Chelmsford Commission was appointed, it was found that Burma, although a province of India, would be excluded from consideration by the Commission. In despair, the young Burmese liberals hastily sent an unofficial delegation to Delhi. Edwin Montagu noted in his report that the Burmese delegates in their colourful dresses were courteous and charming, but he did not recommend that Burma should be included in the system of reforms to be granted to the rest of India. So, when the Westminster Parliament passed the Government of India Act of 1919, Burma was left out.

In Burma there was a storm of protests, resulting in the boycott of all English goods. Young Buddhist monks, for the first time in the history of Burma, entered the political arena, going about armed with small canes, with which they beat anyone found using English goods. Then, in 1920, Rangoon College was raised to the status of a full university. On paper the new university was to be a residential university, on the model of Oxford and Cambridge. But to the nationalists the real aim seemed clear: the Government was determined to prevent the University of Rangoon from becoming another Calcutta, with young men running wild, shouting for political rights and reforms, and instead to turn it into an institution intended, not to give a liberal education, but to discipline Burmese youths and teach them obedience and loyalty. The result was a strike by the students of the new university, which soon spread to all the schools, and became a nation-wide movement for political freedom. There were wholesale expulsions of students, parents who happened to be officials were severely reprimanded for failing to control their sons and daughters, and the

20 George Orwell with a native sword,
a souvenir of his Burmese days.

Government even played with the idea of calling in the army to force the striking students back into the classrooms. But the fever of nationalism remained unabated and the Government was soon forced to make concessions, cancel all expulsions, and amend the University Act. The strike was called off, but many of the striking schoolboys and schoolgirls refused to go back to the government schools, and for them private schools, called National Schools, came to be established all over the country. A National University was also founded, but, lacking resources to compete with the University of Rangoon, it soon faded away.

In 'Shooting an Elephant' and *Burmese Days*, Orwell described the 'grinning yellow faces' of young Burmese students jeering at all Englishmen; evidently the English officials never forgave Burmese boys and girls for participating in the great national strike of 1920. In *Burmese Days*, one of the main characters, Ellis, hated all coloured people, especially the Burmese. One day he passed a group of Burmese boys who seemed to be laughing and jeering at him. Losing his temper, he hit one of the boys with his stick, inflicting an injury which led indirectly to the boy's blindness. The other boys fought him with stones and brickbats, but Ellis escaped into the sanctuary of his office. This incident was based on a personal experience of Blair's in which I also was involved. It was November 1924. I was a freshman at University College, Rangoon, and Blair was serving at a small town across the river from Rangoon. One afternoon, at about 4 p.m., the suburban railway station of Pagoda Road was crowded with schoolboys and undergraduates, and Blair came down the stairs to take the train to the Mission Road station, where the exclusive Gymkhana Club was situated. One of the boys, fooling about with his friends, accidentally bumped against the tall and gaunt Englishman, who fell heavily down the stairs. Blair was furious and raised the heavy cane which he was carrying, to hit the boy on the head, but checked himself, and struck him on the back instead. The boys protested, and some undergraduates, including myself, surrounded the angry Englishman. Although undergraduates, we were not much older than the schoolboys, for the age of admission to the university was sixteen. The train drew in and Blair boarded a first-class carriage. But in Burma, unlike India, first-class carriages were never taboo to natives, and some of us had first-class season tickets. The argument between Blair and the undergraduates continued. Fortunately, the train reached Mission Road station without further incident, and Blair left the train. He must often have pondered on the tragic consequences that could have followed had he not controlled himself. Blair was, of course, merely reflecting the general attitude of his English contemporaries towards Burmese students, especially those from the National Schools. This was to have serious consequences on the later history of Anglo-Burmese relations, because the National Schools, from being merely pro-Burmese, gradually became anti-English, and most of the leaders of the national movement for freedom after about 1930 were products of those schools. In 1924, U Nu had just entered the University from a National School, General Aung San, U Ba Swe and U Kyaw Nyein were studying in the middle forms in the National Schools of their native towns, and General Ne Win was studying in a government school only because the National School in his native town had closed down.

The University of Rangoon never recovered from the initial blow inflicted on it by the strike of 1920, and came to be looked upon as an alien institution. If the English professors (there were no Burmese) had been dedicated teachers, they could have moulded their students in such a way that they would become less hostile to the English, without making them less nationalistic in outlook. Unfortunately the professors belonged to the Imperial Educational Service, and considered themselves officials rather than teachers. They stayed aloof from their students, and behaved as if they were avenging the strike of 1920. The gulf between the professors and the students became wider and wider until in about 1931 the *Thakin* movement started in the dormitories of the University. The stern and unbending attitude of the English professors resulted in the second upheaval, the university strike of 1936, which ended with the two student leaders, Maung Aung San and Maung Nu, joining the *Thakin* movement.

The national demand for reforms became more and more persistent, and in 1923 the Westminster Parliament was finally constrained to extend the dyarchy reforms to Burma. But the delay was fatal to the success of the reforms, because by this time the national leaders in India itself were dissatisfied with the working of the reforms. In Burma, some of the liberal leaders were having second thoughts and were no longer too enthusiastic; they were beginning to wonder whether their trust and confidence in the intentions of the Government were really justified. So, when the elections were held, the country was divided between those who would cooperate with the British Government in working the reforms and those who would not. One result of the reforms was the direct recruitment of young Burmese into the Imperial services. There were also promotions of senior Burmese officials from the provincial services. Thus the opportunity was given for the English officials in Burma to welcome their Burmese colleagues on an equal footing. Instead, they showed resentment. They looked down upon the older Burmese who were promoted to higher services as old-fashioned and corrupt, and upon the young Burmese who received direct appointments as arrogant and conceited. This was reflected in *Burmese Days*, where Orwell made the senior Burmese magistrate the villain of the piece and depicted him as corrupt, cruel, ambitious and scheming, behaving as a tyrant over the simple villagers of his district.

As one of the new policies connected with the dyarchy reforms, the English Governor required the exclusive European clubs in the districts to extend their membership to one or two senior Burmese officials. This was considered to be a great concession by the English officials. Young Blair obviously agreed, for in *Burmese Days* election to the district European club was depicted as the highest ambition of all Burmese officials. In actual fact, it was not so. At the time when the instructions from the Governor went out all over Burma, the Burmese officials who were senior enough to be invited to join the clubs were all over the age of fifty, and not having been educated abroad they considered European club life to be frivolous and time-wasting. My father, U Pein (the Burmese have no family names), who was the additional district magistrate at Pegu in 1923, was the first Burmese to become a member of a district club and I can well remember him making a wry face when he received a letter from the club president, the district magistrate, informing him of his election; my father went to the club only once a month and always considered it an unpleasant social duty.

The Governor's instructions did not apply to the Gymkhana Club at Rangoon. Burmese officials who had received direct appointments to the senior services resented the fact that while their English colleagues, as young and junior as themselves, were invited to join the club, they were never so invited, because they were not Europeans. My eldest brother, U Tin Tut, who was the first Burmese to receive a direct appointment to the Indian Civil Service had, in 1924, an unpleasant experience. The Gymkhana Club always fielded a strong rugby team, but, as the Burmese never took to rugby football, the Gymkhana team usually had only one opponent, a team from the English regiment on garrison duty at Rangoon. That year, however, there were not enough players from the regiment, so a team was formed with players from the regiment and reserve players from the club itself. This team was weak, and some of the players invited my brother to bolster it up, which was not surprising in view of the fact that he had gained his colours at Dulwich, and later captained the Cambridge rugby team. As was the custom in Burma, the players, including my brother, went to the field already dressed for the game, and so at this stage there were no complications. After the match, however, when my brother walked with other players towards the club premises to have a shower and change, his way was barred by the club secretary, who came running out and told him that as he was not a European he could not come into the building. Naturally that was the last game of rugby that my brother ever played. He received personal apologies from individual players, but not an official apology either from the club rugby captain or from the club itself. The incident caused quite a stir among the Burmese officials, and Burmese newspapers were not slow to point out that as U Tin Tut, who besides being a member of the Indian Civil Service had been called to the English bar, and had held a King's commission in the (British) Indian Army, was considered not good enough to be given the privilege of taking a shower in the Gymkhana Club washrooms, it was obvious that the Burmese were considered by the English to be an inferior people, not to be granted Dominion status. It may be noted that even in 1924 the limit of Burmese nationalist aspirations was still merely Dominion status.

The Burmese peasants had never really accepted British rule, and there had been sporadic rebellions from 1886 onwards. Orwell described one such rebellion in *Burmese Days*, emphasizing their futility and pathos. The rebels were armed only with pitch-forks and home-made guns, and a few shots from the military police usually put them to flight, the leaders being caught and later hanged for treason. The educated Burmese deplored these rebellions, and tried to restrain the people, always believing that political freedom could be regained only through negotiation. This was considered weakness by the English officials. In 'Shooting an Elephant', Orwell criticized the Burmese nationalists for lacking even 'the guts to raise a riot'. And in *Burmese Days*, hundreds of Burmese who had besieged the club, demanding the surrender of Ellis who had beaten the schoolboy, dispersed hurriedly when a few shots were fired over their heads. The growing disillusion of the Burmese liberals with the political intentions of the Government, and the dissension among themselves, weakened their restraining hand on the peasants, and in 1930 a nation-wide peasants' rebellion broke out. Armed only with swords and sticks, they fought the English and Indian garrisons to a standstill; a whole division of British and Indian troops had to be called in from India, and even then it took the Government full two years to suppress the rebellion. In the unequal combat the peasants died in hundreds, and many of those who survived were hanged. During the rebellion, the Gymkhana Club again came into the picture. The centre of the rebellion was in a district some fifty miles away from Rangoon, and after the skirmishes of the day the English government officials and army officers drove back to Rangoon in the cool of the evening to dine and dance at the Gymkhana Club, which, for its part, naturally made special efforts to show hospitality to those officers who had been brought in from India. So every night became a gala night. Had the club been multi-racial, the guests would have included Burmese and Indian police and military officers, and no misunderstanding could have resulted. Since, however, only the English officers were entertained, it appeared to the

Burmese masses that the English were celebrating the massacre of the Burmese peasants. The rebellion changed the nature and tempo of Burmese politics. The peasants amidst defeat and disorder realized that all they needed was modern arms, and a dream of winning full political freedom by force of arms began to take shape. The Burmese liberals were discredited, and lost their leadership of the nationalist movement. Into the vacuum stepped the young *Thakins*, who were products of National Schools and had studied at the University, but had not been educated in the West. Dressed in the same wooden slippers and the home-spun clothes that had singled them out among the university students, they travelled from village to village, urging the people to take heart and prepare for the day when the yoke of colonial rule would be broken. Thus, in the rebellion, both the British Government and the liberals were the real losers.

By that time, Eric Arthur Blair was with laboured steps walking the pilgrim's way of his own choosing, that led from Mandalay through Paris to Wigan Pier, in expiation of his feelings of guilt at serving the cause of imperialism, and in compassion for the poor, the distressed, the defeated and the downtrodden. Where did that metamorphosis from policeman to pilgrim take place? It was at Moulmein, perhaps by the old pagoda looking eastward to the sea. At Mandalay, the shock of his disillusionment, his youthfulness and the strange sights and sounds of a tension-torn town prevented Blair from reflecting on those aspects of colonial rule which later created in him a 'gnawing sense of guilt'. While serving in the riverine towns to which he was later posted, he spent his leisure hours in nearby Rangoon where he was lost amidst the large English community, and where, with his unpractised eyes, he was unable to discern clearly the Burmese in the cosmopolitan population of the city. But he was diligently learning the Burmese language – unlike his grandmother, who, as he later told Miss Tennyson Jesse, 'lived forty years in Burma and at the end could not speak a word of Burmese'. By 1922, in addition to the granite wall of racial prejudice, there stood the iron barrier of language. The English officials no longer cared to learn the Burmese language well; they merely studied to pass the examination, compulsory for all officials, in elementary Burmese, a Burmese so elementary that it was barely adequate to order servants to bring food and drink. The first Commissioner of Lower Burma, Sir Arthur Phayre, and G. E. Harvey, a pre-1922 member of the Indian Civil Service, spent long hours studying the language so that they could read the Burmese sources and write their histories of Burma. In 1922, however, even at the University of Rangoon, Burmese history was being taught by those who could not read the Burmese sources and who could not even understand the sarcastic remarks in Burmese made by the undergraduates, commenting on the lectures.

By the time Blair had completed his probationary period and was transferred to Moulmein, he had become quite proficient in Burmese. At Moulmein, he observed at close quarters the handful of fellow English officials, and found them wanting. He looked over the racial wall at the Burmese, and found them wanting also. The darkest period of his life was reflected in the two essays 'Shooting an Elephant' and 'A Hanging', both of which belonged to Blair's Moulmein years. 'Shooting an Elephant' was an essay of intense bitterness against both the Burmese and the English. Like the rogue elephant, which had ceased to belong to its herd and at the same time had become an enemy of human beings, Blair felt himself utterly alone, and in killing the elephant he felt as if he was killing a part of himself. When Blair witnessed the hanging, his mood of despair had become somewhat brightened by his growing compassion for the natives, drowning helplessly in the cruel sea of alien laws. In *Burmese Days* also, the fearful cynicism of the novel was relieved by his compassionate description of the criminals languishing in the local jail.

Although Eric Blair disapproved of the Burmese nationalists, George Orwell was sympathetic towards them. He retained this sympathy for the Burmese throughout the war years, as can be seen from scattered references to Burma in his contributions to *Tribune* during this period. The following extract from his 'As I Please' article published in the issue of that journal for 16 February 1945 contained a plea on behalf of the Burmese and also a prophecy:

For a year or two after the Japanese have gone, Burma will be in a receptive mood and more pro-British than it has been for a dozen years past. Then is the moment to make a generous gesture. I don't know whether Dominion status is the best possible solution. But if the politically conscious section of the Burmese ask for Dominion status, it would be monstrous to ... refuse it in a hopeless effort to bring back the past ... Whether these people remain inside the British Commonwealth or outside it, what matters in the long run is that we should have their friendship – and we *can* have it if we do not play them false at the moment of crisis.

If such magnanimous words could have been spoken in 1922 the English and the Burmese would have remained friends. For that matter, if Blair had stayed on in Burma a little longer, surely he and the Burmese would have become friends. In 'Shooting an Elephant' he said that the Burmese hated him. Yet when I went round Moulmein in 1935 after reading *Burmese Days*, I found that only a handful of people could recollect anything about him, and they remembered him merely as a sporting and skilful centre-forward who scored many goals for the Moulmein police team. To add a personal note, I would like very much to have known him, for on that train, when we shouted and argued and quarrelled, he addressed his explanations mostly to me; perhaps he saw in my eyes a gleam of understanding and sympathy, because only a year before I was running across the playing fields of Dulwich pursued by a huge crowd of English school-boys, jeering and shouting 'Tally ho! Catch that young Gandhi!' It was most unfortunate for Anglo-Burmese relations that Blair was too young when he lived in Burma. Had he been older, had he been George Orwell already, he would doubtless have written a different version of *Burmese Days*, which would have influenced English public opinion to become more favourable towards the nationalistic aspirations of the Burmese, in the same way as E. M. Forster's *A Passage to India* did with regard to those of the Indian people.

John Gross
IMPERIAL ATTITUDES

ORWELL was a child of the British Raj, and his original choice of career suggests at least in part a willingness to conform to family tradition. One of his grandfathers had served in the Indian Army as a young man the other was a teak merchant in Burma; his father worked in the Opium Department of the Indian Civil Service; he himself was born in Bengal, and spent the first four years of his life in India. Beyond this, the reasons which prompted him to fall in with his father's wishes and join the Indian Imperial Police when he was nineteen can only be guessed at; what is certain is that by the time he resigned his commission, five years later, he had become bitterly disillusioned, and that despite some inevitable shifts of emphasis in the changed political climate of the nineteen-thirties and forties he never subsequently wavered in his rejection of the whole imperial set-up.

The fullest direct account of how his attitude took shape can be found in Chapter 9 of *The Road to Wigan Pier*, where he describes how he gradually came to see a colonial regime, whatever its incidental benefits, as a 'monstrous intrusion', an oppressive system from the point of view of those who were subjected to it and, in more subtle ways, those who helped to administer it as well. Almost every Anglo-Indian official, he decided, was secretly troubled by a sense of guilt, a gnawing conviction that he had no right to be lording it over the inhabitants of a foreign country; and whether or not this was a valid generalization as far as his colleagues were concerned, it undoubtedly held good for Orwell himself. On his own showing, he was not so much argued as shamed out of his earlier imperial assumptions. The incident which he selects by way of illustration – it is also the basis of an episode in *Burmese Days* – took place while he was inspecting a police station where one of his subordinates, in order to establish that a suspect was an old offender, was forcing him to display his bamboo-scarred buttocks. A local American missionary who had just then chanced to wander into the station remarked, 'I wouldn't care to have your job', and Orwell was mortified: 'So *that* was the kind of job I had! Even an ass of an American missionary, a teetotal cock-virgin from the Middle West, had the right to look down on me and pity me!' The clear implication is that he felt himself trapped in a role which, contrary to its conventional rating, was essentially unmanly; and when he finally broke free, he recoiled to the opposite extreme. In an unjust world, his place was with the victims, and the four years following his return from Burma saw him repeatedly submerging himself in the lower depths. (At one point, as recounted in the sketch entitled 'Clink', the ex-policeman deliberately did his best to get taken into custody.) Then, towards the end of this period, he began writing *Burmese Days*, the book in which he set out to rid himself of his festering colonial memories.

32

Burmese Days demands to be judged as a novel, and a good one, rather than as a pamphlet with fictional trimmings or a thinly-disguised memoir. The hero, Flory, is a complicated and rounded individual, whose malaise is of a kind not likely to be cured by a simple change of socio-economic scenery. Nevertheless the main thrust of the book is unmistakably political, and if Orwell reaches out beyond narrow autobiography – Flory is a timber-merchant, while the one police officer who makes an appearance is a colourless, fairly peripheral character – it is in good measure so that he can arraign imperialism as a whole, and not just its law-enforcers. In general his phase of pure anarchism was short-lived: since his sense of reality was even stronger than his sense of guilt, he found it hard to suppose for long that any society this side of the Millennium could permanently dispense with its policemen. True, in *The Road to Wigan Pier* he still speaks bitterly of having done 'the dirty work of Empire', but the phrase is double-edged. Given that the system existed, it was arguably less discreditable to take on the unpleasant jobs and incur the odium than to keep one's hands clean and go on drawing one's dividends at a safe distance. At all events, no imperial policeman, no Empire – and in *Burmese Days* Orwell's quarrel was with the Empire.

The main points in his indictment are straightforward. Imperialism is a system which enables one kind of man, if so minded, to kick another kind of man (literally kick him) with impunity. Its primary aim is profit, and since few imperialists can bring themselves to admit this openly, or at any rate officially, it also involves an endless amount of humbug. Those advantages which it has conferred on the natives, usually for reasons of self-interest, can never outweigh the resentment which all occupying powers are bound to arouse, even when they come bearing the gifts of sound administration and modern technology. Moreover, the civilization of the white sahibs, as Orwell presents it, is a shoddy and unattractive affair. Its characteristic products are such things as the Bonzo cartoons adorning the clubhouse, or an inane popular hit like 'Show me the way to go home': Orwell's loss of faith in an imperial mission is part of a wider post-World War One sapping of confidence in Western society's achievements generally. And yet although injustice, exploitation and philistinism are common enough back home, they inevitably tend to be accentuated in a situation where one race is imposing its will on another. However much the more enlightened variety of imperialist may try to persuade himself that he is working towards an eventual goal of equality between the races, in European imperialism as it has actually developed there is an ineradicable core of racial supremacy, aptly symbolized in the novel, as it so often was in real life, by the bristling exclusiveness of the club. (Not long after Orwell left Burma, a native Burman, Sir Joseph

Maung Gye, was appointed acting Governor, but he was still barred from membership of the three principal clubs in Rangoon.)

The Englishmen who congregate in the club in *Burmese Days* are stock types – the old soak, his nagging wife, the ponderous Deputy Commissioner, and so forth; but then Orwell makes it clear that a few years spent in such a place would be enough to turn anybody into a stock type. The one character who seems to hint at deeper potentialities is the young girl Elizabeth, partly because she is a newcomer, partly because Flory romanticizes her; and by the end of the book she too has grown into her allotted role, 'the position for which Nature had designed her from the first, that of a *burra memsahib*'. Of the other English characters the most memorable – for their virulence, not their complexity – are Verrall, the polo-playing lieutenant temporarily quartered in the town, and the timber-merchant Ellis. Verrall is breath-takingly selfish and callous; he is also the youngest son of a peer, a fact which soon gets around in a society where *memsahibs* study the Civil List as intensively as Sir Walter Elliott studied the Baronetage, and it is the local Europeans who bear the brunt of his arrogance. The natives scarcely exist for him, though God help them if he were ever turned loose on them with orders to shoot. Fortunately he only embodies one limited aspect of the Raj. The Deputy Commissioner, who is not a bad sort at heart, comes across as a more central, more representative figure. But the Verrall aspect exists, and it is a dangerous one. Equally, a colonial situation is always liable to throw up a horror like Ellis, fairly bursting with malevolence and racial prejudice. In another context his venom would no doubt be concentrated on other targets (he has a particularly nasty way of talking about women, for instance), but in Burma it is quite inevitable that he should take it out on 'the niggers'. His hostile feelings verge on the pathological, and in the end he precipitates a full-scale riot when he cracks his cane across the face of a Burmese schoolboy who has been provoking him, and the boy is partially blinded.

There is a potential Ellis lurking in all of us, and in creating him Orwell was plainly getting some poisonous matter out of his system. Dr Htin Aung (see Chapter 3) has revealed that the caning episode is based on an incident in which Orwell was personally involved (though fantasy exaggerates the offence: he actually hit his victim across the back), and even without this knowledge it could reasonably be surmised that the passage has autobiographical undertones. The language used to describe the schoolboys who goad Ellis is very close to that used by Orwell in 'Shooting an Elephant' to describe the bystanders who jeered at him in Moulmein; and while his own feelings of hatred may not be made to sound as ugly as those of Ellis, the reader is left in no doubt that they are essentially a judgment on the political system which he serves.

Or so one would have supposed – but Conor Cruise O'Brien, in an essay on Orwell which appears in his collection *Writers and Politics*, has contrived to put the matter in a somewhat different light. Since in other respects Dr O'Brien writes in the guise of a warm admirer, his comments are worth pausing over. Orwell, he remarks,

seldom wrote about foreigners, except sociologically, and then in a hit-or-miss fashion otherwise unusual with him; he very rarely mentions a foreign writer and has an excessive dislike of foreign words; although he condemns imperialism he dislikes its victims even more. Indeed he sometimes goes beyond dislike; he rises to something like hysteria. In 'Shooting an Elephant', he records fantasies about sticking a bayonet into the belly of a sniggering Buddhist priest. This is the kind of fantasy that Orwell himself found sinister in *No Orchids for Miss Blandish*. It is really more disquieting in 'Shooting an Elephant': not that sadistic fantasies are unusual, even in good and gentle men, but that quite unmistakably Orwell was much more likely to have this kind of fantasy about a Burmese than about an Englishman.

And a little later we are told that Orwell

turned towards foreigners, especially Asians, that part of his mind which brooded darkly about sandals, beards and vegetarians. He could not 'think himself into the mind' of any kind of foreigner and he seldom tried to do so.

It is tempting, but it would take too long, to analyse the various distortions and logical glissades in this rather desperate effort to demonstrate that the author of *Down and Out in Paris and London* was morbidly Anglocentric, and that the author of *Homage to Catalonia* was notably insensitive to the plight of mere foreigners. What is more immediately relevant is the reference to fantasies about butchering Buddhist priests. In 'Shooting an Elephant' these take up precisely half a sentence, a sentence which reads in full: 'With one part of my mind I thought of the British Raj as an unbreakable tyranny, as something clamped down, *in saecula saeculorum*, upon the will of prostrate peoples; with another part I thought that the greatest joy in the world would be to drive a bayonet into a Buddhist priest's guts.' In the following sentence Orwell adds that such feelings are 'normal by-products of imperialism', while earlier in the same paragraph he has made it plain that he is describing his reactions as a raw young man, unhappy, perplexed, struggling to adjust to a painfully-acquired conviction that imperialism was 'an evil thing'. No one who was anxious not to misrepresent him could cite such a passage as an instance of the hysteria to which he 'sometimes' succumbed without giving any indication of its context and of where it belongs in his career.

Then what of the alleged dark thoughts about Asians and other non-Englishmen elsewhere in his work? To concede that as a novelist he was not very successful at getting inside the minds of foreigners (how many novelists have been?) is of course very different from saying that as an essayist and political journalist he wilfully refused to see their point of view. And in *Burmese Days,* his one novel with a foreign setting, he at least goes out of his way to show how much he deplores unyielding English insularity (as typified by Elizabeth's frigid behaviour at the folk-play and in the bazaar), to say nothing of making an Asian, Dr Veraswami, the most honourable character in the book. True, the deep-dyed scoundrel whose machinations provide the mainspring of the plot is another Asian, the Burmese magistrate U Po Kyin. Whether or not he is the product of a fevered xenophobic imagination must remain a matter of individual judgment; my own view is that while his presence in the story may suggest an undue determination to avoid idealizing the natives, he is a stage villain rather than a genuinely disturbing stereotype. But even if some readers do find the manner in which he is portrayed objectionable, he is very much an exceptional case. To insinuate that Orwell was habitually haunted by racist fantasies, let alone racist fantasies of a Miss Blandish-type violence, is nothing short of grotesque: anyone who set out to go through his work for solid evidence of such a theory would have a very long search indeed ahead of him. What the records do reveal, on the other hand, are repeated condemnations of racial prejudice, unswerving support for Indian independence, and a lively awareness of Indian susceptibilities, whether they were being affronted by official propaganda or slanted reporting, by a 'ghastly' diehard speech from Leo Amery or some flippant answers in an interview with Bernard Shaw. (Before he contracted tuberculosis, incidentally, Orwell had been planning to go back to India to take up a post with a newspaper in Lucknow.) As for imperialism at large, a good example of the anger which it continued to arouse in him is 'Not Counting Niggers', his fierce denunciation of a proposal for a union of Western democracies which had simply left colonial grievances out of account; and at his most extreme he was capable of writing (in an article in *Tribune* in July 1944) that there was 'quite a strong case' for saying that British imperialism was 'actually worse than Nazism'.

At other, calmer moments he would have recognized such a statement for the intemperate fling that it was, and he could also talk, for instance, of the 'exceptionally high traditions of the Indian Civil Service'. This last remark occurs in a review of Maurice Collis's *Trials in Burma*, an excellent book which, read alongside *Burmese Days*, provides both a partial corrective and basic corroboration. Collis was a magistrate in Burma in the late twenties and early thirties. His picture of the official English community has more lights and shades than Orwell's, and his fine record on the bench is a tribute to the

[margin, handwritten] !! use it to agree w/him on Indian police services

theoretical ideals of the system which produced him as well as to his own personal integrity. But in the end, as Orwell didn't fail to note in his review, he was faced with an impossible dilemma, a double commitment to the impartial dispensing of justice and to the maintenance of British political supremacy. As an individual, he was able to hand in his notice; for the community at large there was no way out short of decolonization.

If Orwell himself, from the mid-nineteen-thirties onwards, was occasionally prepared to tone down his criticisms of the Empire, it was because at heart he never seriously doubted that it was far less vicious than the new streamlined tyrannies which were threatening to take its place – and because at least one of these tyrannies was being stridently defended by all too many educated people who claimed to be champions of freedom and social justice. The Indian Imperial Police, whatever the blots on its record, was not exactly in the same class as the Gestapo or the OGPU; nor is it likely that by the end of the last war many Burmese would have agreed that the Japanese security forces, the kempetai, were a preferable alternative. However, for Orwell the moral of all this was not that the Empire should be preserved, but that once former colonies had been given their freedom they should be offered military and economic assistance. There could be no question, as far as imperialism went, of using the greater evil to justify the lesser; and that he felt this no less strongly when the greater evil was Stalinism is spelt out (though it could in any case be readily inferred from his work as a whole) in a letter which he sent to the Duchess of Atholl in November 1945, declining to speak for the League of European Freedom:

... I cannot associate myself with an essentially Conservative body which claims to defend democracy in Europe but has nothing to say about British imperialism. It seems to me that one can only denounce the crimes now being committed in Poland, Jugo-slavia etc. if one is equally insistent on ending Britain's unwanted rule in India.

While the problem of dismantling the Empire remained one of his immediate political concerns, it is true that by the last years of his life it no longer deeply engaged his imagination as a creative writer. He was looking further ahead, and in *Nineteen Eighty-Four* he portrays a world in which an altogether more pervasive and more implacable form of imperialism has triumphed, with no prospect of its being overthrown. The three superpowers endlessly jostle and change partners, although actual warfare only takes place along their fluctuating frontiers: the disputed areas of the globe are tropical Africa, the Middle East, southern India and South-East Asia, which pass from conqueror to conqueror and which are treated as an immense reservoir of what is virtually slave labour.

37

On the other hand it is accepted that the basic territory of the Big Three is sacrosanct, since any invasion 'would violate the principle, followed on all sides though never formulated, of cultural integrity'. Eurasia could easily seize control of the British Isles, Oceania could just as easily overrun Western Europe, but in either case the population, if it were not simply wiped out ('a task of great physical difficulty'), would have to be absorbed into the system – and contact with former enemy citizens who turned out to be sympathetic fellow-creatures was the surest way of sowing subversive ideas and endangering the monolithic unity of the warfare state.

In some respects this is inspired prophecy as well as brilliant satire. According to the book's chronology, for instance, it finally becomes apparent that Eastasia is a superpower in her own right and that the world struggle is essentially three-sided around 1960, the year of the decisive open breach between Moscow and Peking. One element which is notably missing from the picture, however, or at any rate blurred, is the impact of nationalism. There is no indication that 'cultural integrity' might be a force to be reckoned with in the Afro-Asian buffer zone, or for that matter within the superstates themselves: although Britain is now 'Airstrip One', it is never felt to be the American dependency which this implies. (To be logical, shouldn't the reigning philosophy of Ingsoc really be called Amerisoc, or at the most Anglosaxsoc?) No doubt Orwell had to simplify for the sake of artistic effect, but the omissions are also in keeping with a certain general reluctance on his part to think the problems of nationalism through. When he emphasizes the pernicious and often horrifying forces which nationalist movements have unleashed, who can disagree? At the same time, it seems to me that he doesn't allow enough for the extent to which among oppressed peoples nationalism may also be the form which an otherwise unaggressive loyalty to country or culture is compelled to assume. Some of what he assails as nationalism could reasonably be described as other people's patriotism, and he was certainly no outright enemy of patriotic feelings as such. In his 'Notes on Nationalism', indeed, he remarks that half the worst follies of nationalism 'have been made possible by the breakdown of patriotism'. A confident distinction like this comes more easily to an Englishman that it would to someone who had been on the receiving end of imperialism, and here at least, I think, Orwell can legitimately be taxed with being unduly Anglocentric in his outlook. Yet once again, the important point is that he never allowed his imperfect sympathies to interfere with his actual judgment of what the situation demanded. A cool response to nationalism was no argument in favour of imperialism; old injustices had to be set right, whatever the new hazards which independence brought in its wake.

Paris

21 Orwell's Paris:
6 rue du Pot de Fer.

23 Free soup being distributed in Paris.

22 Down and out in Paris.

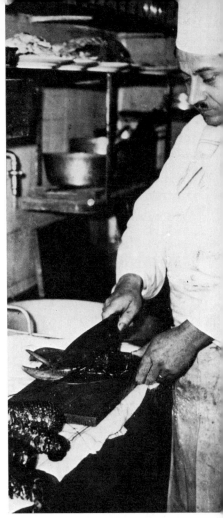

Richard Mayne
A NOTE ON
ORWELL'S PARIS

D

I N the spring of 1928 I went to Paris, to live cheaply while I wrote a couple of novels – I'm sorry to say they were never published – and also to learn French. One of my Paris friends found me a cheap hotel room in the working-class district I describe in the first chapter – any wideawake Parisian will no doubt recognize it. By the summer of 1929 I had written my two novels, but the publishers had rejected them and I was almost penniless and in urgent need of a job. At that time it wasn't illegal – or at any rate not seriously illegal – for foreigners living in France to take jobs, and it seemed more sensible to stay where I was rather than go back to England, where there were then about two and a half million unemployed. So I stayed on in Paris, and the events I describe in the book took place in the late autumn of 1929.

This comes from George Orwell's introduction to *La Vache enragée* ('Roughing It'), the French edition of *Down and Out in Paris and London*. If it sounds a little awkward, this is because it's a retranslation, based on the still lamer version in Orwell's *Collected Essays, Journalism and Letters*: the English original, if any, hasn't survived. But it makes some points that are worth looking at. Orwell's Paris, and his use of it, may shed light on Orwell himself.

First, its matter-of-factness. Since Orwell's death, both his detractors and his defenders have stressed – and to my mind overstressed – his sense of guilt and his *nostalgie de la boue*. Some have seen in him an urge for self-destruction like that ascribed to Ernest Hemingway. Perhaps in both cases it was there towards the end. But even Orwell's decision to settle in the Hebrides was partly a matter of self-preservation; and his move to Paris as a young man was surely both reasonable and fairly typical. As he himself said in his essay on Henry Miller, 'During the boom years, when dollars were plentiful and the exchange-value of the franc was low, Paris was invaded by such a swarm of artists, writers, students, dilettanti, sight-seers, debauchees and plain idlers as the world has probably never seen.' True, Orwell was two years too late for the 1926 bonanza, when the franc dropped to 178 to the pound, then plunged to nearly 250. But when he lived in Paris it was still at 120, and life was far from expensive. Paris even now is a good place to write, if you can afford it; so why look for occult, unadmitted motives? Yet critics continually discount Orwell's practicality. 'He goes to Paris,' wrote Tom Hopkinson in his British Council pamphlet on Orwell, 'ostensibly in order to write books and articles, but no one wants the books and articles of an unknown writer in a foreign country and it is clear his real motive must be different.' What was it? 'To plunge himself into the destructive element he has been brought up to dread: to experience failure in its most painful form; to rub shoulders with mankind at its lowest and dirtiest; to commit an act of public defiance against the money-values of the present-day world, and particularly of those wealthier than himself by whom he had been surrounded at his schools.' Hopkinson went on to add three further motives: identification with the underdog, the relief of no longer struggling to avoid rock-bottom poverty, and the latent desire to record a new experience. All these, it seems to me, become more plausible when applied to Orwell's roughing it in England; but to suggest that he went to Paris looking for squalor and failure is too much. Living 'abroad' is one way of buying time, freedom, and detachment. Twenty-five years after Orwell's stay in Paris, I myself went to Rome 'ostensibly in order to write books and articles'. Being 'an unknown writer in a foreign country', I too ran out of money for a while, and did unexpected jobs; but so have innumerable young men in their twenties, and so they do still.

Secondly, Orwell's phrase 'a working-class district'. In the putative original, this may have been 'a poor district' – which is more accurate, although still a little strong. Orwell's Paris street, called in the book 'the rue du Coq d'Or', was in fact the rue du Pot de Fer in the *5ième arrondissement*, running between the rue Mouffetard and the rue Lhomond, with the gloomy-sounding Monge as its nearest métro station.

'It was a very narrow street', Orwell tells us,

a ravine of tall, leprous houses, lurching towards one another in queer attitudes, as though they had all been frozen in the act of collapse. All the houses were hotels and packed to the tiles with lodgers, mostly Poles, Arabs and Italians. At the foot of the hotels were tiny *bistros*, where you could be drunk for the equivalent of a shilling. On Saturday nights about a third of the male population of the quarter was drunk. There was fighting over women, and the Arab navvies who lived in the cheapest hotels used to conduct mysterious feuds, and fight them out with chairs and occasionally revolvers. At night the policemen would only come through the street two together. It was a fairly rackety place. And yet amid the noise and dirt lived the usual respectable French shop-keepers, bakers and laundresses and the like, keeping themselves to themselves and quietly piling up small fortunes. It was quite a representative Paris slum.

Not, I suspect, by the standards of Belleville, Ivry, or La Villette. Orwell was living in what Hemingway had earlier called 'the best [i.e. most typical] part of the Latin Quarter'; and it's characteristic that most of the people he mentions are North Africans, foreign workers, immigrants or transients – not ordinary French representatives of the industrial proletariat. Again, in England, it was tramps whose life he shared and studied; even in *The Road to Wigan Pier*, he dealt with coalminers rather than factory workers, characteristically seeking the typical in the extreme. A hostile critic might accuse him of 'romanticism'; and there was certainly a touch of the bohemian in his otherwise realistic account of Paris. The rue du Pot de Fer, admittedly, has changed in the last forty years. The whole *5ième arrondissement* has become a haunt of students, driven out of

Saint-Germain-des-Prés by tourists and rising prices. Next door to Orwell's old hotel at No. 6, there's now one of several modest but excellent restaurants, candle-lit and crowded. The hotel has become an office and workshop, with flats and bed-sitters above it; the bistros are fewer, and the old *bals musettes* have gone. Here and there along Orwell's street are a few new shop-fronts, a few square metres of fresh paint. But the small shopkeepers are still small, although their fortunes may be bigger; and the actual buildings are unchanged – not particularly tilted, no more 'leprous' than any of the peeling stucco, tall old-fashioned windows, and dark-grey leaded roofs in the rest of René Clair's Paris. There's a barracks at one end of the street: but not far from the other is – and was – the Ecole Normale Supérieure. Nearby are the Panthéon and the Jardin des Plantes. In the Introduction already quoted, Orwell claimed that he had 'exaggerated nothing except in so far as all writers exaggerate by selecting'. I don't doubt his word in matters of fact: it was, in his day, a pretty tough area. But its appearance is a different matter. In this respect, I imagine, some of the atmosphere that Orwell found in Paris was his own very English reaction to a French norm. 'Hectic shabbiness' was the rather apt malapropism that another writer – Peter Green in *The Expanding Eye* – used to convey his own first impression of Paris. Parts of the city still strike the English or American visitor as both 'leprous' and 'rackety'; but this doesn't make all of them 'representative slums'.

'The events I describe in the book took place in the late autumn of 1929.' By then, Orwell had been in Paris eighteen months. As he says himself, he was not completely alone. Another Englishman, called 'R.' in the book, spent half the year in the same hotel, drinking four litres of wine a day; the other half he spent with his parents in Putney. The editors of the *Collected Essays, Journalism and Letters* point out that Orwell's aunt, Nellie Limouzin, was living in Paris throughout his stay there. In the summer of 1928, although he may not have known it, the Scott Fitzgeralds were only twenty minutes' walk away, at 58 rue Vaugirard opposite the Luxembourg Gardens. A year later, the Hemingways stopped in Paris on their way back from Spain: earlier in the twenties, Hemingway had lived only five hundred yards from Orwell's street; and Jake Barnes, the mutilated narrator of *The Sun Also Rises*, actually walked along it in Chapter 8. Henry Miller, whom Orwell admired for his portrayal of Parisian squalor and for his 'notable effort to get the thinking man down from his chilly perch', didn't arrive until after he had gone back to England: their meeting later, according to Miller's friend Alfred Perlès, was awkward and shy. But Elliot Paul was then still living in his own 'narrow street', the rue de la Huchette, in the same *arrondissement* down by the river near the Place Saint-Michel; and once, at the Deux Magots in 1928, Orwell thought he saw James Joyce. Little of this emerges in *Down and Out in Paris and London*: there, Orwell's life seems quite cut off. And well it may have been, because he was extremely busy. By the summer of 1929, he had written not only his two unpublished novels – now vanished – but also a 'ballade', at least three short stories, and something like a dozen articles, several of which appeared in French. It was hardly the work-load of someone out to 'experience failure': nor, so far as a judgment is now possible, was Orwell's aim primarily political. In later life, he admitted that he might have liked to be an old-fashioned country parson, and in *Coming Up For Air* he produced a hymn to country childhood. Like many politically committed writers, he felt the tug of 'pure' literature of an almost Georgian kind. In Paris, he may well have produced some. His first published writing there, an article on 'La Censure en Angleterre' in Henri Barbusse's paper *Monde*, might be called 'politico-literary'; so might another, on Galsworthy. In *Progrès Civique* he wrote on unemployment, tramps, beggars, and Burma; in *G. K.'s Weekly*, where his work first appeared in English, he attacked a quasi-giveaway newspaper, the right-wing *Ami du Peuple*. But if pieces like these foreshadowed his later writing, the lost 'ballade' and the titles of the equally lost short stories suggest something different – 'The Sea God', 'The Petition Crown', 'The Man in Kid Gloves'. Even *Down and Out in Paris and London* steers clear, for the most part, of mentioning national politics. While Orwell was in Paris, the Maginot Line was started, Poincaré retired, Aristide Briand proposed a Union of Europe, and the world rocked to the Wall Street crash; but although Orwell read and wrote for French newspapers, he stayed close to the world he knew. In the end, he couldn't avoid politics: his sense of common humanity was too strong. It wasn't this alone, however, that gave his political writings their force and vivid-ness – it was also his 'literary' care for language and his 'subjectively' keen alertness to things around him. In this sense, his apprenticeship as a novelist wasn't wasted. And yet, as an ordinary novelist, he remained amateurish: although in all his novels the thrust of his ideas and his personality survived the fabricated characters and 'plots', even *Nineteen Eighty-Four* and *Burmese Days* shared some of the weaknesses of *A Clergyman's Daughter* and *Keep the Aspidis-tra Flying*. Conceivably, Orwell might have continued further along this false trail, trying to be a rather 'Georgian' novelist and nevertheless say something urgent about politics and society, if his Paris experience hadn't forced him to be more direct.

As so often, he found his *métier* by what at the time seemed bad luck. In February 1929, weakened by cold, overwork, and probably underfeeding, he caught pneumonia and was taken to the nearby Hôpital Cochin. He was there for several weeks. He described the ordeal seventeen years later in 'How the Poor Die' – the bureaucratic admission routine, the prison-like indifference, the slatternly nurses, the unspeakable food, the dirt, the vermin, the smell. He left as soon as he could. Then, in the autumn, came a further blow, described in *Down and Out in Paris and London*: he was robbed, he says, of some 200 francs, saved up from writing and from giving English lessons. All he had left was forty-seven francs, or seven and tenpence. It was then, as he wrote, that his experience of real poverty began.

It lasted about ten weeks – little enough by comparison with his eighteen months of modest living at a rent of about thirty-five shillings a month. But intensity can make up for brevity: D. H. Lawrence, after all, wrote *Sea and Sardinia* after only a week on the island. And Orwell's experiences were just as grim as his spell in the Hôpital Cochin: the gripe of real hunger; physical weakness and desperation; the humiliated pretence that nothing was wrong; at length, greasy salvation as a washer-up in a smart hotel and then in a fancy restaurant. When *Down and Out in Paris and London* was published, a certain M. Humbert Possenti, who described himself as 'a *restaurateur* and *hôtelier* of 40 years' experience', wrote to *The Times* to protest on behalf of the French hotel industry. Orwell replied, rather primly, that he had merely reported what had happened in one hotel and one restaurant. The restaurant, presumably, has long since vanished; the hotel may still be in existence. Which they were, however, it's possible only to guess. The hotel was 'near the Place de la Concorde' and also near – or perhaps in? – the rue de Rivoli. 'One of the dozen most expensive hotels in Paris', it was 'a vast, grandiose place with a classical façade, and at one side a little, dark doorway like a rat-hole, which was the service entrance'. Several surviving establishments might fit this bill, but for fear of libel actions Orwell covered his tracks most carefully, and it's best to leave them effaced. At the time, no doubt, his picture of life below stairs was accurate – although, as suggested by the phrase about the rat-hole, it was coloured by his own repugnance.

Until I re-read the book in order to write about it, the image that Orwell's 'Hôtel X' conjured up was always that of the roast chicken dropped by mistake down the lift-shaft. It landed in 'a litter of broken bread, torn paper and so forth at the bottom' – and then was wiped and sent back up again, to be carried in with great ceremony to the waiting guests. Looking out this memorable story, I found that it was only an aside, told in two sentences, and that I'd actually made up the bit about the chicken's being carried in with extra pomp to disguise its misadventure. On reflection, too, the accident seemed less horrifying: similar mishaps often occur at home. Why, then, had the episode stayed so vivid? The reason, I think, is that it's emblematic. It sums up very neatly Orwell's inside knowledge, his relish at revealing behind-the-scenes squalor, his curious and characteristic mixture of contempt for the wealthy guests and outrage on their behalf. The force of the story is our own delighted horror, our own shock; and this is true of a great deal of Orwell's later writing. He was always taking the lid off things – poverty, parlour Socialism, life in a coal mine, prep-school tyranny, the Empire, the Spanish Civil War, the Russian Revolution, the political misuse of language. He might well have echoed W. H. Auden: 'All I have is a voice/To undo the folded lie.' But although of the same generation, he lacked Auden's or Graham Greene's sense of fatality: he was still hopeful enough to be shocked. However 'low' he might sink, an important part of him remained with the hotel guests and reacted as they might, to the swearing and the smell.

It seems fair, then, to see Orwell's Paris experience as his most decisive spell as a kind of 'gentleman ranker' – and it's tempting to suggest that there was therefore something dilettante about his poverty. Certainly, he worked in a service industry rather than in a factory; certainly he got out, at the end, with a £5 loan from a friend in England. Some critics have made much of these facts. But it's worth while noting that the evidence in both cases comes from Orwell's own admission. He wasn't pretending; and I don't think, myself, that he was deliberately playing at poverty. He was what he was – an educated, fastidious man with a strong conscience who set out to write and became poor mainly by accident. Afterwards, in the French Introduction to *Down and Out in Paris and London*, he spoke of Paris as 'a city of which I have very happy memories'. The remark was doubly justified. Paris had not only given him intense private experience; it had also, almost literally, plunged him into the concerns that made his career as a writer. Until then, he had been a potential latter-day Galsworthy, going on East-End 'expeditions' from a room in Notting Hill. Now, he had shared the life that he had looked at. In this sense, although he chose his pen-name three years later, Paris helped to make George Orwell out of Eric Blair.

Dan Jacobson
ORWELL'S SLUMMING

ORWELL himself would have disapproved of the title of this essay. He wrote with nothing but distaste of people who went 'slumming'. His reasons for doing so are hardly mysterious. The word has almost inescapable associations with snobbery, with patronage, with the uncharitable distribution of charity, and, perhaps worst of all, with sensation-seeking, the pleasure that can be derived from seeing at the closest possible quarters the sufferings of others. None of these attitudes or predispositions can fairly be ascribed to Orwell during his periods as a down and out, or when he investigated living conditions among the unemployed in the north of England, or even when he made briefer excursions into the slums with a single objective in mind – for example, his attempt to get himself arrested (described in 'Clink' in Volume One of the *Collected Essays, Journalism and Letters*) or simply 'to see how the Embankment sleepers get on in winter'. The slummer, we feel, is one who makes daytrips into the lower depths, and then hastens back, positively refreshed by what he has seen, into the security and comfort of the middle classes. Orwell, by contrast, lived in those depths; he worked as a *plongeur* in Paris, he tramped the roads around London with his friend Paddy, he worked as a hop-picker, he spent months as a lodger in the houses of unemployed coal-miners.

Yet he was an intellectual, an Etonian, a member of the 'lower-upper-middle classes', a writer. Was he, then, merely 'seeking experience' or 'gathering material' in the slums? And if so, can this not be considered a form of slumming subtly but unmistakably allied to the kind he despised and disliked? Well, there is an obvious distinction to be made here between works like *Down and Out in Paris and London* and *A Clergyman's Daughter* on the one hand, and a directly commissioned book like *The Road to Wigan Pier* on the other. In the latter case Orwell never pretended to the reader or to himself to be anything but a reporter, carrying out a particular job of investigation with the immediate purpose of writing about it subsequently. Oddly enough, this appears to be a relatively unambiguous, direct way of going about things; rightly or wrongly we nowadays accept the reporter's role as an altogether legitimate one. It is, rather, the earlier books, the ones in which Orwell is writing wholly from within the world of the dispossessed and poverty-stricken, or as if from wholly within it, about which we might feel it necessary to press the questions asked above.

If we do so, however, we realize that a degree of ambiguity about how a serious writer 'gathers material' for his work is inherent in the very nature of the craft or art. If we are ready to acquit an author of a charge of role-playing, or even of vampirism, it is never because one manner of coming by potential subject-matter is morally more pure than another, but because of the depth and disinterestedness of his response to his subject, whatever it may be. We know, in

48

fact, that the confrontation between a man and the necessities of his own nature, out of which all first-class work springs, simply cannot be produced *ad hoc*.

In Orwell's case, the long duration of his immersions into poverty and destitution is in itself a sign of how deep were the compulsions he was obeying during those periods of his life. His journeys through the lower depths were indeed natural and necessary to him; they could not be avoided; he owed them to himself for reasons that were stronger than any immediate or more distant ambitions he might have had as a writer, let alone stronger than any concern for his own health and welfare. (And who can say just how much permanent damage was done to his health by those episodes?) His own explanation of his motives is given clearly enough in a well-known passage from *The Road to Wigan Pier*. He had been, he explained, a functionary in what he called an 'evil despotism' – namely, British imperial rule in Burma.

For five years I had been part of an oppressive system, and it had left me with a bad conscience. Innumerable remembered faces . . . haunted me intolerably. I was conscious of an immense weight of guilt that I had got to expiate . . . I had reduced everything to the simple theory that the oppressed are always right and the oppressors are always wrong: a mistaken theory, but a natural result of being one of the oppressors yourself. I felt that I had got to escape not merely from imperialism, but from every form of man's dominion over man. I wanted to submerge myself, to get right down among the oppressed, to be one of them and on their side against the tyrants.

If only it were true for everyone that the 'natural' result of being cast in the role of oppressor is to make one want to identify oneself with the oppressed! Orwell's response to his career in Burma was 'natural' only to himself; and it is no derogation of the honour due to his passionate sense of justice to say that the 'weight of guilt' he had to expiate had deeper roots in his own character and history than his spell in the Imperial Police, and that his readiness to take upon himself all the signs and burdens of the most painful forms of deprivation was beyond any rational explanation he could offer. Indeed, in his memoir of his prep-school days, *Such, Such, Were the Joys*, he makes it clear that an over-whelming sense of his own worthlessness, as one doomed to 'failure, failure, failure', was by far the strongest conviction about himself that he carried from his childhood into his adolescence. 'I had no money, I was weak, I was ugly, I was unpopular, I had a chronic cough, I was cowardly, I smelt . . . The conviction that it was *not possible* for me to be a success went deep enough to influence my actions until far into adult life.' Moreover, it seems hardly fanciful to describe Orwell's years at that expensive, dreadful prep school as his first real experience of slum-life; much of the essay about the school is devoted to descriptions of the physical squalors and discomforts of the school as he vividly recalled them:

At almost every point some filthy detail obtrudes itself. For example, there were the pewter bowls out of which we had our porridge. They had overhanging rims, and under the rims there were accumulations of sour porridge, which could be flaked off in long strips. The porridge itself contained more lumps, hairs, and unexplained black things than one would have thought possible . . . And there was the slimy water of the plunge-bath . . . and the always-damp towels with their cheesy smell; and, on occasional visits in winter, the murky sea-water of the local Baths, which came straight in from the beach and on which I once saw floating a human turd . . . It is not easy for me to think of my schooldays without seeming to breathe in a whiff of something cold and evil-smelling – a sort of compound of sweaty stockings, dirty towels, faecal smells blowing along corridors, forks with old food between the prongs, neck-of-mutton stew, and the banging doors of the lavatories and the echoing chamber-pots in the dormitories.

With very few changes, a passage like the above could be about one of the casual wards in which he was to sleep, or about the hospital in Paris in which he was to see how the poor die; some of the phrases in the passage are actually word-for-word repetitions of those he had used in his early writing to describe more recent experiences.

There was only one way Orwell could confront and overcome his own conviction that he was doomed to be a worthless failure. That was by failing. The ex-policeman, ex-public schoolboy, could disprove the harshest judgments he had ever made against himself, and believed others to have made, only by voluntarily taking it on himself to serve out the harshest sentence society could impose upon those it rejected and condemned. Then, like Edgar in *King Lear* (another member of the upper class, it is worth recalling, who is suddenly transformed into a verminous beggar and bedlamite) he could say, 'The lowest and most dejected thing of Fortune . . . lives not in fear.' Down and out, he had become a free man.

Hence the fact that in some respects Orwell's chronicles of destitution are his gayest books. In saying this, I do not wish to be misunderstood: the conditions of life which are presented in these chronicles are appalling, and Orwell does not want his readers to be able to blink at any of the facts he is describing. There is nothing sentimental, nothing wishful, nothing romantic in his approach to poverty, either as a general condition or in the detail in which it is embodied. Furthermore, his intention in all these works, in a novel like *A Clergyman's Daughter* almost as much as in a work of reportage like *The Road to Wigan Pier*, is a reformatory one; the books are written with an openly avowed political purpose; and this in itself would have restrained any tendency to glamorize or soften the people and events depicted. But the ugliness, the filth, the bedbugs, the smells, the physical hardships and the tiny physical consolations of life in the slums – all these become, in the very fullness with which they are presented to us, occasions for a most paradoxical display of zest, of high spirits, of an affectionate appreciation of eccentricity, of an unabated interest in how people actually live and see their lives.

The point is worth stressing, and not only in the perhaps unexpected context of the kind of work under discussion here. Orwell's pessimism, which was both political and beyond politics – his dread of a totalitarian future for us all, and his belief that even under the best of circumstances 'on balance life is suffering, and only the very young or the very foolish believe otherwise' – this pessimism of his has tended to overshadow in the minds of most readers how keen his appetite for life was, how vigorous his delight even in aspects of it that other people, other intellectuals not least, would find intolerably degrading, or at best would regard with a blank, undifferentiated distaste. It is precisely for this reason that he remains the best critic of popular English culture we have yet had; why so much of the day-to-day journalism he wrote for his column in *Tribune* is still so engaging and refreshing today; why young readers respond so immediately to much of his work. And it is this, too, I believe, which gives the works I have mentioned, as well as the related essays and journals, much of their vitality and relevance today.

Two bad days followed. We had only sixty centimes left, and we spent it on half a pound of bread, with a piece of garlic to rub it with. The point of rubbing garlic on bread is that the taste lingers and gives one the illusion of having fed recently. We sat most of that day in the Jardin des Plantes. Boris had shots with stones at the tame pigeons, but always missed them, and after that we wrote dinner menus on the backs of envelopes. *(Down and Out in Paris and London)*

Deafie was a queer old man, and a poor companion after Nobby, but not a bad sort. He was a ship's steward by profession, but a tramp of many year's standing, and as deaf as a post . . . He was also an exhibitionist, but quite harmless. For hours together he used to sing a little song that went 'With my willy willy – *with* my willy willy', and though he could not hear what he was singing it seemed to cause him some kind of pleasure. He had the hairiest ears Dorothy had ever seen. *(A Clergyman's Daughter)*

Beggars do not work, it is said; but then, what is *work*? A navvy works by swinging a pick. An accountant works by adding up figures, A beggar works by standing out of doors in all weathers and getting varicose veins, bronchitis etc. It is a trade like any other; quite useless, of course – but then, many reputable trades are quite useless. And as a social type a beggar compares well with scores of others. He is honest compared with the sellers of most patent medicines, high-minded compared with a Sunday news-paper proprietor, amiable compared with a hire-purchase tout.

(Down and Out in Paris and London)

In their qualities of compassion and mettlesomeness, passages like these, chosen pretty much at random, are perfectly continuous with the more eloquent denunciations of the human waste, exploitation, and callousness he encountered in his wanderings. They are continuous with this passage, for example, which I know has often been quoted before, but which deserves repetition:

At the back of one of the houses a young woman was kneeling on the stones, poking a stick up the leaden waste-pipe which ran from the sink inside and which I suppose was blocked. I had time to see everything about her – her sacking apron, her clumsy clogs, her arms reddened by the cold. She looked up as the train passed, and I was almost near enough to catch her eye. She had a round, pale face . . . and it wore, for the second in which I saw it, the most desolate, hopeless expression I have ever seen . . . For what I saw in her face was not the ignorant suffering of an animal. She knew well enough what was happening to her – understood as well as I did how dreadful a destiny it was to be kneeling there in the bitter cold, on the slimy stones of a slum backyard, poking a stick up a foul drainpipe. *(The Road to Wigan Pier)*

Social conditions have of course changed greatly since Orwell wrote. The changes that have taken place affect most obviously certain parts of *The Road to Wigan Pier*; I would say that some of his large-scale assertions about the nature of class-prejudice in England have little more life in them today than the tables of statistics in the book. But what is surprising is how little, not how much, of the work which sprung from his experiences in the slums has dated. They present us with the vivid picture of a man, and of the life he shared with other men: as such they can hardly be outmoded. And it is legitimate that they should also retain for us the special interest of representing the opening phase of what was to become one of the exemplary careers in the history of twentieth-century literature.

In this connection, there is a most curious couple of sentences in an article, written late in Orwell's life, about Winwood Reade's rationalist, anti-religious history of mankind, *The Martyrdom of Man*: an article which may appear remote enough from the present subject, but which Orwell himself brings into startling relevance. Praising Reade's ironic rationalism, his puncturing of religious pretension, Orwell chooses as an example of the kind of deflating assertion he greatly admired when he first came across it, the following description of the typical Hebrew prophet: 'As soon as he received his mission, he ceased to wash.' Yes, one feels, that is quite a funny aphorism, a genuinely cutting remark. But one's pleasure in it must turn, on reflection, into a wonder at the guile of the subconscious mind: Orwell's mind, that is. Why did this particular sarcasm make such an impression on him? Why did he recall it with so much relish after so many years?

Ian Hamilton
ALONG THE ROAD
TO WIGAN PIER

IN 1935, few of George Orwell's friends, even those closest to him, would have found it easy to predict the future course of his career. Eton, Burma, the down-and-out experiences: these he had written about and seemed to be done with, both in art and life. The book he was completing, *Keep the Aspidistra Flying*, was based fairly directly, it appeared, on his current situation as impoverished bookseller and spare-time author and reviewer. It was, moreover, a rancorous, almost whining, testament; an unloading of deep feelings of failure and exclusion.

Orwell had decided, in that clear-cut, totalistic way in which he usually decided things, that he was going to be a writer. There was no problem about his powers of industry – he worked extraordinarily long hours – but there was some doubt about his talent. His first books had been greeted respectfully, though with more praise for their interesting factuality than for any imaginative distinction, and his reviews, whilst they were always common-sensical and lucidly composed, did not augur great critical originality. Even the loyal Richard Rees, about to be rather cruelly caricatured in *Keep the Aspidistra Flying*, could not predict much 'creative' success for his intelligent protégé.

If the prospect of Orwell becoming primarily a political writer had been considered at the time, it too would probably have been viewed with some scepticism. Through his association with the *Adelphi*, Orwell had dealings with middle-class Socialists and he had surely measured their goals and behaviour against his own first-hand experience of the lives of tramps and destitutes. Just as his own middle-class origins and education made it impossible for him actually to become a tramp, so the fact that he had, though briefly, pretended to become one made it impossible for him to talk about the poor with mere abstract goodwill. Of his down-and-out days, Orwell wrote: 'At that time, failure seemed to me the only virtue. Every suspicion of self-advancement, even to "succeed" in life to the extent of making a few hundreds a year, seemed to me spiritually ugly, a species of bullying.' (*The Road to Wigan Pier*.) Although, as an energetic writer wishing to rid himself of the distractions of poverty, Orwell was now in pursuit of at any rate a measure of success, he still felt a long way from achieving it; the notion of burying a still relished sense of aggrieved isolation in some forward-looking group activity would have been thoroughly abhorrent to him. To other, more purposeful leftists, there must have seemed a fair chance that Orwell's identification with the shunned, the victimized, would turn into something sour and negative.

And so it might have done. Like many who steer clear of groups, Orwell persistently thought in terms of groups, of castes and types, and in 1935 he was nurturing quite a few ominously ripe prejudices: against Roman Catholics,

London

27 Singing hymns in a Salvation Army hostel.

28 (*Left*) Down
and out in
London.
29 (*Below left*)
Living conditions
in Limehouse.

30 (*Above right*)
Hop-picking in
Kent.
31 (*Right*) The
other half lives it
up.

The north

32 (*Opposite left*) Orwell on Southwold beach, 1934.
33 (*Opposite right*) Eileen Blair whom Orwell married in 1936.
34 (*Opposite below*) The house at Southwold where Orwell's parents lived.

35 (*Below*) Miner and his wife.   36 (*Overleaf*) Lancashire industrial landscape.

Scotsmen (or 'Scotchmen', as he enjoyed calling them), homosexuals, vegetarians. Summer-schooling Socialist intellectuals were relatively recent additions to the list, but well on the way – the more he saw of them – to becoming his favourite targets of ill-will. And yet, through Rees's patronage, Orwell was probably closer to this group than to any other literary formation. Had he stuck with them for very much longer, the bile simmering in secret, it is just possible that he would eventually have become completely alienated, not just from Socialists, but from Socialism.

Late in 1935, Victor Gollancz offered Orwell £500 to undertake an investigation of working-class conditions in the industrial north, and to write up his findings for the Left Book Club. The offer could not have come at a better time, and – for Orwell's particular situation – could hardly have been a better *kind* of offer. The money, a really sizeable payment for those days, would enable him to give up his crushing bookshop job, marry Eileen O'Shaughnessy, and rent the village store at Wallingford. The book itself, when it came out, would almost certainly bring him more fame than any of his earlier books had managed to; Left Book Club choices were distributed to forty thousand readers. But even more importantly, the commission would allow him to enrich, give political substance to, those beliefs and sympathies which he was finding it so hard to find a public role for. Feeling already that he knew more about real poverty than most so-called Socialists would ever know, he would yet have been obliged to acknowledge that his experience to date had brought him in touch mainly with the eccentric poor and hardly at all with the true working-class predicament. If nothing else, he would find out from his northern excursion just how much of a Socialist he was. He would also learn how to focus, with authority, his distate for those whose Socialism was never subject to such doubts.

Orwell's sojourn in the north is often spoken of as if it were a heroic act of self-sacrifice; as if, even, Orwell's suffering were as significant as the suffering he went to study. It is worth remembering that the whole trip lasted slightly less than two months, and that for a fair part of it he stayed in relatively comfortable (what he would call 'clean and decent') lodgings. It is also worth noting that he did not go there in working man's disguise. Richard Rees provided him with letters of introduction to various Independent Labour Party contacts, and he was not at any time left to fend for himself. These points should be kept in mind, not to disparage Orwell but merely to stress the distinction between his *Wigan Pier* project and the self-abasing escapades of his down-and-out-days. In Wigan, Orwell's exposures of himself to the squalid and uncomfortable were strictly utilitarian and at their worst they were as brief as he could make them.

37 (*Above*) Pit disaster in the 1930s.
38 (*Below*) In a coalmine near Wigan.

Orwell left for the north of England on 31 January 1935. He went via the Midlands, passing through Coventry, Birmingham and Wolverhampton, making overnight stops in or near each of these towns. He notes in his diary the 'vistas of mean little houses' and (an apt simile for one so fresh from the metropolis) 'the potbanks like monstrous burgundy bottles', but made no real attempt to begin his investigations there; it was as if he needed a fairly gradual acclimatization before getting down to it. There is a suggestion of this too in the proudly listed 'miles walked' and the register of minimal expenses. In the five days it took Orwell to reach Manchester, he spent just over £1 (he slept in youth hostels) and walked forty-four miles.

In Manchester, he stayed with the first of Rees's recommended contacts, Frank Meade, the treasurer of a local ILP fund. (Orwell notes of Meade that he displays the middle-class accretions typical of working-class escapees; noting such accretions in the few politically self-conscious workers that he met up north was to become one of Orwell's more troublesome reflexes.) Meade directed him to Wigan and by 11 February Orwell was installed in the first of his *bona fide* workmen's digs. These lodgings were found for him by Joe Kennan, an electrician at the local pit:

> There was a knock at the door on Saturday afternoon. We were just having tea. I opened the door and there was this tall fellow with a pair of flannel bags on, a fawn jacket and a mac. And he told me he had two letters, one from Middleton Murry, wanted me to find him lodgings of a lower class type, practically of a slum character. ('The Road to the Left', T.V. Script, 1970)

Such accommodation was easily got hold of, and that same day Orwell found himself sharing a room with an unemployed railwayman, digging (though somewhat disgustedly; for all his anti-vegetarianism, he was to be generally appalled by the 'astonishing ignorance about and wastefulness of food among the working-class people here') into a monstrous plate of stewed beef, dumplings and potatoes, and washing at the scullery sink. Within twenty-four hours, he was able to record in his diary a detailed analysis not just of the appearance and character of his landlord's family, but also of their entire income and expenditure. He had also found time to take a look round Wigan and to attend a political meeting.

The speed with which Orwell set to work is significant, because it suggests an answer to those who have found something bogus and unpleasant in the notion of this old Etonian insinuating himself into the lives of the impoverished (and it suggests an answer too to those who believe that Orwell was enjoying himself): there was clearly no pretence about what he was there for, and he rightly saw that the best approach was to be as brisk and business-like as possible.

He had been introduced to the lodgings by a member of the Union of Unemployed Workers who had evidently thought them to be usefully typical, and
his landlord (himself an unemployed miner) certainly knew, when he took
Orwell in, that he, his home and family were going to be used as 'samples'.
Orwell himself recognized, and indeed was to build the whole argument of his
book around this recognition, that it would be futile to attempt any 'true intimacy' with these people he was visiting: 'However much you like them, however interesting you find their conversation, there is always that accursed itch of
class difference, like the pea under the princess's mattress.' He had come to
Wigan as, at best, a sympathetic middle-class investigator and the last way
to get results was to pretend that he was otherwise. One of *The Road to
Wigan Pier*'s less obvious touches of authenticity is to be found in Orwell's easy,
unguilty use of posh-pejoratives like 'dreadful', 'frightful', 'fearful', 'monstrous',
'unspeakable', 'beastly' and so on. He knew that, whatever else the working
man might be fooled by, he was not going to fall for a scrupulously dropped
aitch.

After four days, Orwell was obliged to move to new lodgings in Wigan. His
landlady had been ill since his arrival and she was now going into hospital. It is
not unlikely that the family was relieved to see the investigator leave. However
open he had been about his motives, there must have been something unnerving
about Orwell's busy scrutiny – even when washing himself in the scullery, he
had been compiling a meticulous inventory of the available provisions: 'A piece
of bacon about 5 pounds. About two pounds of shin beef. About a pound and a
half of liver (all of these uncooked). The wreck of a monstrous meat pie . . .
etc. etc.'

Orwell's new home was the one made famous by his book: the room above
the tripe shop. These were by far the most squalid lodgings he had to endure
during his stay up north: the house itself was over-crowded, filthy, the food was
meagre and repugnant, the landlord and his wife were crooked and disgusting.
In no sense could these lodgings be said to be characteristic of the town. The
landlord was an ex-miner, but was now enjoying full employment selling ageing
tripe to the out-of-work and letting insanitary accommodation to commercial
travellers and to pensioners forced from their families' homes by the Means Test.
Orwell loathed both landlord and landlady, and was pretty much repelled by
his co-lodgers (though he took the chance to cull useful northern data from the
commercial travellers), and he was well aware that the whole set-up was viewed
by the locals with at least something of his own distaste. And yet, in *The Road to
Wigan Pier*, he gives more prominence, more detailed description, to this
establishment than to any other single place he stayed in. The landlord's black

thumb-print on the bread, the blue-bottles in the shop window, the chamber-pot in the kitchen, the landlady's vile habit of surrounding her bed with soggy, screwed up tissues: these rank among the book's most memorable images; but distortingly, as Orwell must have known. The distortion, one suspects, arose less from polemical cunning than from a novelist's susceptibility to the spectacular, but even so it is worrying; particularly when one finds, in the argumentative second section of the book, Orwell using the chamber-pot episode as if it *were* typical.

Needless to say, Orwell did not last long at the tripe shop (about two weeks altogether) but it was during his stay there that he made his all-important first visit to a coal-mine. Orwell's own description of what he saw and felt there is well-known, and is the most impressive long stretch of writing in the book. It is therefore worth recording here an account of the same visit by Joe Kennan:

We hadn't gone more than 300 yards when Orwell just didn't duck his head quick enough. It knocked his helmet off and knocked him down. He was flat out. When we revived him, got him round, we travelled further in and the further in we travelled the lower the roof and I would think he travelled the best part of ¾ mile bent absolutely double. When we got there, he was absolutely exhausted. And I remember him lying on the coal on the floor and I said to him, 'It's a so-and-so good job they don't know what you're down here for, to write a book about mining, otherwise the whole roof would come down on top of you.' ('The Road to the Left', T.V. Script, 1970).

Such details give an extra edge to Orwell's heartfelt assertion that 'By no amount of effort or training could I become a coal-miner. The work would kill me in a few weeks.' Having met the unemployed and seen the misery in which they were living, Orwell was now brought face to face with the misery (or, to him, the almost superhuman difficulty) of their jobs; and yet all they wanted was their jobs.

The experience had a lasting emotional effect on Orwell; its physical effects were temporary, but severe. Kennan has recorded that after going down the mine, Orwell disappeared for three days and when he eventually reappeared 'he said he'd stayed in bed the whole of the time'. This was not in fact the case, though perhaps it should have been. The day after his subterranean ordeal, Orwell took a train to Liverpool (it was now 25 February) and visited another contact, Mary Deiner. Mrs Deiner has recalled that Orwell appeared on her doorstep in a state of collapse and had to be put to bed more or less immediately. He refused to allow a doctor to be called and, although he must still have been very shaky, was the next day touring Liverpool in the company of George Garrett (a dock-labourer who, unknown to Orwell, had contributed to the *Adelphi* under the pseudonym Matt Lowe), inspecting the docks, and admiring the new blocks of corporation flats. Garrett, it should be noted, was one of the very few working-class activists for whom Orwell had a good word, and the only one he accepted as an intellectual equal. At a political meeting, for example, it would be 'the same sheeplike crowd – gaping girls and shapeless middle-aged women dozing over their knitting' that would attract Orwell's attention; he rarely took anything that was *said* seriously. And, although he spent most of his time in the north in the company of politically active workers there is remarkably little mention of their ideas or beliefs. Again, it is worth inserting a quotation from Joe Kennan:

> Several of the boys really on the Left very much doubted Orwell's sincerity. Because he was very cynical and he certainly never expressed any thanks for anything that was done for him. For instance he had one full meal, he had several snacks on other occasions. But he never showed any appreciation of hospitality, or anything like that. He was kind of up in the air and a snob in some ways, and was trying to come down to earth and find what things was really like. ('The Road to the Left', T.V. Script, 1970.)

Kennan, over thirty years after Orwell's visit, was still hurt that he had never been sent a copy of *Wigan Pier*: 'I thought, well what a peculiar type. Wasn't the money I was thinking about or anything like that. But I'm not surprised at anything he did.'

From Liverpool, Orwell returned to Wigan for a couple of days and then moved on to Sheffield, where he stayed until 5 March – finding the city 'one of the most appalling places I have ever seen' – and from there he travelled to Leeds, where he visited his sister Marjorie and her husband, Humphrey Dakin. Orwell makes no mention of the state of his health during these last few days, though he does complain of having a 'long and exhausting' day being shown round Sheffield by a jargonizing ILP man, but it seems likely that he was still feeling the effects of Wigan, and that the visit to the Dakins was partly recuperative. At any rate, it was not until 13 March that he moved on to Barnsley, and he evidently enjoyed the 'elbow room' of the Dakins' middle-class menage. He also spent some time in his brother-in-law's country cottage – though this was not the bracing rural intervention that he was perhaps hoping for: 'the smoky look peculiar to this part of the country seems to hang about everything' – and visited the Brontë Museum at Haworth Parsonage.

It was now over a fortnight since Orwell had been down the mine, and he was probably keen to get back to work. As in Wigan, it is only twenty-four hours after his arrival in Barnsley that he records in his diary an analysis of his new landlord's living conditions and financial situation. The house itself, like the one he had stayed in at Sheffield, was clean and comfortable ('my room the best I have had in lodgings up here. Flannelette sheets this time') but the weather was brutally cold, and a clear note of despondency and weariness appears in Orwell's diary entry for 14 March:

> I . . . do not think I shall pick up much of interest in Barnsley. I know no one here except Wilde, who is thoroughly vague. Cannot discover whether there is a branch of the NUWM here. The public library is no good. There is no proper reference library and it seems no separate directory of Barnsley.

One sees here the extent to which Orwell was dependent, throughout his northern tour, on local assistance. In Barnsley, Orwell had taken strongly against his guide, an official of the South Yorkshire branch of the Working Men's Club and Institute Union, and disliked the idea of working with him; nonetheless, it does not occur to Orwell (or if it does, he dismisses the idea) to go it alone. As it turned out, Barnsley proved more fruitful than he anticipated; he went with Wilde to a meeting of the Club and Institute Union and also to a 'sort of smoking concert' at the Radical and Liberal Club. Noting that Wilde's accent 'becomes much broader when he is in these surroundings', Orwell was also disdainful of the clubs he represented (though this disdain appears only in the diary and not in *Wigan Pier* itself where he speaks with respect of the working men's clubs) finding in most of their – usually relatively well off – members a sinister lack of political awareness: 'One can foresee the germs of a danger that they will be politically mobilized for anti-Socialist purposes.' Which is to say that Orwell found them more depressing than the purposeful Socialist workers he had come across.

On the following night, Orwell attended a Mosley meeting and – though he noted the bullying tactics of the Fascist flunkies – was more depressed by the audience's apparent sympathy with Mosley: 'After the preliminary booing the (mainly) working-class audience was easily bamboozled by M speaking from as it were a Socialist angle.' On the other hand, though Orwell himself does not record the argument in his diary, it has been claimed that he disapproved of those few workers who *did* heckle Mosley. Tom Degnan, a Communist worker who was ejected from the meeting has described a dispute he had with Orwell; according to Degnan, Orwell's attitude was: 'O it was no danger and you ought to be British, fair play and all that kind of thing. He didn't understand what Mosley was doing at the time.' Against this, though, should be set the fact that Orwell took pains to contact a worker who had been beaten up by Mosley's men so that he could inspect his bruises and write an authoritatively angry letter to the papers. The truth of the matter would seem to be that Orwell was repelled by the violence and thought it pointless to invite it; a tenable position, though again one might have wished for Orwell to have taken a less sceptical view of working-class political activity.

Orwell's remaining days in Barnsley were spent more or less on the Wigan pattern; he teamed up with an unemployed miner called Ellis Firth (Firth has described Orwell as 'a lad after me own heart' and clearly welcomed his arrival as a relief from the boredom of unemployment) and went with him on a tour of slum houses. At each house, Firth recalls, Orwell briskly produced his tape measure and his questionnaire: 'He reminded me of a detective, trying to find the missing link.' Firth also took him to the local pits, but Orwell's incursions this time were more cautious than in Wigan.

On 23 March, two days before he was due to leave the north for good, Orwell went with Firth to visit a particularly notorious row of slum houses. In his diary, Orwell writes:

In the row called Spring Gardens we found public indignation because the landlords have served about half the row with notices to quit for arrears of, in some cases, only a few shillings . . . The people took us in and insisted on our seeing their houses. Frightful interiors. In the first one old father, out of work of course, obviously horribly bewildered by his notice to quite after 22 years and turning anxiously go F and me with some idea that we could help him. The mother rather more self-possessed. Two sons aged about 24, fine big men with powerful, well-shaped bodies, narrow faces and red hair, but thin and listless from obvious under-nourishment and with dull brutalized expressions. Their sister, a little older and very like them, with prematurely lined face, glancing from F to me, again with some idea that we might help.

In this passage, one sees the merits of *Wigan Pier* itself; the accurate, concise observation, the compassionate refusal either to inflate or aestheticize the ugly facts. But there is also that 'idea that we could help' which he attributes to both father and daughter. Orwell had one more day to serve up north. He was going back to marriage, probable fame and an invigorated sense of political purpose. Without being censorious, is it possible to wonder if here was one instance in which (without ensuing complications) he might in fact have 'helped'? He does not seem even to have thought of doing so. As usefully as anything in *Wigan Pier* itself, this diary entry demonstrates the extent to which Orwell's impartiality took strength from his impersonality. It neatly reminds us that one of the reasons why we tend to believe what Orwell tells us is that he never tried to persuade us (or Victor Gollancz, or the summer schools) to befriend him. He does not seem even to have thought of doing so.

Raymond Carr
ORWELL AND
THE SPANISH CIVIL WAR

THE Spanish Civil War produced a spate of bad literature. *Homage to Catalonia* is one of the few exceptions and the reason is simple. Orwell was determined to set down the truth as he saw it. This was something that many writers of the Left in 1936-9 could not bring themselves to do.

Orwell comes back time and time again in his writings on Spain to those political conditions in the late thirties which fostered intellectual dishonesty: the subservience of the intellectuals of the European Left to the Communist 'line', especially in the case of the Popular Front in Spain where, in his view, the party line could not conceivably be supported by an honest man.

To the Comintern, Popular Fronts were instruments of Soviet diplomacy, the means by which France and Britain might be aligned against Germany in a common defence of 'democracy' against Fascism. Hence they must run from bourgeois democrats through Socialists to Communists. As we now know, it was the Communist aim to 'manipulate' the fronts in the diplomatic interests of the Soviet Union – a pardonable strategy – and to hunt out as heretics all who sought to resist such manipulation.

This manipulation was first evident in Spain. The Popular Front parties had won a majority in the election of February 1936 and it was against the Republican, non-Socialist Government it supported, harassed by extremists of the Right and Left, that the army conspirators rose in the name of order in July 1936. Since the workers' organizations had played an important part in defeating the military rising, above all in Madrid and Barcelona, the Socialists and the Communists and the anarcho-syndicalist CNT entered the Government (September-November 1936) and remained the real force of the Republic at war.

It was the policy of the Communists and the purpose of Comintern propaganda to present the Republican Government as a bourgeois democratic concern. A 'Red Spain' supported by the Soviet Union would merely scare away France and Great Britain from a common anti-Fascist policy. Now, the workers' organizations, particularly in Catalonia, had brought off a spontaneous social revolution: factories and farms had been 'collectivized' i.e. brought under various forms of workers' control. Communist policy therefore demanded that this revolution be damped down, if not reversed.

This reaction could be presented as a demand for an efficient war effort, as an essential process if non-workers were to be kept loyal to the Republic, and as the condition for the supply of arms to a weapon-starved Republic by the respectable bourgeois West. However there were elements in the Republic, especially the militants of the CNT and the POUM (a revolutionary Marxist but *not* Trotskyite party) which were uneasy at the destruction of the workers' revolution implicit in the Communist presentation of the Popular Front as a bourgeois democratic government. Using their relatively undimmed prestige and the leverage given through the supply of arms by the Soviet Union, the Communists set out to destroy all those who 'opposed' the orthodox Popular Front line. Most of the European Left supported them uncritically.

Once Orwell had seen the Communists at work on their political enemies in Spain with the suppression of the POUM during the summer of 1937 and once he had sensed the failure of the pro-Communist Left to protest against this political persecution, he could not suppress a disillusionment that amounted to nausea.

Literary subservience, in the late thirties, was either direct or indirect, the latter depending on the peculiar and temporary alignment of the literary establishment. Koestler has described the results of direct subservience of a Communist writer to the Communist line: the telling of blatant lies for propaganda purposes. 'The Red militia issue vouchers to the value of one peseta. Each voucher is good for one rape. The widow of a high official was found dead in her flat. By her bedside lay sixty-four of these vouchers.' 'That, Arturo, is propaganda.'*

More sickening to Orwell and Victor Serge was the way that the non-Communist Left abandoned truth in the same fashion as the Communists. Party members at least had a theory to cover their torturing of the truth – that truth itself was class conditioned and objective truth a bourgeois virtue to be superseded by historically correct proletarian truth – and a psychological need for the emotional supports of Party life at whatever the cost.

Orwell, I think, is unfair and unbalanced in his insistence that the flight of the left intellectuals from truth was conditioned by the attractions of power, i.e. the Soviet Union. He underestimates the almost hypnotic qualities of the Popular Front. It was no doubt morally reprehensible and profoundly mistaken to swallow the Communist version of the Spanish War entailing, as it did, the deliberate destruction of convinced anti-Fascists whose views were inconvenient to Stalin. But it was easy. Only in Spain was Fascism being resisted and only the Soviet Union was supplying that resistance, for whatever purposes of its own, with arms. To criticize the role of the Communists in the Popular Front was to weaken it and thus help the victory of Fascism. Thus it was, to use the language of the dialectic, 'objectively' Fascist. The mystique of the Popular Front was tremendous – one can sense it even in the writing of the Soviet journalist Koltsov.† Many Communist intellectuals – Koestler, Regler and

---

* The propagandist was Willi Münzenberg. The episode is described in Arthur Koestler's *The Invisible Writing* (London, 1954) p. 334.

† See A. Garosci *Gli intellettuali e la guerra di Spagna* (1959) p. 282 ff.

Münzenberg among them – who knew more about the purposes of Stalin than did their left-wing allies, were on the point of leaving the Party. The prospect of a victory over Fascism in Spain brought them back for a short second honeymoon. Stalin was a lesser evil than Hitler. To Communists in doubt and to the Left in general – even after the Moscow Trials – this was the fundamental political equation of the late thirties.

Only a few strong souls, Victor Serge and Orwell among them, could summon up the courage to fight the whole tone of the literary establishment and the influence of Communists within it. They were therefore boycotted. Orwell's articles on Spain were refused by the *New Statesman*; Victor Serge's account of the murder by the GPU of Ignacio Reiss was banned by the Paris press. It was this refusal of the left-wing literary establishment to face up to unpalatable truths, to defend human dignity and decency, that nauseated Orwell and Serge. Koestler quoted to an audience of Communist sympathizers Thomas Mann's phrase, 'In the long run a harmful truth is better than a useful lie'. The non-Communists applauded; the Communists and their sympathizers remained icily silent.

It is almost as if Orwell fought in the Civil War by accident. He arrived in Barcelona when the 'spontaneous revolution' which had defeated the generals' rising of July in the streets was still a reality. The anarchist-syndicalist CNT, the revolutionary Marxist POUM were still resisting the Communist social and political 'counter-revolution'. In December 1936 Barcelona was 'a town where the working class were in the saddle'. There was no tipping – this impressed Orwell deeply; no 'well-dressed people' in the streets. The workers' militia, the collectivized factories and workers' control still functioned. After class-ridden England the impression was overwhelming. Coming to write newspaper articles, he joined the militia 'because at that time and in that atmosphere it seemed the only conceivable thing to do . . . there was much in it that I did not understand, in some ways I did not like it, but I recognized it *immediately* as a state of affairs worth fighting for'.

It is precisely the immediacy of his reaction that gives the early sections of *Homage* its value for the historian. Kaminski, Borkenau, Koestler came with a fixed framework, the ready-made contacts of journalist intellectuals. Orwell came with his eyes alone; his descriptions of militia life from the inside are not merely unforgettable, they are historically invaluable. Yet how reliable *were* those eyes on that treacherous frontier where direct observation borders on political analysis?

That he joined the POUM militia was likewise an accident; he happened to be sponsored by the ILP. Yet his whole account of the Civil War, as he himself recognized (for no one had a stronger sense of the subjective element in the writing of history) would have differed had he joined another group. Take for instance his defence of the militia system and 'revolutionary discipline', both articles of faith in POUM battalions.

Individual courage is useless in war which demands organized courage, and it is one of the saddest spectacles in history to see spontaneity worn down and defeated by discipline. Orwell saw the idiocies of militia training and amateur soldiering; but he could not believe generals – the dolts of 1914–18 – really knew anything special about winning wars. Nor could he believe that the organized Popular Army, built up in accordance with Communist advice, was any better than the militia it displaced. This was false. It is true, as he asserts, that the militia held (inactive) lines while the Popular Army with its officers, salutes, differential rates of pay, smart uniforms – all the things Orwell hated – was built up. But only the Popular Army could have fought actions like Teruel or the Ebro. His own solution – a reorganized efficient militia under the direct control of the trades unions – would have perpetuated those very military vices which the Popular Army to some extent cured: inability to deploy troops according to military necessity, failure to make the best use of scarce resources. Distribution of his combat forces in accordance with logistical necessity was the supreme advantage of Franco; and the dominance of political criteria and the pull of local issues the fatal weakness of Republican strategy.

Consider Orwell's verdict on the Anarchist militia – 'notoriously the best fighters among the purely Spanish forces'. The word 'notoriously' is interesting; it gives to an emotional judgment the status of an obvious truth.

Orwell's admiration for the militia derives, not from the military value of revolutionary discipline but from his own dislike of privilege. In the militia there was no saluting, no uniforms with badges of rank, no higher pay for officers, 'no bootlicking'; the militias 'were a sort of microcosm of a classless society . . . where hope·was more normal than apathy or cynicism . . . where political consciousness and disbelief in capitalism were more normal than their opposites'. Dislike though he did the physical hardships of dull trench warfare, his time in the militia on the Aragon Front (January–May 1937) was therefore 'of great importance to me'. Here was an egalitarian society 'unthinkable in the money-tainted air of England'. 'The effect was to make my desire to see Socialism established much more actual than it had been before.' He had seen it work in human terms. 'At last I really believe in Socialism which I never did before'. (Letter to Cyril Connolly, 8 June 1937)

When Orwell arrived back in Barcelona from the Aragon Front the face of the city had changed. The Communists and their Catalan Republican allies were pushing the spontaneous revolution out of sight. Expensive restaurants, tipping, smart clothes had returned; the black market flourished, shopwalkers cringed. The spontaneous revolution was revealed as a mixture of hope and camouflage.

Whereas seasoned anti-Stalinists like Victor Serge knew how the Communists would act, Orwell was surprised. It took him some time to grasp the political changes that underlay this social counter-revolution. He confessed that the 'political side of the war had bored him'. Characteristically he reacted against the views he heard around him: the POUM insistence on the maintenance of the revolutionary conquests of July (the militia and collectivization) as a pre-condition for victory against Franco. Hence he tended to sympathize with Communists' criticism of the CNT and the POUM and their pleas for getting on with the war and letting the revolution take second place to organizing for victory over Fascism.

Once street fighting had broken out on 3 May 1937, between the Catalan Government, dominated by the Communist line, and the POUM together with their supporters in the CNT, Orwell was forced to analyse the struggle of the factions. Part of the Communist case, though misguided in his view, was respectable; it could be argued the indiscipline of the militia and the chaos of industry under workers' control was too high a price to pay in wartime for socialism.

What he could not tolerate was the 'dull blind spite' of the Communist vendetta against the POUM; their determination to put the workers' revolution into reverse as a price for continued arms supplies from the Soviet Union, supplies that they could threaten to turn on or off as it suited their political convenience. He did not recognize – and most subsequent historians have followed him – any validity in the Communist case. The POUM appear as political innocents first mangled by dull terrorists and bureaucrats and then slandered by a controlled press.

There was, however, an arguable case. The Communists believed that the Popular Front was the *only* way to provide a political basis for fighting the war: the bourgeoisie must be kept on the side of the Republic at the cost of post-poning, indeed of crushing, the workers' revolution; only a 'respectable' Republic could hope for arms supplies from the capitalist West. Only very occasionally did party unanimity collapse. In *Mundo Obvers* (28 March 1938) a Madrid communist questioned the idea of a Spain neither Socialist nor capitalist as a necessary condition of victory. He was promptly slapped down by José Díaz, the party secretary; democratic unity was the *only* way to resist Fascism etc. 'War first, Revolution after' was their slogan. The POUM reversed the priorities. Fascism, the POUM paper *La Batalla* argued, cannot be opposed by the bourgeois democracy of the Popular Front which is only another name for Fascism itself: 'The only alternative to Fascism is workers' control and this can only be secured by the workers' militias'.

The POUM 'line', if implemented – and it is hard to see how such a small party could have hoped to implement anything – would have brought disaster: POUM's declared aim 'to put an end to the bourgeoisie and the reformists' would have put an end to the Popular Front and any hopes of resistance. This result of 'revolution first' Orwell refused to face; and to him the Popular Front was a 'pig with two heads', a sham combination of socialists and capitalist-democrats with as much right to exist as a Barnum and Bailey monstrosity.

Orwell was one of the few commentators who understood the dilemma which was to tear the CNT apart. The CNT could not accept the POUM analysis because it demanded seizure of *political* power. In spite of the realization of the CNT leaders that it was necessary to join the government and in return sacrifice some of the 'revolutionary conquests' of July (e.g. the militia), the militants considered that the leadership had made a bad bargain and therefore sympathized with POUM's insistence on the workers' retention of their only guarantee (the militia). Orwell saw the alliance between the POUM and the CNT was circumstantial – common fear of Communist domination. It could not be one of principle.*

Orwell knew that, however sound the objections to the POUM line, the Communists were acting as they did for other reasons. The leaders of the POUM, above all Andrés Nin who had been active in the Left Opposition in the Soviet Union, were the only Spanish politicians ready to resist every advance of the Communists within the 'bogus' Popular Front Government. One cannot analyse Communist policy in Spain without remembering that the Civil War overlapped the Moscow Trials and that the Popular Front line was a necessary part of Soviet diplomacy. To harp on the Moscow Trials would destroy the image of a Liberal-Socialist-Communist alliance in defence of bourgeois freedom. The POUM leaders had no hesitation in denouncing Stalin's domestic tyranny in the pages of *La Batalla*. They must be silenced. The opportunity came in May 1937.

So acute were the tensions between the Communists and the POUM by 1 May

* For the differences between the POUM and CNT attitudes to political power see Julián Gorkín *Canibales políticos* (1940) p. 67 ff.

that the traditional Labour Day parades had to be called off. Barcelona became the only non-Fascist city in Europe with no celebrations. On 3 May 1937, fighting broke out after an attempt by the Catalan security forces to seize the Telephone Exchange, manned since July by the CNT.

The civil war within the Civil War which followed is the core of *Homage to Catalonia*: Orwell's eye-witness account is the prime source for our knowledge of the fighting. It has filtered into every subsequent history book.

Two points are of exceptional importance. Orwell's account reveals how the POUM was utterly unprepared for a contest (and therefore could not be accused of wanting one) and that no one at the time understood what was happening. There were only sixty rifles at the POUM headquarters, and the POUM leaders were 'furious at being dragged into the affair', which they felt had been brought on them by the resistance of the CNT at the Telephone Exchange. The fighting appeared at first sight as a struggle between the police and the CNT. Orwell was puzzled in a battle where the fighting seemed to be defensive 'on both sides'; people simply stayed in buildings and blazed away at the people opposite. His reaction was characteristic. 'When I see an actual flesh and blood worker in conflict with his natural enemy, the policeman, I do not have to ask which side I am on.' Again, as in his declaration of the motives which led him to join the militia, one is startled by the immediacy of the re-action. Like generals and journalists (except those of the *Manchester Guardian*) policemen, for Orwell, must always be on the wrong side.

Many Englishmen – at least in the thirties – found policemen unsympathetic and had a soft spot for anarchists; and indeed, favourable treatment for the CNT is one of the most marked features of Anglo-Saxon historiography of the Civil War. It is not the sympathy but the judgments based on it which dis-concert one. Thus Orwell argues that the CNT *gained* in its struggle with the Communists by its half-hearted participation in the May riots. True he calls this 'pure guesswork'. But it was a bad guess. After May the CNT was eliminated from the Government and its power destroyed; it spent the rest of the war licking its wounds and hoping for *political* power – a strange fate for anarcho-syndical-ists. The CNT was caught out by the war, badly split between leaders who were ready to make compromises for the sake of power for the movement and militants who would make no compromises but preferred to go down fighting. And go down they did.

Orwell was affected less by the May fighting than by the ruthless use the Communists made of a political post-mortem in order to destroy their enemies.

Nothing could excuse, in his eyes, the terrible Robespierrian techniques employed to achieve the suppression of the POUM. The 'line' was set down by

Spain

39 Demonstration against Fascism in Barcelona.

40 Fascist troops on their way to Bilbao.

41 On the Aragon front at Huesca, March 1937: Orwell is the tall figure standing in the centre, Eileen is crouching in front of him.

42 Historic church at Briones, burnt and pillaged by revolutionaries.

43 Military guard at the central post office, Barcelona.

44a Red artillery being brought into position.

Eine Abteilung antimarxistischer spanischer Truppen aus Marokko
wird an der Küste bei Cordoba ausgeschifft.

General Franco,
der Führer der spanisch-nationalen
Militärgruppe.

Rechts:
Ein Soldat zerstört ein Straßenschild.
Die Straßen vieler spanischer Städte trugen Namen marxistischer Politiker. Ein Soldat der Gegenrevolution vernichtet unter dem Beifall der Menge die Aufschrift eines Schildes.
Aufnahmen: Presse-Photo (3).

Bürgerkrieg
in Spanien

Links: Angehörige der marxistischen
Volksfronttruppen mit einem
Maschinengewehr.

Bei den Straßenkämpfen dienten aufgetürmte Pferdeleichen
als Barrikaden.

44b (*Opposite*) Official German reporting of the Spanish Civil War, 1936.

45 (*Above*) Republican poster.

46 Revolutionaries in
Barcelona.

47 Fighting near Sara-
gossa: Red telegraphists.

the party secretary, José Díaz, on 9 May. 'Our principal enemies are the Fascists. However, these not only include the Fascists themselves, but also the agents who work for them . . . Some call themselves Trotskyites . . . If everyone knows this, if the Government knows it, why doesn't it treat them like Fascists and extermin- ate them pitilessly.'* The POUM leaders were accordingly denounced as Trot- skyites and as Fascist *agents provocateurs*: the Barcelona fighting was presented, not as the violent outcome of tensions over disagreements in policy, but as a deliberate insurrection against the Government, engineered by the POUM in order to help Franco by creating chaos on the home front.

Jesús Hernández, a Communist Republican minister, at the time claimed that the Barcelona troubles were provoked by *Communist* agents (Antonov-Ovseenko and Ernö Serö) in order to force the reluctant Largo Caballero to liquidate the POUM by implicating them in a revolt. When the Prime Minister refused to suppress a workers' party at the behest of the Communists, he was 'dismissed' in favour of the more pliant Negrin. Though obedient to Moscow, most *Spanish* Communists were, according to Hernández, 'disgusted' with the liquidation of the POUM; the exception was that most obedient tool of all, La Pasionaria.†

Time and again Orwell insists that there was no preparation; that there was really no planned 'rising' but a 'bloody riot'; above all that it was monstrous to label a genuine working-class party Fascist. He was appalled at the treatment of the May days as a 'Trotskyist Revolt' in papers like the *News Chronicle* which simply swallowed uncritically the Communist line; or Ralph Bates' report in the *New Republic* that POUM militiamen were playing football with Fascist troops. He was deeply depressed at his failure to get his own views across and the readiness with which the Communist version was accepted by the Left. The *New Statesman* refused his articles and reviews; *Homage to Catalonia* was written rapidly, with great passion, before the news of the murder of Andrès Nin by the Communists had leaked out. Gollancz rejected *Homage* without reading it. In the prevailing climate it sold 'damn all'.

Given this *supresio veri* by interested parties, how could true history be written? Propaganda would pass as truth; 'facts' could be manipulated. Those who monopolized communication could create their own history after the event – the nightmare of *Nineteen Eighty-Four*.

'Very hostile to the CP since 1935'. (Letter to Stephen Spender, 1938) Orwell's Spanish experiences turned hostility to loathing. He had lived his last

---

* Quoted in Burnett Bolloten, 'The Parties of the Left and the Civil War' in *The Republic and Civil War in Spain*, ed. Raymond Carr (1970) p. 144.

† For a summary of Hernández' view see Robert Conquest, *The Great Terror* (1968) pp. 438–440.

few weeks in Spain as a hunted fugitive, sleeping out of doors, in constant fear of arrest, his wife's room searched by secret police, immersed in the 'horrible atmosphere of political suspicion and hatred'. All this he knew to be part of the Communist police heresy hunt of the POUM.

He was left with a twin legacy. He had *felt* what Socialism could be like in the militia. At the same time he was profoundly disillusioned with the intellectuals and parties of the Left who were the official proponents of Socialism. All his generation were marked by the Great War and it is clear that his 'model' for the journalists of the Left was in some sense derived from a memory of war journalism; people were deceived by their 'anti-Fascist stuff exactly as they were deceived by the gallant little Belgium stuff'. [Letter to Rayner Heppenstall, 31 July 1937.] The 'screaming lies and hatred' did not touch the men at the front; Communist militiamen did not call him a Trotskyist or a traitor. That was left for the journalists who had not seen a shot fired in anger and who concocted stories of babies' bodies used as barricades.

Faith in the workers remained. Throughout his work in Spain runs a belief that the workers' revolution and a revolutionary militia might have been a better instrument for an anti-Fascist war than the Popular Front of the politicians or the Popular Army of Communist military advisers. Hence a series of what must now appear as political misjudgments, characteristic of Orwell as a short-term political prophet. Would, as he asserts, a truly revolutionary Spain have inspired the working class of Europe to strikes and boycotts and therefore changed the policies of, say, Chamberlain? Would the image of a workers' republic have set off a 'real popular movement in Franco's rear'? Would the capitalist bourgeois of the Popular Front have come to terms with Franco? Was it true to say that 'every swing to the Right' weakened the Republic? Orwell concluded that 'perhaps the POUM and the Anarchist slogan: "The war and the revolution are inseparable" was less visionary than it sounds'. This is a cautious judgment, but curiously enough it remained with him. In 'The Lion and the Unicorn' the theme that a Socialist Britain was not merely possible in 1940 but alone could win the war is an echo of the old POUM slogan.

With time his vision of Spain had become indistinct. Whereas *Homage* shows the apathy and indifference to the war that came with the return of privilege and class distinction in 1937, Orwell maintained in 1940 that *the main reason the Republic could hold out for two and a half years was that there were no gross contrasts of wealth* ('The Lion and the Unicorn').* The need to prove

* Orwell's description of the apathy and indifference of 1937, in contrast to the enthusiasm of 1936, has not gone unnoticed by historians sympathetic to the Nationalist cause e.g. Ramón Salas Larrazábal in *Aproximación histórica a la Guerra Española* (Madrid, 1970) p. 247.

that England must become a reasonably egalitarian society to win the war, that Fascism could not be defeated by an English Popular Front, which would 'lead England up the garden path in the name of capitalist democracy' forced Orwell towards what, at other moments, he would stigmatize as an intellectual vice: the rewriting of history in a manner which suited the demands of the moment.

This is a harsh judgment; it can be stated in other terms. Orwell's vision of Spain was blurred by a romanticism that could lapse into political naïveté. He was, here, within a well-established tradition: that of the literary traveller, stunned by the contrast between supposed Spanish simplicity and sincerity and the complex compromises and materialism of life at home. Spain seemed to hold a mirror up to Western man in which to observe the imperfections of modernity; never more so than to anti-Fascists who visited Republican Spain before the grey days of defeat and discord, when the impact of the 'natural' democracy of Spanish manners was heightened by the defence of democracy as such.

John Wain
IN THE THIRTIES

MOST of what seem to be the paradoxes in Orwell's thinking and writing can be explained by the fact that he was born into an age in which the really suffocating nonsense was talked by reactionaries, and lived on into an age in which it was talked by progressives.

Orwell was born into the Edwardian age and seems to have started his life with an unusually thorough and unpleasant immersion in the character-forming processes of that age at their silliest. The relevant documents here are the autobiographical sections of *The Road to Wigan Pier* (i.e., chapters 8 and 9) and the essay 'Such, Such Were the Joys' (1947), describing his prep school. The portraits of 'Sambo' and 'Flip', the headmaster of 'St Cyprian's' and his wife, are good enough to stand as a classic case-history of English snobbery of the kind that flourished in the afterglow of Victorian confidence and died out only sporadically, being still alive in pockets well into the nineteen-fifties and probably not entirely extinct, in a duck-billed platypus sort of way, even now. Their ministrations enabled Orwell to go to Eton by means of a scholarship, which presumably did him some good or at least no harm but on the other hand they placed on his back a psychological load which he had to spend years trying to shake off.

Beyond this personal grievance there lay a wider rejection of the whole glittering world of social and material success which Flip and Sambo were supposed to be putting within the grasp of their fortunate *protégés*. Looking back, he saw them as 'a couple of silly, shallow, ineffectual people, eagerly clambering up a social ladder which any thinking person could see to be on the point of collapse'. But even if that ladder had been eternal, the happy land to which it led was repulsive to Orwell. In view of the current tendency to see the Edwardian age as a golden afternoon, it is worth recalling how it appeared to Orwell, who had, as a clever schoolboy of the scholarship-winning type, experienced that age almost as it might have been experienced by a member of the working class – that is, as a series of burdens laid on his back in the name of nothing very much.

There never was, I suppose, in the history of the world a time when the sheer vulgar fatness of wealth, without any kind of aristocratic elegance to redeem it, was so obtrusive as in those years before 1914. It was the age when crazy millionaires in curly top-hats and lavender waistcoats gave champagne parties in rococo house-boats on the Thames, the age of diabolo and hobble skirts, the age of the 'knut' in his grey bowler and cutaway coat, the age of *The Merry Widow*, Saki's novels, *Peter Pan* and *Where the Rainbow Ends*, the age when people talked about chocs and cigs and ripping and topping and heavenly, when they went for divvy week-ends at Brighton and had scrumptious teas at the Troc. From the whole decade before 1914 there seems to breathe forth a smell of the more vulgar, un-grown-up kinds of luxury, a smell of brilliantine and *creme-de-menthe* and soft centred chocolates – an atmosphere, as it were, of eating everlasting strawberry ices on green lawns to the tune of the Eton Boating Song. The extraordinary thing was the way in which everyone took it for granted that this oozing, bulging wealth of the English upper and upper-middle classes would last for ever, and was part of the order of things. ('Such, Such Were the Joys'.)

The same note is struck in the essay on Wells (1941):

When Wells was young, the antithesis between science and reaction was not false. Society was ruled by narrow-minded, profoundly incurious people, predatory business-men, dull squires, bishops, politicians who could quote Horace but had never heard of algebra. Science was faintly disreputable and religious belief obligatory. Traditionalism, stupidity, snobbishness, patriotism, superstition and love of war seemed to be all on the same side; there was need of someone who could state the opposite point of view. Back in the nineteen-hundreds it was a wonderful experience for a boy to discover H. G. Wells. There you were, in a world of pedants, clergymen and golfers, with your future employers exhorting you to 'get on or get out', your parents systematically warping your sexual life, and your dull-witted schoolmasters sniggering over their Latin tags; and here was this wonderful man who could tell you about the inhabitants of the planets and the bottom of the sea, and who *knew* that the future was not going to be what respectable people imagined.

As if the kind of upbringing we glimpse here were not enough, the young Orwell went straight from Eton into the Imperial Police in Burma, where he had to do the dirty work of Empire with his own hands. Five years of this were enough: on his first home leave, he resigned. Once again, he sums up for us with great penetration the nature of what had been done to him:

I was conscious of an immense weight of guilt that I had got to expiate. I suppose that sounds exaggerated; but if you do for five years a job that you thoroughly disapprove of, you will probably feel the same. I had reduced everything to the simple theory that the oppressed are always right and the oppressors are always wrong: a mistaken theory, but the natural result of being one of the oppressors yourself. I felt that I had got to escape not merely from imperialism but from every form of man's dominion over man. I wanted to submerge myself, to get right down among the oppressed, to be one of them and on their side against their tyrants. And, chiefly because I had had to think everything out in solitude, I had carried my hatred of oppression to extraordinary lengths. (*The Road to Wigan Pier.*)

As a picture of Orwell in 1927, this is entirely credible. Behind him were the austerities of his 'lower-upper-middle-class' home, Flip and Sambo, Eton; and then Burma, the monsoons, the convicts, the hangings, the mindlessly rigid society at the Club, and the endless involvement in futile situations such as that captured so perfectly in 'Shooting an Elephant'.

It was these experiences that gave Orwell the head of steam that drove him into the thirties. Books like *Down and Out in Paris and London*, *Burmese Days*, *A Clergyman's Daughter*, are straight expressions of the resentment, the guilt, the stinging pity for those pinned to the earth by 'the system', that one would expect to see engendered by these means in a young man whose mind was both strong and sensitive. And during these years it was very natural that Orwell should identify the enemy as being on the Right. Socialism was the answer, if an answer in political terms was to be found at all. And Orwell was determined that it could and must. Throughout his life he never wavered from his attitude of stern contempt for those who claimed that the nobler destiny was to be above the battle. A decent society would never come unless men got down and worked for it – even, if necessary, fought for it.

This was the Orwell who saw himself unequivocally as a man of the Left, and who felt it his duty as a writer to champion the underdog in the rich and technically advanced societies of the West. Naturally, he had misgivings, but these were of a personal, temperamental nature. To identify yourself with any cause is, inevitably, to be dismayed at some of the people you find yourself trying to cooperate with. Hence the amusing knockabout at the end of *The Road to Wigan Pier*. Orwell had been conscientiously trying to fit himself into the framework of Socialism, and he had found a good deal of smugness, evasiveness, selective blindness, and sheer muddle there – as one finds in any mass movement. In addition, there was the usual disagreement about objectives. Orwell was for a simple version of Socialism which boiled down to (a) fairer distribution of wealth and resources and (b) large-scale concerted resistance to international Fascism. And he rightly realized that many people describing themselves as Socialists, and holding influential positions within the world of Socialism, were lukewarm about these objectives and seemed to have other, unconfessed objectives of their own:

> Sometimes I look at a Socialist – the intellectual, tract-writing type of Socialist, with his pullover, his fuzzy hair, and his Marxian quotation – and wonder what the devil his motive really *is*. It is often difficult to believe that it is a love of anybody, especially of the working class, from whom he is of all people the furthest removed. The underlying motive of many Socialists, I believe, is simply a hypertrophied sense of order. The present state of affairs offends them not because it causes misery, still less because it makes freedom impossible, but because it is untidy; what they desire, basically, is to reduce the world to something resembling a chessboard. (*The Road to Wigan Pier*.)

Orwell's misgivings about the Left, however vigorously he expressed them, had by the beginning of 1937 not yet attained the status of a 'disillusion'. We can, indeed, already see the tiny hair-line cracks which were soon to open out into major rifts. But, for the moment, it is a matter of disagreement about emphases rather than opposing structures of values. The Introduction which Victor Gollancz was fain to provide before *Wigan Pier* could be trusted into the hands of Left Book Club members is still part of that world of innocent knockabout. Orwell's suspicion of Stalin's methods, for instance, provokes Gollancz to a plaintive 'look-here-I-say' that reminds one of Boswell's protest that Johnson was surely going too far in condemning the slave trade. Noting Orwell's 'general dislike of Russia', Gollancz goes on wonderingly: 'He even commits the curious indiscretion of referring to Russian commissars as "half-gramophones, half-gangsters".' Such was the state of mind of the British intelligentsia at that time. Russia was a country calling itself 'Socialist' and Russia was industrializing rapidly, so Russia *had* to be right. To see the commissars for what they were was at worst a counter-revolutionary crime and at best a 'curious indiscretion' like swearing in front of some white-haired old vicar.

The time was now approaching, however, when Orwell's condemnation of totalitarian methods within the Left was to go beyond the realm of the 'curious indiscretion'. Up to 1937, Orwell saw the world struggle as between Left and Right, with the goodwill and the good arguments on the side of the Left, if only they could get rid of the tiresome hangers-on who came 'flocking towards the smell of progress like bluebottles to a dead cat'. After 1937, he saw it in terms of democracy *versus* totalitarianism, and he no longer cared whether the totalitarianism called itself Left or Right.* What changed his outlook was his Spanish experience. *Homage to Catalonia* is the most important book for anyone who wants to understand Orwell's mind. It is a book that describes the hinge of a man's life.

Every tyranny is resisted by two quite distinct groups of people. There are those who resist the tyranny in the name of freedom, and there are those who resist it in the hope of replacing it by a rival tyranny in which they themselves will enjoy power.

Orwell's experiences in the Spanish Civil War gave him an inside view of this process actually at work. When that war broke out in 1936, left-wingers throughout the world felt a sense of exalted dedication. This was the beginning, the first in that series of battles which would sweep Fascism from the earth and leave peace, brotherhood and Socialism. In fact, many of those who died were to be casualties not in the war against Fascism, but in the struggle for power

* Cf. the essay on Arthur Koestler (1944): 'The sin of nearly all left-wingers from 1933 onwards is that they have wanted to be anti-Fascist without being anti-totalitarian.'

within the structure of the Left. The Communists, directed from Moscow, had never any intention of losing that struggle.

Orwell left a Spain on which the night of a police-state had fallen. He got back to an England where nobody wanted to hear his story. To the Right, still busily retailing stories about how government forces employed their leisure time in raping nuns, he was discredited because he had fought on the Socialist side. To the Left, he was merely a nuisance, a tactless fool who was determined to put his foot in it. It was Gollancz's 'curious indiscretion' again. So that Orwell, still weak and ill from his wound and shaken with rage and pity by the fate that had overtaken men he loved and admired, was met by frustration and delaying-tactics when he tried to tell his story to an English public. Gollancz would not take the book. He rejected it without reading it – before it was finished, even – on the strength of the fact that Orwell had been fighting with the anarchist militia, the POUM, rather than with an orthodox Communist outfit like the International Brigade. And when Orwell brought it out with another publisher, the more independent-minded Secker and Warburg, he had to endure such indignities as being lectured by V. S. Pritchett in the *New Statesman*. To Pritchett (and, doubtless, to his editor Kingsley Martin) Orwell's appetite for the unvarnished truth was 'perverse'. (*New Statesman and Nation*, 30 April 1938.) Small wonder that in the months that followed Orwell went through a bad crisis of depression and discouragement: not about himself, but about the society he was living in. I base this judgment not on anything that is established about his personal life, which for all I know was outwardly normal, but on the manifest despair and disgust that arises, as physically and concretely as a smell, from *Coming Up For Air*, his most depressing book, which was published in 1939 and therefore presumably written in 1938, during the aftermath of the Spanish experience.

The best way to see clearly the new dimension of horror and despair that came into Orwell's mind after the events of 1937–8 is to set two novels side by side: *Coming Up For Air*, written, as we saw, in the trough that followed his return from Catalonia, and *Keep the Aspidistra Flying* (1936), the last novel, though not the last book, he wrote before going there.

To take the earlier book first: *Keep the Aspidistra Flying* is not a good novel, a fact which Orwell very soon came to appreciate, though he remained firm in his (correct) judgment that *A Clergyman's Daughter* (1935) was 'even worse'. (*Burmese Days*, 1934, in some ways a better book than either of them, is not quite germane to our present discussion because of its specialized theme.) The faults of *Aspidistra* are many. Its style is nagging and repetitive. Its story is not well told, being clotted with great lumps of essay-material and moving its figures about like puppets. Its characterization is all too often two-dimensional. Ravelston, for instance, is the nice rich sensitive man, so everything he does and says has to be in complete consistency with this formula; he is a 'humour', but without the vitality that makes some humours (Holmes and Watson, for instance, or Welch in *Lucky Jim*) amusing to read about.

These faults can be tolerated in a book which offers so much that is vital and hard-hitting. A much more serious defect is that the whole story is blurred by what seems to be a fundamental indecision in the author's mind. It is very much a novel with a purpose; but *what* purpose? No one in his senses would demand that a novel should preach – but if it starts out with an evident *wish* to preach, we are entitled to ask that it should preach one sermon at a time and do so coherently.

For about the first half of the book, the theme seems to be the familiar one of the artist struggling to be fertile in a sterilizing money-society. Gordon, wishing to develop his gifts as a poet, has thrown up a well-paid but shame-making job with an advertising agency and taken work as a bookseller's assistant. The idea is to get free of the poisoned air of competitive money-making and then let his imagination shape something beautiful. The trouble is that, amid the shabby-genteel miseries of his existence, his imagination switches itself off. In the limbo represented by Mr McKechnie's bookshop and Mrs Wisbeach's boarding-house, he is like a wraith between two worlds. If he were still in advertising he would at least have money and pleasant surroundings; if he were poor enough to sink into the slums, his life would at least be free of dreary respectability and the battle for 'appearances'. Everything in his life, as well as his work, seems to be hanging fire. Rosemary, who tells him with evident sincerity that she loves him, has never become his mistress, and he cannot even make a whole-hearted play for her because Mrs Wisbeach will not have 'young women' in the house.

Stalemated as he is, Gordon must move, if anything is to happen in the story one way or the other. The novel fails because Orwell cannot, in the last analysis, make up his mind which way to move him. It looks, for a time, as if he had decided to push Gordon decisively *downwards*. After a drunken spree in which he disgraces himself and loses his job, Gordon gets a similar job at a much lower level; he takes a room in a real slum, gives up all social and intellectual pretensions, and frankly accepts himself for what he is – a drop-out. Here Orwell was at a cross-roads. If he had decided to make Gordon Comstock a real artist, a poet of genuine power, the novel could have finished strongly on his self-recovery. Away from the aspidistra of mincing respectability, down among the frowzy freedom of bugs and the bailiffs, he might have written a handful of great sonnets. What he actually does is to seduce Rosemary, more or less absent-mindedly, get her with child, and then suddenly realize that *this*, for him, is the positive path. Marriage, responsibility, children, and back to the advertising agency.

This, too, might have made a strong finish, but as the book actually stands it does not. There is a muted, half-hearted quality about it, as if Orwell, while wishing Gordon Comstock well in his new life of fatherhood and office hours, feels regret at having to shrug off all the tirades in the first half of the book. All that splendid denunciation of the money-world, the swindle of advertising, the slow choking to death of an acquisitive society: and then Gordon, in the end, decides that it is humanly preferable to join that world rather than lick it! Will a life spent in making up advertising slogans to unload fake products on to the public really be better than working in the bookshop and trying to write poems? Well, but there is the embryo in Rosemary's womb, proof at last that 'once again, things were happening in the Comstock family'. With that, we have to be content. But we can't be content. It is not stated strongly or lyrically enough.

The failure is interesting because, like most failures, it is symptomatic. Orwell really was undecided on this point. On the one hand, he disliked the type who makes 'artistic' pretensions a licence for selfishness and irresponsibility. He very much preferred 'ordinary' people, who had jobs and families and paid their debts, to 'bohemians' who were above such trivialities. Indeed, his references to the literary and artistic fringe of society, where bohemians are to be met with, are always venomously hostile. 'Shrieking poseurs', 'verminous little lions' – such expressions abound. On the other hand, as he could not help being aware, there *have*, now and again, been real artists who have lived a shiftless life, without any money except what they cadged from friends and usually spent on drink, who have in the end repaid everything by producing great work. Just as there have been real artists who, without being bohemian, have sunk below the level of respectable shabbiness into genuine, proletarian poverty, and found its climate fertilizing to their work. When William Faulkner was short of money, in 1929, he took a job shovelling coke at the town power-station of Oxford, Mississippi, and wrote *As I Lay Dying* during the slack period of midnight to 4 am, improvising a writing-desk from a wheelbarrow.

Orwell did not allow Gordon Comstock to come up this way. He did not, that is to say, allow him to be a genuine artist. And of course, if he was not a genuine artist, if his was merely the kind of half-baked talent that produces a slim volume and then dies a quiet death, then a job and marriage and fatherhood were, for him, the proper way back to self-respect. But what if he *had* been a genuine artist? Well then, *Aspidistra* would have been a different book. And, I think, a more interesting one. For among the problems that Orwell never got round to solving was the problem of the artist; what kind of life he should be allowed to live, how much special privilege he should be allowed, whether he should be encouraged to think of himself as 'altogether exceptional' ('Benefit of Clergy') or to keep his feet on the ordinary earth.

Orwell's mind was never made up. All that *Aspidistra* really succeeds in saying is that if Gordon had had plenty of money, his lack of real talent would not have prevented his making a reputation as a poet and being lionized in literary *salons*. Which is true enough. And also that, since he did not possess the poetic gift of a Baudelaire, the best thing for him was to straighten up and fly right. Which again is true enough. But the story seems trivial when it is set against the lurid back-projection of a dying civilization. The book's vitality comes from Orwell's passionate rejection of capitalist society, 1934 model. The background is stronger than the foreground, if only because we cannot believe that Gordon Comstock would have been worth bothering about even if he had lived in an age of flourishing art and high civilization.

It is evident that the state of mind that produced the ending of *Aspidistra* was still very much with Orwell a few months later, when he wrote his review of Cyril Connolly's *The Rock Pool* (*New English Weekly*, 23 July 1936). He finds fault with Connolly for his choice of subject-matter, the adventures of a young would-be writer who is sucked into 'one of those dreadful colonies of expatriates calling themselves artists that were dotted all over France in the late nineteen-twenties'. He goes on:

. . . even to want to write about so-called artists who spend on sodomy what they have gained by sponging betrays a kind of spiritual inadequacy. For it is clear that Mr Connolly rather admires the disgusting beasts he depicts, and certainly he prefers them to the polite and sheeplike Englishman; he even compares them, in their ceaseless war against decency, to heroic savage tribes struggling against western civilization. But this, you see, only amounts to a distaste for normal life and common decency, and one might equally well express it, as so many do, by scuttling beneath the moulting wing of Mother Church. Obviously, modern mechanized life becomes dreary if you let it. The awful thraldom of money is upon everyone and there are only three immediately obvious escapes. One is religion, another is unending work, the third is the kind of sluttish antinomianism – lying in bed till four in the afternoon, drinking Pernod – that Mr Connolly seems to admire. The third is certainly the worst, but in any case the essential evil is to think in terms of *escape*. The fact to which we have got to cling, as to a life-belt, is that it *is* possible to be a normal decent person and yet to be fully alive.

This is the Orwell who had some faith left, some hope that the day-to-day quality of life, even in a rotting society, would be tolerable because the decency of ordinary people would make it tolerable. He condemned 'escape' just as the orthodox Communists condemned it, though from a different point of view; by 'escape' they meant refusal to toe the Party line, whereas to him 'escape' could take a number of forms – of which, indeed, such line-toeing was one. He was, at this time, prepared to advocate a whole-hearted policy of involvement in everyday living. Fittingly, it was in this year that he married Eileen O'Shaughnessy, who is said to be the original of Rosemary in *Aspidistra*, and took her to live in the little grocery shop he was running in a Hertfordshire village.

But other doubts stirred in his mind, as one can see from the very respectful assessment of Henry Miller which came four years later, in the essay 'Inside the Whale'. Orwell's account of Miller begins by praising him for making just that same descent into real poverty that Gordon Comstock made without effect. Miller is writing about the literary and artistic world of Paris, 'but he is dealing only with the underside of it, the lumpenproletarian fringe which has been able to survive the slump because it is composed partly of genuine artists and partly of genuine scoundrels'. This seems to me a revealing sentence, admitting as it does that if the genuine scoundrel is not swept away by the crash of the Stock Market and the disappearance of *rentier* incomes, neither is the genuine artist. In other words, Gordon Comstock was neither.

The central issue of *Aspidistra*, then, insofar as we reach it through the story's main character, is blurred. The foundation of thinking and feeling in which Orwell embedded this issue, however, is very clear. His targets are very much what they remained for the next year or so, during the writing of *The Road to Wigan Pier*. It is the heartlessness, witlessness and gutlessness of a money-society, as seen by someone whose experience of that society has been sited mainly, though not exclusively, on the underside of the upper crust, among the people whose gentility makes them unfit to join in the scramble and sweat of everyday working life while not providing them with the means to rise definitely above it.

This society, as Orwell sees it in the novel, is undermined and threatened. It cannot survive – does not deserve to, indeed. On the other hand, the enemy that threatens it is only partly identified. There is, of course, the overhanging threat of war, which makes itself felt in the first chapter when Gordon gazes out of the bookshop window and imagines the drone of bombing-planes – 'a sound which, at that moment, he ardently desired to hear'. The death-wish of a stale and unjust society is caught in that phrase. But the nightmare is still in the present rather than the future. The stench arises from the habit-ridden, crumbling society, phosphorescent with decay, that is capitalism in its final stage. And at the end, when Gordon has found his positive aims in life, the whole question of what will happen to that life is quietly shelved.

Turn now to *Coming Up For Air*. This again is not a success in novelistic terms. George Bowling, the fat and rather beery-minded *homme moyen sensuel*, is made to voice Orwell's opinions a little too directly. A man like Bowling in actual life might very well agree with Orwell on most essentials, but he would be unlikely to express his views in such an Orwellian way. His voice would come to us, so to speak, through a layer of fat. Once again the vitality of the book is to be found in its hinterland, in the wide-angle view of Western capitalist society it presents to us.

In his short but extremely penetrating essay on *Helen's Babies* (1946), Orwell says that nineteenth-century America was fortunate in being 'a rich, empty country which lay outside the main stream of world events, and in which the twin nightmares that beset nearly every modern man, the nightmare of unemployment and the nightmare of State interference, had hardly come into being'. In *Aspidistra*, the first of these nightmares is vivid and actual: everybody fears the sack, hankers for more money and security, cringes to the boss. But only to the boss at work, the economic boss. The Commissar, 'half-gangster, half-gramophone', is not yet on the scene. To that extent the world of George Bowling is worse – colder, crueller, more inescapable – than the world of Gordon Comstock. When Bowling thinks of the future, he fears not only the ever-present financial insecurity, the endless work, work, work with the gutter only a few steps away; he fears also the new breed of tyrants, the myrmidons of totalitarianism, the leader and his strong-arm boys. Visiting his public-school-Oxford-classically-educated friend Porteous (a figure who belongs much more naturally to Orwell's background than to George Bowling's), he reflects:

Old Porteous's mind, I thought, probably stopped working at about the time of the Russo-Japanese war. And it's a ghastly thing that nearly all the decent people, the people who *don't* want to go round smashing faces in with spanners, are like that. They're decent, but their minds have stopped. They can't defend themselves against what's coming to them, because they can't see it, even when it's under their noses. They think that England will never change and that England's the whole world. Can't grasp that it's just a left-over, a tiny corner that the bombs happen to have missed. But what about the new kind of men from eastern Europe, the stream-lined men who think in slogans and talk in bullets? They're on our track. Not long before they catch up with us. No Marquis of Queensberry rules for those boys. And all the decent people are paralysed. Dead men and live gorillas. Doesn't seem to be anything between.

Bowling is caught between the dead past (which, like Orwell, he loves as much as any of its professional defenders) and the all too menacingly alive future. In between, there is a third region of nightmare. It concerns what we have since learnt to call 'the environment'. Part of Bowling's despair comes from the fact that he lives in a smirched, scribbled-over, cheapened England.

Once again we can take a perspective from 1946. In one of his *Tribune* pieces of that year, 'Thoughts on the Common Toad', Orwell pulls himself up after an entrancing description of the toad and its habits at various stages of the yearly cycle, and asks:

Is it wicked to take a pleasure in spring and other seasonal changes? To put it more precisely, is it politically reprehensible, while we are all groaning, or at any rate ought to be groaning, under the shackles of the capitalist system, to point out that life is frequently more worth living because of a blackbird's song, a yellow elm tree in October, or some other natural phenomenon which does not cost money and does not have what the editors of left-wing newspapers call a class angle? There is no doubt that many people think so. I know by experience that a favourable reference to 'Nature' in one of my articles is liable to bring me abusive letters, and though the key-word in these letters is usually 'sentimental', two ideas seem to be mixed up in them. One is that any pleasure in the actual process of life encourages a sort of political quietism. People, so the thought runs, ought to be discontented, and it is our job to multiply our wants and not simply to increase our enjoyment of the things we have already. The other idea is that this is the age of machines and that to dislike the machine, or even to want to limit its domination, is backward-looking, reactionary and slightly ridiculous. This is often backed up by the statement that a love of Nature is a foible of urbanized people who have no notion what Nature is really like. Those who really have to deal with the soil, so it is argued, do not love the soil, and do not take the faintest interest in birds or flowers, except from a strictly utilitarian point of view. To love the country one must live in the town, merely taking an occasional week-end ramble at the warmer times of year.

This last idea is demonstrably false. Medieval literature, for instance, including the popular ballads, is full of an almost Georgian enthusiasm for Nature, and the art of agri- cultural peoples such as the Chinese and Japanese centres always round trees, birds, flowers, rivers, mountains. The other idea seems to me to be wrong in a subtler way. Certainly we ought to be discontented, we ought not simply to find out ways of making the best of a bad job, and yet if we kill all pleasure in the actual process of life, what sort of future are we preparing for ourselves? If a man cannot enjoy the return of spring, why should he be happy in a labour-saving Utopia? What will he do with the leisure that the machine will give him? I have always suspected that if our economic and political problems are ever really solved, life will become simpler instead of more complex, and that the sort of pleasure one gets from finding the first primrose will loom larger than the sort of pleasure one gets from eating an ice to the tune of a Wurlitzer. I think that by retaining one's childhood love of such things as trees, fishes, butterflies and – to return

Pre-war years

48 A demonstrator against unemployment being led away, 1936.

50 (*Above*) Members of the British Union of Fascists, at their Chelsea headquarters.

49 (*Below*) Watching a football match between unemployed miners and Etonians, 1938.

51 (*Below right*) Mosley at a Blackshirt rally in Hyde Park.

52 (*Overleaf*) Hunger marchers in Hyde Park.

53 (*Left*)
Independent
Labour Party
summer school,
1937. Orwell
second from
right.

54 and 55 (*Right
above and below*)
Registration
cards, Marrakech,
1938.

Taille I.82
Front moy.
Nez rect.
Bouche moy;
Menton rond
Visage ovale
Cheveux cht.
Barbe rasée
Corpulence moy.
Yeux cht.
Teint clair

Marques particulières apparentes

Nom et prénoms de la femme :
Ellen Maud O'SHANGHNESSY
Prénoms des enfants âgés de moins de 18 ans :

G 21202

SIGNALEMENT

Taille In 65
Front bombé
Nez rect.
Bouche moy.
Menton rond
Visage ovale
Cheveux chat.
Barbe
Corpulence moy.
Yeux ch.
Teint clair

Marques particulières apparentes

Nom et prénoms ~~de la femme~~ l'époux
BLAIR Eric Arthur
Prénoms des enfants âgés de moins de 18 ans :

56 Orwell in Marrakech.

to my first instance – toads, one makes a peaceful and decent future a little more prob-able, and that by preaching the doctrine that nothing is to be admired except steel and concrete, one merely makes it a little surer that human beings will have no outlet for their surplus energy except in hatred and leader worship.

What makes *Coming Up For Air* so peculiarly bitter to the taste is that, in addition to calling up the twin spectres of totalitarianism on the one hand and workless poverty on the other, it also declares the impossibility of 'retaining one's childhood love of such things as trees, fishes, butterflies', and so forth – because it postulates a world in which these things are simply not there any more.

Everyone who has even glanced through *Coming Up For Air* will remember the remorseless way in which the forty-five-year-old insurance salesman, sneak-ing away from his semi in the suburbs to go back to his country boyhood at Lower Binfield in the Thames Valley, is dragged through one miry ditch of disappointment after another. The town has been swamped in raw red brick, the river has been polluted, the trees have been cut down, the house where he grew up is now Wendy's Tea-Shop, and so on through a grisly catalogue that would almost convict Orwell of exaggeration if it were not so manifestly a true account of what has happened to virtually the whole of south-east England. For two days Bowling wanders about, suffering. But one inner sanctuary remains. 'The pool at Binfield House', a deep, dark pond accessible only by those adventurous enough to trespass and hardy enough to tear themselves on thorn-bushes, that pool where he had lain in wait for enormous fish and which had remained through the years the node of his most powerful fantasies – it might, just *might*, be still there. Of course, the reader knows the kind of thing that is coming. In such a pitiless novel, a harmless fat man will not be left with his crumb of happiness *à la recherche du temps perdu*. There is a new, superior housing estate. The pond has been drained and used for a rubbish-dump. Standing nearby is a simple-lifer, the kind of person Orwell had attacked in the closing chapters of *The Road to Wigan Pier*:

He began to show me round the estate. There was nothing left of the woods. It was all houses, houses – and what houses! Do you know these faked-up Tudor houses with the curly roofs and the buttresses that don't buttress anything, and the rock-gardens with concrete bird-baths and those red plaster elves you can buy at the florists?' You could see in your mind's eye the awful gang of food-cranks and spook-hunters and simple-lifers with £1,000 a year that lived there. Even the pavements were crazy. I didn't let him take me far. Some of the houses made me wish I'd got a hand-grenade in my pocket. I tried to damp him down by asking whether people didn't object to living so near the lunatic asylum, but it didn't have much effect. Finally I stopped and said:

o

87

'There used to be another pool, besides the big one. It can't be far from here.'

'Another pool? Oh, surely not. I don't think there was ever another pool.'

'They may have drained it off', I said. 'It was a pretty deep pool. It would leave a big pit behind.'

For the first time he looked a bit uneasy. He rubbed his nose.

'Oh-ah. Of course, you must understand our life up here is in some ways primitive. The simple life, you know. We prefer it so. But being so far from the town has its inconveniences, of course. Some of our sanitary arrangements are not altogether satisfactory. The dust-cart only calls once a month, I believe.'

'You mean they've turned the pool into a rubbish-dump?'

'Well, there *is* something in the nature of a ——' he shied at the word rubbish-dump. 'We have to dispose of tins and so forth, of course. Over there, behind that clump of trees.'

We went across there. They'd left a few trees to hide it. But yes, there it was. It was my pool, all right. They'd drained the water off. It made a great round hole, like an enormous well, twenty or thirty feet deep. Already it was half full of tin cans.

I stood looking down at the tin cans.

'It's a pity they drained it', I said. 'There used to be some big fish in that pool.'*

We can, it seems to me, trace the temperature-chart of Orwell's thoughts and feelings after this fashion:

1910–27: the normal rebellious feelings of a spirited and intelligent schoolboy, forced against his will into an obsolete pattern of governing-class values in an unjust world.

1927–37: bitter disgust with the state of the world, particularly that part of it about which he could speak from experience; sense of living 'in the wreck of a civilization', wrecked by industrialism with its ugliness and capitalism with its greed. These feelings tempered, but not very strongly and not consistently, by a feeling that 'Socialism' was capable of building a better world.

1937–40: subsidence into a state very close to total despair, after the snuffing-out of the hope that had flared briefly in revolutionary Catalonia. The realization (in Spain) that the Left was too split, and too sheep-like in its acceptance of totalitarian methods, to do any effective good in the world; realization (in England) that the propaganda-machine was already strong enough to drown individual honest testimony.

* Before leaving the subject of *Coming Up For Air* it is fair to chronicle the fact that some stout-hearted readers have found it not at all dismaying – good high-spirited fun, in fact. Sir Richard Rees in *George Orwell*: *Fugitive From the Camp of Victory* (1961), says of this book that it was written in a mood 'blithe and sometimes even optimistic' and that its 'peculiar buoyancy and vigour is due to the stimulus he received from the comradeship and idealism of the POUM militiamen'. Hoorah for comradeship, idealism and the Boy Scouts.

1940–50: a rallying of the spirits caused partly by the fact that action, how-ever painful, is better than waiting for action, and partly by the winning of the war.

Hitler and the Gestapo were defeated, even at the cost of strengthening Stalin and the NKVD, and what is more they were defeated largely by the courage and resolution of Orwell's beloved 'common humanity'. So the long years of semi-starvation and discouragement had not, after all, broken England's spirit. What is more, the war – though it did not produce the sweeping social changes that Orwell predicted in 1940 and 1941 – did help to dynamite some entrenched class-attitudes, particularly the serene confidence of the conservative business community in their own financial policies. (As Orwell noted with grim satisfac-tion: 'Hitler will at any rate go down in history as the man who made the City of London laugh on the wrong side of its face.') On the evidence of his work, *passim*, I think it is clear that Orwell's spirits rose during the war years. He emerged into the Cold War period in a more positive mood. It is true that his last two books, and the essays he wrote after the 1946 collection, still show a mind very preoccupied with the dangers that threatened the world. But a satirist, almost by definition, is not a man in despair. Despair breeds inertia. And while both *Animal Farm* and *Nineteen Eighty-Four* are sombre in mood (the second, of course, more so than the first, which still has some playfulness), they show Orwell striking two mighty blows for the things he loved against the things he hated. 'Pessimistic' they may be, but to the extent that they are strongly motivated they are constructive. There is no sign here of 'the sickness unto death'.

In the nineteen-thirties, however, Orwell came close to that sickness. He saw democracy, rotted inwardly by the poison of greed and irresponsibility, facing a ruthless totalitarianism sworn to destroy it. The Spanish effort had failed, and with it had gone – as he could not help but believe – the last hope that men of good will might cooperate to save the world. He was prepared to sell his life dearly, but he had, I think, no hope.

Naturally I am not so complacent as to make it a point *against* Orwell that he experienced despair as the thirties ebbed away. That decade had seen so many lights go out, and the new ones that were to offer our present gleams of hope were as yet so far in the future, that any man who combined imagination with decency would find that, together, they added up to despair. Orwell's own image for the thirties was 'a riot of appalling folly that suddenly becomes a nightmare, a scenic railway ending in a torture-chamber'. In such a situation, despair can be the only honourable reaction. Such, at any rate, was the view taken at that time by E. M. Forster, who remarked almost parenthetically, in a book review [*New Statesman and Nation*, 10 December 1938] that 'there is nothing disgraceful about despair. In 1938–9, the more despair a man can take on board without sinking, the more completely he is alive.'

Orwell never sank under his load of despair. But it must have been, at times, a near thing. His work abounds in passages – usually thrown off, like Forster's remark quoted above, more or less by the way – which reveal an intimate knowledge of suffering and self-doubt. The road from the Depression to Cold War was a long one for everyone, but it must have been specially long for him, with his capacity to identify with suffering and to feel it in his own blood and bones.

As I write, it is once more the fashion to decry Orwell, as it was in the thirties. Now as then, his truth-telling is dismissed as 'perverse', and his warnings are shrugged off by what he himself called 'the huge tribe known as "the right left people"'. Now as then, the most vicious digs at Orwell come from men whose basic intellectual position is totalitarian, the sort of people who are always ready to point out the flaws in an untidy democracy, but see nothing disturbing in the dreadful tidiness of, say, a classroom of North Vietnamese children squeaking in unison: 'No one loves Uncle Ho more than the children!' We are plagued with these people now, as we were in the thirties, and for much the same reasons.

It is a testimony to the continuing vitality of Orwell's work that totalitarian-minded critics hate him so much. They hate him because he is a thorn in their flesh. May he stay there for ever.

William Empson
ORWELL AT THE BBC

ON the day when a stranger offered me his hand and said 'I am George Orwell', we were both students at the start of a six-week course in what was called the Liars' School of the BBC: my future wife was also a student there, and it seems to me now a time of great happiness. He must have been writing *Animal Farm* while employed by the Corporation, but he never discussed work in progress, and had resigned some time before it was published. We remained friends afterwards, and sometimes had dinner together; but practically speaking, as I went back to China soon after the war, the Indian Editor of the BBC Eastern Service was the only Orwell I knew.

It is interesting to consider why he was there, a question which would not occur to us at the time. My future wife and I, come to think of it, represented the two main types of student at the 1941 session (the School was a yearly event). I had served an apprenticeship, working for a year on the big daily Digest of foreign broadcasts, and towards the end writing earnest memos recommending myself as a propagandist to the Far East (the Digest staff acted as a kind of pool for the propaganda expansion); whereas Hetta, like many other high-minded people at the time, had been dubious about working directly for the Government until Hitler attacked Russia, though it had been all right to drive lorries or ambulances through the London blitz. Orwell was the only student who jeered at those who expressed pleasure at having recently acquired the powerful ally. One might expect this to have annoyed people, and maybe it would have done but for another recent event, slightly earlier; the Battle of Britain had been won, so that we were no longer afraid, in a furtive and astonished manner, of losing the war, as we had been for a year, since the fall of France. (There was a night when the figures of German aircraft shot down over Britain, chalked up on a blackboard in the sub-editors' room of the Digest, rose so high that no one's bet was anywhere near, and the sweepstake had to be given to charity. Maybe the figures were wrong, but they were decisive for many people, and Hitler decided the same way.) During that year before I met him, Orwell though quietly growing food in the country, had been to do with an official scheme planning resistance after a successful German invasion. Survivors of the Spanish War were being taken seriously, by some elements of the British Army, as advisers on how to organize a *maquis*. I did not ask about this, but realized that he would love teaching the British Army how ignorant it was. Still, he would not do even that for mere pleasure, and now the immediate occasion for it had stopped. He would have liked to be a war correspondent, but his health stood in the way. 'I hold what half the men in this country would give their balls to have,' he was accustomed to remark, 'a yellow ticket' (or whatever colour it was, meaning that he could not be conscripted), 'but I don't want it.' In writing this I paused and searched my memory, feeling that another bright phrase should come next; but no, he did not sustain his rhetoric, though he would use a phrase intending it to glitter. He was indignant at being told he was too ill to go abroad. 'The impudence of it, when they know perfectly well I'm too ill to stay here. Probably save my life to go to North Africa. But if it didn't, they might have to give the widow something, d'you see.' No doubt he would have enjoyed being a war correspondent. But radio propaganda to India might offer a more important role. If Hitler broke right through Russia to the Persian Gulf, and India joined Japan, the Axis might win after all. And then again, if Churchill won, he might prevent the liberation of India. As it happened, Orwell was Indian Editor at the time when these major questions became settled, though he could not have been sure they were settled when he resigned. He always regarded his work in a high manner, not to say a self-important one, as many of us were prone to do.

It was lucky for me that George thought I was all right, as I admired him and wanted his friendship, and he might easily have decided I was not. I had come back from China voluntarily for the war, and no doubt this made me sufficiently unlike the types he was denouncing. 'I don't know people like that,' he was soon remarking about Kingsley Martin, who (it seemed) had printed a picture in the *New Statesman* of how much gold would make a US dollar, so as to help rats to rat. George, I thought, sounded a bit like what one had read of Lord Curzon, another isolated ailing and public-spirited Etonian who had cultivated a funny accent. I had returned feeling that the defeat of Hitler was of immense importance, to be sure, but also feeling reasonably confident that I would be allowed an interesting war by being let into the propaganda machine; and, then again, I was protected by my obscurity, unlike the poet Auden who, I still think, was right in refusing to become the laureate of Churchill. For that matter, my Chinese university had simply assumed that I would require indefinite wartime leave (the Chinese were already regarding our war as a part of their war); it would have been embarrassing to act otherwise. Having practically remained on my tram-lines, I felt it was a rather undeserved bonus to be approved by Orwell. But we never cleared this point up either; he was not a man who asked personal questions.

When the two editors were settled in, which took another year or so of the gradual expansion (I rather think we each had a brief period as Burmese Editor, but it was I who held the office during the fall of Burma), they worked among many others on the open space of a whole floor of an Oxford Street shop, in offices separated by partitions about nine feet high; one of these lay between us, so that I could hear parts of his interview with the Indian propagandists whom he was vetting or briefing – or rather I could hear the bits which he said in a special tone of voice, as a rule one standard sentence. At first the visitor would do most of the talking, with George increasing his proportion gradually; no doubt he had to lure the visitor into providing an entry for the tremendous remark which one learned to expect towards the end of the interview. 'The FACK that you're black,' he would say, in a leisurely but somehow exasperated manner, immensely carrying, and all the more officer-class for being souped up into his formalized Cockney, 'and that I'm white, has *nudding whatever to do wiv it.*' I never once heard an Indian say 'But I'm not black', though they must all have wanted to. This no doubt was a decisive part of the technique; if he had used the phrase to actual Negroes, from an official position, they would be likely to object, and he would have to stop; but the Indians, who of course chatted to a variety of people in the basement canteen, were clearly in no mood to complain. They thought he was a holy saint, or at least that he must be very high-minded and remote from the world. Nobody ever mentioned, to my knowledge, that this dread sentence was being pronounced; I never even mentioned it privately to George. In his writing, of course, he often uses shock tactics, but I actually did feel a bit shocked to hear them put into practice. (Naturally the Chinese Department had an entirely different lay-out, having to handle so different a situation.)

One can see, however, that the tactics might have an important function. George was intensely devoted to the liberation of India (though the discovery that his Number Two was working for an independent Pakistan came as a great shock) – so much so that he felt Hitler's war would be worth while if it spelt the end of the British Raj, as it was likely to do if properly handled; but the 'advanced' Indians who imagined they would secure this result by helping Hitler to win were (he was convinced) disastrously deluded. Actually, most of the Englishmen you could have found for the job would have held these opinions (though Churchill insisted that he himself did not), but to political thinkers from the subject countries the English attitude was incredible; and it could only be made credible by someone who was plainly not mealy-mouthed. George would be uniquely good at this rather odd line of work. However, for all his skill, he found himself having to allow broadcasts to go out to India, from speakers too important to offend, which he thought likely to do more harm than good; well then, the great organization should accept the advice of an Editor, and simply tell the engineers to switch off the power. The man would be thanked and paid as usual, and could be told later if necessary that there had been an unfortunate technical hitch. He seemed genuinely indignant when complaining that the BBC had refused; surely we could not expect to defeat Goebbels, if we were so luxuriously honest as all that. (The stories about

Milton when he was a propaganda chief amount to saying that he behaved as George wanted to do, very charitably in a way, so I won't believe that they are merely libels, as is always assumed by critics with no propaganda experience.) The Liars' School, I should perhaps explain, had only dealt with lies in passing, and only under the form of warning us against the methods of the enemy. I chiefly remember two young disc jockeys who put on a very saucy turn with two gramophones and two copies of a record by Churchill; the familiar voice was made to leave out all the negatives, ending with 'we will (hic) surrender'. Towards the end of his time with the BBC, Orwell brought out a volume of specimens of the political reflections by Indians which he had provided for India, with part of a speech by Hitler as a contrast; and at this late hour he was really pleased to discover that Hitler too was receiving his due royalties, forwarded to him by the Royalty Department through neutral Sweden. The modern world, it now occurs to me, is liable not to realize how high-minded the whole affair was; George and the Corporation were both leaning over backwards, though in rather different directions.

'The working classes smell' was one of his famous debunking pronouncements, printed in italics if I remember; and this was a settled enough assumption in his mind to make him feel that only tramps and other down-and-outs were genuinely working class. It was a serious weakness in his political judgment, otherwise very good, and it clearly resulted from deep internal revulsions. I judged it to be connected with his firmly expressed distaste for homosexuality: at that time, or when we were both a bit younger, many young gentlemen who loved the Workers did it practically, and would explain to you that the ruling classes, owing to their vices and their neuroses, were the ones who stank. You may think I should have confronted George with someone who said this, but it would have been worse than useless. For the truth is that he himself stank, and evidently knew it – well, his (first) wife talked to mine about it quite frankly, and she would be unlikely to treat her husband to a frozen silence on the matter. It was the rotting lungs that you could smell, not at once but increasingly as the evening wore on, in a confined room; a sweetish smell of decay. Maybe I will be told that this does not happen, and indeed I have never met it in other TB patients. But then, Orwell told me more than once that he hadn't got TB; he had an allied lung disease; and as he made no bones about the threat of death I expect some doctor had really told him this. Most other doctors would call his disease merely a variety of TB, while agreeing that the condition of the lungs was unusual. Bodily disgust, or rather a fear that a good man may at any moment be driven into some evil action by an unbearable amount of it, is deeply embedded in his best writing; and at the time I thought all this was easy to

97

explain – he just hated his own smell. But surely, he wouldn't be likely to live many years with his lungs in so extreme a condition. Much more likely, when he was putting himself through the experience of being down-and-out, or among down-and-outs, he smelt quite all right. It would be like what they say to children pulling faces, 'you'll grow like that'; and, in a way, it would suit his expectations, as the later writing became more and more confidently grim.

Whether because of this background of suffering or from his very active experience of life, he had a great power to make you feel ashamed of yourself, or, if your moral resistance held firm, to feel sorry that poor George felt ashamed of you. My wife and I ran into this at a quite unexpected point. At that time the Government, or Churchill himself probably, had put into action a scheme for keeping up the birth-rate during the war by making it in various ways convenient to have babies, for mothers going out to work; government nurseries were available after the first month, I think, and there were extra eggs and other goodies on the rations, clearly a reward for Mum, or even Dad, since they could not be digested by baby. We took advantage of this plan to have two children; it seems rather athletic, looking back, as one or other parent had to retrieve them from the nursery as soon as the official worktime stopped, and the arrangements in case of illness were left to be improvised. I was saying to George one evening after dinner what a pleasure it was to cooperate with so enlightened a plan when, to my horror, I saw the familiar look of settled loathing come over his face. Rich swine boasting over our privileges, that was what we had become; 'but it's *true*, George', I cried out piteously, already knowing that nothing would alter his mind. True, that is, that these arrangements had been designed for the whole population, and did apply to all factory workers. He did not refer to the subject again, but at the time his disapproval was absolute.

And yet, as so often when one brushes up an old anecdote, I am not sure now that I did not get him wrong. Not long after that his wife died, and he resigned his job. They had adopted a child, which needed attention during the day, and so did the two goats, living in his garden to supply the child with proper milk. Writing articles for *Tribune* was all right, because he could do that at home, but he could no longer spend most of the day at an office. This looks as if he thought the Government arrangements inadequate rather than too luxurious, but perhaps he was objecting to something else in what I had said altogether. Also it looks as if he was not quite so devoted to his high duties as I had presumed (in writing this, I felt so baffled to understand why he had resigned that I asked John Morris, who was our boss at the time; but now I feel sure that George had told us what he told John Morris). He can hardly have decided that the problems of India had been solved, but they had become less explosive, and

I dare say these goats were partly a polite excuse; he might well feel, as well as wanting a change, that the postwar election would be decisively important and was beginning to loom up, so that writing internal propaganda for Labour in *Tribune* was the most important duty now before him. Also he had at last found a publisher for *Animal Farm*.

The experience of being Indian Editor continued to work on him, and the early parts of *Nineteen Eighty-Four* were evidently conceived as farce about it, so that one expects the book to be gay. Many people get the impression that the author merely chose, for some extraneous personal reason, to make the later parts as horrible as he could. But one cannot understand either book without realizing that he considered having to write them as a torture for himself; it was horrible to think of the evil men, stinking Tories, who would *gain* by his telling the truth, let alone jeer about it triumphantly. But tell it he must, he could do no other. Awful, though, for instance, to think of Hetta reading *Animal Farm*; 'it is like cutting off the baby's arm', he said. (So far as I could tell, she did not feel any of the distress he feared, because she did not believe him.) 'Anyway *Animal Farm* won't mean much in Burma,' he said to me one day with timid hope, 'because they won't know what it is about; they haven't got mixed farming there, like the English mixed farming.' A year or two later, when I passed that area on my way back to China, every detail of English mixed farming was being explained to the Burmese on a comic strip of a vernacular newspaper, solely in order that they might relish to the full the delicious anti-Russian propaganda of Orwell. And though he was rather anti-aesthetic, indeed one might sometimes think Philistine on purpose, he was inclined to retreat into an aesthetic position when the book first came out. With all the reviews ablaze he stayed cross about the reception of the book, so that we said: 'What more do you want, George? It's knocked them all right back. They all say its terrific.' 'Grudging swine, they are', he muttered at last, when coaxed and stroked into saying what was the matter; 'not one of them said it's a beautiful book.'

John Coleman
THE CRITIC OF
POPULAR CULTURE

ORWELL'S life – as we know it through his books, journalism and letters – was exceptionally of a piece. Between the end of 1934 and the beginning of 1936, he worked as a part-time assistant in a Hampstead bookshop. Meanwhile he was writing his third novel, *Keep the Aspidistra Flying*. Its jaundiced hero, Gordon Comstock, seems to have shared some of his author's experiences:

Much of the time, when no customers came, he spent reading the yellow-jacketed trash that the library contained. Books of that type you could read at the rate of one an hour. And they were the kind of books that suited him nowadays. It is real 'escape literature', that stuff in the twopenny libraries. Nothing has ever been devised that puts less strain on the intelligence; even a film, by comparison, demands a certain effort.

Comstock sinks lower yet:

He read nothing nowadays except twopenny weekly papers. *Tit Bits, Answers, Peg's Paper, The Gem, The Magnet, Home Notes, The Girl's Own Paper* – they were all the same . . . Some of them were as much as twenty years old.

Yet the tone of voice is susceptible of change:

For casual reading – in your bath, for instance, or late at night when you are too tired to go to bed, or in the odd quarter of an hour before lunch – there is nothing to touch a back number of the *Girl's Own Paper*.

The last quotation comes from a short article, 'Bookshop Memories', that Orwell wrote for the *Fortnightly* in 1936, and it sounds much more amiable than poor Comstock ever did. Two years earlier, in a letter to a friend, Brenda Salkeld, the following bit of news was retailed:

I also bought for a shilling a year's issue of a weekly paper of 1851, which is not uninteresting. They ran among other things a matrimonial agency, and the correspondence relating to this is well worth reading.

At the time when Orwell was breaking into a career in letters, this would not have been generally regarded as the intellectually muscle-building stuff required. As always, he was his own man.

Certainly there had been a few highbrow precursors in the study of 'popular' literature and its adjuncts, notably Q. D. Leavis with her *Fiction and the Reading Public* (1932) and F. R. Leavis and Denys Thompson in *Culture and Environment*, published a year later and used in my sixth-form days as a sort of Bible against the evils of advertising. The point about Orwell is that he appears, when speaking *in propria persona*, positively to have enjoyed the forms of popular

The war years

57 'All the latest', September 1940.

58 Writing for *Horizon*.

Horizon
A REVIEW OF LITERATURE AND ART

HOW FIRM IS THE ATLANTIC HANDCLASP?
by BEATRICE LEEDS

THE PUPIL
by ROLLO WOOLLEY

POETRY IN 1941
by STEPHEN SPENDER

RUDYARD KIPLING
by GEORGE ORWELL

FRAGMENT OF AN AUTOBIOGRAPHY—VI
by AUGUSTUS JOHN

POEM *by* GEORGE BARKER
REVIEW *by* BRINSLEY FORD

LETTERS *from* VERONICA WEDGWOOD, ARTHUR CALDER-MARSHALL
AND HUGH SLATER

LONDON NIGHT. FOUR PHOTOGRAPHS *by* BILL BRANDT

MONTHLY: ONE SHILLING AND SIXPENCE NET
FEBRUARY VOL. V, No. 26 1942

Edited by Cyril Connolly

59 Page from Orwell's private war diary, 1942.

14.3.42. I reopen this diary after an interval of about 6 months, the war being once again in a new phase.

60 BBC Eastern Service broadcasters, including Orwell, T.S. Eliot,
Tainbimuttu (second from left), and William Empson (third from right) 1942.

Crash ! "Yoo-hoop !" roared Bunter. "Wow ! Oh crikey ! My jaw's broken ! Ow ! Wow !" "What is this ?" thundered Mr. Quelch. "I will keep order in this class ! Who threw that book ? Was it you, Vernon-Smith ?" The Bounder glared.

66 Membership
card, 1943.

67 Letter to Gleb
Struve.

NATIONAL UNION OF JOURNALISTS

7 John Street, Bedford Row, London, W.C.I

'Phone:
HOLborn 2258

Telegrams:
Natujay Holb, London

This is to certify that

Mr. GEORGE ORWELL

of The Tribune

is a member of the T. & P.
Branch of the National Union of Journalists.

Leslie R. Aldous Branch Sec.

(Address) 66. Priory Gans. N.6.

Member's Sig.

10a Mortimer Crescent
London NW 6
17.2.44

Dear Mr Struve,

Please forgive me for not writing
earlier to thank you for the very kind gift of "25 Years of Soviet
Russian Literature", with its still more kind inscription. I am
afraid I know very little about Russian literature and I hope your
book will fill up some of the many gaps in my knowledge. It has
already roused my interest in Zamyatin's "We", which I had not heard
of before. I am interested in that kind of book, and even keep making
notes for one myself that may get written sooner or later. I wonder
whether you can tell if there is an adequate translation of Blok?
I saw some translated fragments about ten years ago in "Life and
Letters", but whether they were any good as a translation I do not
know.

I am writing a little squib which might amuse you when it
comes out, but it is so not O.K. politically that I don't feel
certain in advance that anyone will publish it. Perhaps that gives
you a hint of its subject.

Yours sincerely

Geo. Orwell

AS I PLEASE: by George Orwell

ARTHUR KOESTLER'S recent article in *Tribune* set me wondering whether the book racket will start up again in its old vigour after the war, when paper is plentiful and there are other things to spend your money on.

Publishers have got to live, like anyone else, and you cannot blame them for advertising their wares, but the truly shameful feature of literary life before the war was the blurring of the distinction between advertisement and criticism. A number of the so-called reviewers, and especially the best known ones, were simply blurb writers. The "screaming" advertisement started some time in the nineteen-twenties, and as the competition to take up as much space and use as many superlatives as possible became fiercer, publishers' advertisements grew to be an important source of revenue to a number of papers. The literary pages of several well-known papers were practically owned by a handful of publishers, who had their quislings planted in all the important jobs. These wretches churned forth their praise—"masterpiece," "brilliant," "unforgettable" and so forth—like so many mechanical pianos. A book coming from the right publishers could be absolutely certain not only of favourable reviews, but of being placed on the "recommended" list which industrious book-borrowers would cut out and take to the library the next day.

If you published books at several different houses you soon learned how strong the pressure of advertisement was. A book coming from a big publisher, who habitually spent large sums on advertisement, might get fifty or seventy-five reviews: a book from a small publisher might get only twenty. I knew of one case where a theological publisher, for some reason, took it into his head to publish a novel. He spent a great deal of money on advertising it. It got exactly four reviews in the whole of England, and the only full-length one was in a motoring paper, which seized the opportunity to point out that the part of the country described in the novel would be a good place for a motoring tour. This man was not in the racket, his advertisements were not likely to become a regular source of revenue to the literary papers, and so they just ignored him.

*　　*　　*

EVEN reputable literary papers could not afford to disregard their advertisers altogether. It was quite usual to send a book to a reviewer with some such formula as, "Review this book if it seems any good. If not, send it back. We don't think it's worth while to print simply damning reviews."

Naturally, a person to whom the guinea or so that he gets for the review means next week's rent is not going to send the book back. He can be counted on to find something to praise, whatever his private opinion of the book may be.

In America even the pretence that hack-reviewers read the books they are paid to criticise has been partially abandoned. Publishers, or some publishers, send out with review copies a short synopsis telling the reviewer what to say. Once, in the case of a novel of my own, they misspelt the name of one of the characters. The same misspelling turned up in review after review. The so-called critics had not even glanced into the book — which, nevertheless, most of them were boosting to the skies.

*　　*　　*

A PHRASE much used in political circles in this country is "playing into the hands of." It is a sort of charm or incantation to silence uncomfortable truths. When you are told that by saying this, that or the other you are "playing into the hands of" some sinister enemy, you know that it is your duty to shut up immediately.

For example, if you say anything damaging about British imperialism, you are playing into the hands of Dr. Goebbels. If you criticise Stalin you are playing into the hands of the *Tablet* and the *Daily Telegraph*. If you criticise Chiang-Kai-Shek you are playing into the hands of Wang Ching Wei—and so on, indefinitely.

Objectively this charge is often true. It is always difficult to attack one party to a dispute without temporarily helping the other. Some of Gandhi's remarks have been very useful to the Japanese. The extreme Tories will seize on anything anti-Russian, and don't necessarily mind if it comes from Trotskyist instead of right-wing sources. The American imperialists, advancing to the attack behind a smoke-screen of novelists, are always on the look-out for any disreputable detail about the British Empire. And if you write anything truthful about the London slums, you are liable to hear it repeated on the Nazi radio a week later. But what, then, are you expected to do? Pretend there are no slums?

Everyone who has ever had anything to do with publicity or propaganda can think of occasions when he was urged to tell lies about some vitally important matter, because to tell the truth would give ammunition to the enemy. During the Spanish civil war, for instance, the dissensions on the Government side were never properly thrashed out in the left-wing Press, although they involved fundamental points of principle. To discuss the struggle between the Communists and the Anarchists, you were told, would simply give the *Daily Mail* the chance to say that the Reds were all murdering one another. The only result was that the left-wing cause as a whole was weakened. The *Daily Mail* may have missed a few horror stories because people held their tongues, but some all-important lessons were not learned, and we are suffering from the fact to this day.

68　A *Tribune* column, 1944.

culture he was subsequently to examine. 'Casual' reading, after all, is not all that casual if you are ready and willing to embark on a longish, critical piece about it. Unless you are a hack or a masochist, there is bound to be something that appealed to you about the subject. Sure enough, in May 1936, Orwell was writing to Geoffrey Gorer:

What you say about trying to study our own customs from an anthropological point of view opens up a lot of fields of thought, but one thing to notice is that people's habits etc. are formed not only by their upbringing and so forth but also very largely by books. I have often thought it would be very interesting to study the conventions etc. of books from an anthropological point of view. I don't know if you ever read Elmer Rice's *A Voyage to Purilia*. It contains a most interesting analysis of certain conventions – taken for granted and never even mentioned – existing in the ordinary film. It would be interesting and I believe valuable to work out the underlying beliefs and general imaginative background of a writer like Edgar Wallace. But of course that's the kind of thing nobody will ever print.

Orwell may have been hedging his bets a little here, an activity he indulged in far less than most journalists, but he manifestly couldn't have known how ripe the times were for his peculiar mixture of obsession and observation. In a grudging essay in her collection *The Writing on the Wall* (1970) indicative of the kind of intelligent hostility Orwell's body of work continues to arouse in some quarters, Mary McCarthy makes an unexpected allowance: Orwell 'virtually invented' the criticisms of popular culture as a *genre*. She instances the crucial essays: 'Boys' Weeklies' (1939), 'The Art of Donald McGill' (1941) and 'Raffles and Miss Blandish' (1944). George Woodcock, in his temperate and useful examination of Orwell and his writings, *The Crystal Spirit*, invokes the same trio: they 'have formed the foundation for a whole branch of contemporary British criticism – represented particularly by Raymond Williams and Richard Hoggart – devoted to the study of popular culture at various social levels'. One can imagine Mr Williams's reservations about this ascription of influence, but it's sure that Mr Hoggart acknowledged a 'general debt', if only to 'Raffles and Miss Blandish', in his important book on the media and the working class, *The Uses of Literacy* (1957).

Since then, of course, we have probably had more analysis of the traffic on the highways and byways of the mass media than we need. Hardly a Sunday supplement goes by without someone sounding off about comic strips or gangster movies or the rise and fall of the music hall. We are in danger now of satiating our appetite for reassurance. For that is what Orwell did in this area. He was a trustworthy writer, *un type sérieux*, and he said it was perfectly all right to enjoy manifestations of low art. He steadily visited the part of us which he described as 'Sancho Panza' – that lazing *alter ego*, somnolent in the bath or 'too tired to go to bed' – and came back with encouraging reports. But it was 'Don Quixote' who produced the reports. I think this duality is verifiable in most people's experience of their inner lives and I suspect it is Orwell's supreme gift to us that he made us aware of it, without shame.

The celebrated essays *are* very good of their inspiriting kind. 'Whereas in papers like *Esquire*, for instance, or *La Vie Parisienne*, the imaginary background of the jokes is always promiscuity, the background of the McGill postcard is marriage' ('The Art of Donald McGill'). This is true and a pretty remarkable insight in its time and place. And, as Orwell moves into his conclusions, there are further clear-headed proposals. 'Society has always to demand a little more from human beings than it will get in practice.' 'On the whole, human beings want to be good, but not too good, and not quite all the time.' This is how the piece ends:

> In the past the mood of the comic postcard could enter into the central stream of literature, and jokes barely different from McGill's could casually be uttered between the murders in Shakespeare's tragedies. That is no longer possible, and a whole category of humour, integral to our literature till 1800 or thereabouts, has dwindled down to these ill-drawn postcards, leading a barely legal existence in cheap stationers' windows. The corruption of the human heart that they speak for might easily manifest itself in worse forms, and I for one should be sorry to see them vanish.

In 'Boys' Weeklies', his very first excursion into quarrying pop, presaged in that letter to Gorer, he also emerges with nuggets. Regarding the *Gem* and the *Magnet*, he suggests 'their basic political assumptions are two: nothing ever changes, and foreigners are funny'. He goes on to delineate the sort of audience for such publications, more extended than one might think. There is an entirely typical, eye-opening aside: 'Recently I offered a batch of English papers to some British legionaries of the French Foreign Legion in North Africa; they picked out the *Gem* and the *Magnet* first.' On reflection, I am astounded by the confrontation, but less astounded than Orwell seems to be by the choice. Exiles in danger presumably need their fantasies more than most and what could be more relieving that the never-never escapades, bloodless and sexless, of bands of posh kids? Doubtless those legionaries had their well-thumbed pornography as well to keep them warm.

To be fair, Orwell would probably have responded to this, after his fashion. He was unblinking about Henry Miller; had written a letter to T. S. Eliot as far back as 1931, putting up a proposed translation of a French novel ('It is the story of a prostitute, quite true to life so far as one can judge, and most ruthlessly told, but not a mere exploitation of a dirty subject'); his down-and-out experiences had left him exposed to plenty of ribaldry and obscenity. Where he reacts most strongly, it is to the pornography of violence. 'Raffles and Miss Blandish' is fundamentally about this. It is concerned with the opposition of two worlds, or concepts of countries: decent, old England, where a crook might still be a near-gentleman and there was honey still for tea, and stomping, tear-away America, where you kicked a man firmly when he was down. (The essay has to do with the concomitant prose, to boot, and Hemingway comes in for an irascible dig or so.) Orwell made rather an item of perverse endings and he closed like this:

Raffles . . . has no real moral code, no religion, certainly no social consciousness. All he has is a set of reflexes – the nervous system, as it were, of a gentleman. Give him a sharp tap on this reflex or that (they are called 'sport', 'pal', 'woman', 'king and country' and so forth), and you get a predictable reaction. In Mr Chase's books there are no gentlemen and no taboos. Emancipation is complete. Freud and Machiavelli have reached the outer suburbs. Comparing the schoolboy atmosphere of the one book with the cruelty and corruption of the other, one is driven to feel that snobbishness, like hypocrisy, is a check upon behaviour whose value from a social point of view has been underrated.

Now this, in its turn, is snobbish nonsense. You don't summon up the crickety gamesmanship of E. W. Hornung to combat the sadistic sex-ploys of the pseudo-American author of *No Orchids for Miss Blandish*: they were always playing in different ball-parks. They were also playing their respective tunes over a time-gap of about forty years. Orwell admits this at the beginning of his article, but loses sight of it during his moral peroration.

He subjected himself to terrible pressures. As late as February 1946, the year he began work on *Nineteen Eighty-Four*, he could write to Dorothy Plowman: 'I am constantly smothered under journalism – at present I am doing 4 articles every week.' What one does notice now, thanks to the four volumes of *The Collected Essays, Journalism and Letters of George Orwell*, is how frequently he used the word 'interesting'. Journalists under stress do. It is shorthand for something meriting attention but unlikely to get the required degree of it. This doesn't mean that journalism is without a function, but it does help to define its scope. Yet, even at his lowest ebb, Orwell was alert. Perhaps there was not enough time or energy to elaborate on certain insights or projections, but they were there, throughout his life's work. 'The first sign that things are really happening in England will be the disappearance of that horribly plummy voice from the radio.' 'Newspapers will presumably continue until television techniques reach a higher level.' Both these prophecies have been at least partially fulfilled.

Orwell could be very astute about contemporary influences on popular culture and was always ready to accuse the overlords of the press and radio of enforcing their own monopolistic tastes on a submissive people. At its most extreme, this pessimistic reading of history found its expression in the concept of 'prolefeed' in *Nineteen Eighty-Four*, 'meaning the rubbishy entertainment and spurious news which the Party handed out to the masses'. Yet his private involvement in what the masses saw or did as ways of amusing themselves turns out to be astonishingly limited in terms of today's free-for-all standards of participation. Most of the essays that have made his reputation as a shrewd observer of popular culture are first and foremost *literary* pieces, examinations of books, magazines, the lewd tag-lines on postcards. Furthermore, as almost everyone has pointed out, they are nostalgic in essence, devolving on enjoyments already being superseded.

With his painful honesty, Orwell recognized an insuperable gap between himself and many of the working-class representatives – as opposed to the genuine down-and-outs – that he met. In a diary he kept before writing *The Road to Wigan Pier*, he complained: 'I cannot get them to treat me precisely as an equal, however. They call me either "Sir" or "Comrade".' Writing to Jack Common [16 April 1936], he exploded: 'Yes, this business of class-breaking is a bugger. The trouble is that the socialist bourgeoisie, most of whom give me the creeps, will not be realistic and admit that there are a lot of working-class habits which they don't like and don't want to adopt.'

George Woodcock records that Orwell 'would often pour his tea into his saucer and blow on it vigorously before he drank it, and if anyone appeared to be shocked, he would be delighted and regard it all as a great joke'. Hoggart gently chastises him for similar self-conscious mannerisms, suggesting that he 'never quite lost the habit of seeing the working classes through the cosy fug of an Edwardian music-hall'. The chasm is real. Sir or comrade: either way, it seems to leave you on an edge. How hopefully Orwell invited admission to the life of most of the people is touchingly established in the much-quoted passage from *Wigan Pier*:

I have often been struck by the peculiar easy completeness, the perfect symmetry as it were, of a working-class interior at its best. Especially in winter evenings after tea, when the fire glows in the open range and dances mirrored in the steel fender, when Father in shirtsleeves sits in the rocking chair at one side of the fire reading the racing finals, and Mother sits on the other with her sewing, and the children are happy with a pennorth of mint humbugs, and the dog lolls roasting himself on the rag mat – it is a good place to be in, provided you can be not only in it but sufficiently of it to be taken for granted.

A stupefying amount is taken for granted here. It may be that such social beati-

THE CRITIC OF POPULAR CULTURE

tudes occasionally furnished their author with a womb-with-a-view. But what did it look out on? What did Father and Mother *do* on their outings away from this rosy scene?

This is where Orwell is far less effective than, say, Richard Hoggart and subsequent writers about largely urban popular culture who were not merely *in* it but very much *of* it from the first. In another long essay, 'The Lion and the Unicorn', Orwell makes a shot at annotating the English character:

We are a nation of stamp-collectors, pigeon-fanciers, amateur carpenters, coupon-snippers, darts-players, crossword-puzzle fans. All the culture that is most truly native centres round things which even when they are communal are not official – the pub, the football match, the back garden, the fireside and the 'nice cup of tea'.

Orwell undoubtedly liked his cup of tea and his pint of beer and he wrote amusingly somewhere about his ideal pub, but I sometimes wonder if he ever went to a game of football in his life: the sport of the masses. He correctly prophesied universal ill-will if anything like a World Cup ever took place. 'There are quite enough real causes of trouble already, and we need not add to them by encouraging young men to kick each other on the shins amid the roars of infuriated spectators.' On cricket he was more expansive, if contradictory. He referred to it three times in 1944. Reviewing Edmund Blunden's *Cricket Country* in April, he pronounced that 'the test of a true cricketer is that he shall prefer village cricket to "good" cricket'; then went on as follows: 'Contrary to what its detractors say, cricket is not an inherently snobbish game . . . Since it needs about twenty-five people to make up a game it necessarily leads to a good deal of social mixing.' In an 'As I Please' in the same month, he retails a scarifying youthful memory of a local squire countermanding the decision of an umpire, presumably one of his tenants. In 'Raffles and Miss Blandish', which appeared in October, he seems to amalgamate these previous statements:

Since cricket takes up a lot of time and is rather an expensive game to play, it is predominantly an upper-class game, but for the whole nation it is bound up with such concepts as 'good form', 'playing the game' etc., and it has declined in popularity just as the tradition of 'don't hit a man when he's down' has declined . It is not a twentieth-century game, and nearly all modern-minded people dislike it.

And that, apart from a glancing reference or two in his schoolday memoir, 'Such, Such Were the Joys', is his last word on the subject.

The cinema would surely figure nowadays in anyone's conception of popular culture, if not as a prime example. Here is poor old Gordon Comstock again:

Gordon halted outside a great garish picture-house, under the weary eye of the commissionaire, to examine the photographs. Greta Garbo in *The Painted Veil*. He yearned to go inside, not for Greta's sake, but just for the warmth and softness of the velvet seat. He hated the pictures, of course, seldom went there even when he could afford it. Why encourage the art that is destined to replace literature? But still, there is a kind of soggy attraction about it. To sit on the padded seat in the warm smoke-scented darkness, letting the flickering drivel on the screen gradually overwhelm you – feeling the waves of its silliness lap you round till you seem to drown, intoxicated, in a viscous sea – after all, it's the kind of drug we need. The right drug for friendless people.

Elsewhere, Orwell (in 'Boys' Weeklies') throws off a semi-political note on *Chapaiev*, writes of seeing Jack Hulbert in *Jack Ahoy* ('which I thought very amusing') and tells Rayner Heppenstall: 'Last night I went with Geoffrey Gorer to see Greta Garbo in *Anna Karenina* – not too bad. Please remember me to the Murrys.' There are a few more scattered indications that he has seen other movies at different times – he must be referring to Lotte Reiniger's silhouette films in one aside – and in answer to a questionnaire from the *Partisan Review* [April 1941] he really sounded off: 'The movies seem almost unaffected by the war, i.e. in technique and subject-matter. They go on and on with the same treacly rubbish and when they do touch on politics they are years behind the popular press and decades behind the average book.' This was in 1941. A year later, he found our people in the big towns becoming more and more Americanized in speech through the medium of the cinema. By 1946 he gloomily foresaw that 'probably novels and stories will be completely superseded by film and radio productions'.

In conversation, Sonia Orwell hesitantly proposed to me that George, with his pretty intense contempt for 'Hollywood' films, felt that the cinema had taken a wrong turn somewhere. He doesn't seem to have registered as much in print, his specific criticism of the medium being, to put it mildly, laconic: but there is one extraordinary proposition, made at some length, in an unpublished article, 'New Words'. (1940? E. J. L. Vol. II.) I only wish I had space to quote the relevant argument in full. Its gist is this: 'Properly used, the film is the one possible medium for conveying mental processes . . . If one thinks of it, there is very little in the mind that could not *somehow* be represented by the strange distorting powers of the film.' He goes on to postulate a millionaire with all the equipment and actors at his beck and call: 'He could explain the real reasons of his actions instead of telling rationalized lies, point out the things that seemed to him beautiful, pathetic, funny, etc. – things that an ordinary man has to keep locked up because there are no words to express them. In general he could make other people understand him . . .' I'm none too sure any millionaire, however hypothetical, would want to go that far, but we have since had Fellini's

8¼ and you probably have your own candidates for men who have at least partially enacted this dream of the cinema's potential.

But what about those radio productions that might be going to replace printed fiction? There's a transcript of a radio discussion between Orwell and Desmond Hawkins, formidably entitled 'The Proletarian Writer' and delivered in December 1940, roughly a year before Orwell took up his service in the Indian section of the BBC. The most revealing and Orwellian exchange came near the end.

HAWKINS: ... And epitaphs, limericks, advertisement jingles – sticking simply to poetry, those are the special literature of the Proletariat, aren't they?
ORWELL: Yes, and don't forget the jokes on the comic coloured postcards, especially Donald McGill's. I'm particularly attached to those. And above all the songs for bugle calls and military marches – those are the real popular poetry of our time, like the ballads in the Middle Ages. It's a pity they are always unprintable.

In a much later essay, 'Poetry and the Microphone' [1943, E. J. L. Vol. II], when Orwell could look back in irritation on his experiences as a talks producer, we get this: 'Indeed the very word "wireless" calls up a picture either of roaring dictators or of genteel throaty voices announcing that three of our aircraft have failed to return. Poetry on the air sounds like the Muses in striped trousers.' By now the radio was felt to be an irremediably upper-class affair, talking down to its captive audience.

And by now Orwell's few but authentic affiliations with popular culture, both that produced for the people and more rarely produced by them, should be easier to enumerate. He reviewed theatre for a short period for *Time & Tide* and one of his pieces has been reprinted, in praise of Max Miller, 'who looks more like a Middlesex Street hawker than ever when he is wearing a tail coat and a shiny top hat, ... one of a long line of English comedians who have specialized in the Sancho Panza side of life, in real *lowness*. To do this probably needs more talent than to express nobility.' There is a characteristic conclusion: 'So long as comedians like Max Miller are on the stage and the comic coloured postcards which express approximately the same view of life are in the stationers' windows, one knows that the popular culture of England is surviving.' 'The Art of Donald McGill', with its nods to Max Miller, appeared in *Horizon* a couple of years after. Orwell did not waste much.

Otherwise, we know that he was very fond of *Macbeth*, thought George Robey could play Falstaff 'if he would sink his own personality', and went to see 'the so-called Blackbirds – a troop of Negro actors – and was bored stiff'. The kind of evening out he is more likely to report on with some geniality would be like this one from *Wigan Pier*: 'There was a sort of smoking concert going on, as these clubs, like the pubs, all engage singers etc. for the week-ends. There was quite a good knockabout comedian whose jokes were of the usual twins-mother-in-law-kippers type, and pretty steady boozing.' Things don't seem to have changed all that much up north in that last thirty odd years.

It has proved impossible to convey some idea of the variety, limitations and contradictions of Orwell's approaches to popular culture without having recourse to copious quotations from his writings: and I make no apology for doing so. Let the man speak directly for himself a couple more times:

> Outside my work the thing I care about most is gardening, specially vegetable garden-ing. I like English cookery and English beer, French red wines, Spanish white wines, Indian tea, strong tobacco, coal fires, candelight and comfortable chairs. I dislike big towns, noise, motor cars, the radio, tinned food, central heating and 'modern' furniture. ('Autobiographical Notes, for 20th Century Authors', April 1940.)

And he did try, all his life, to get away from the great urban agglomerations, often for reasons of health but mainly from choice. 'For man only stays human by preserving large patches of simplicity in his life, while the tendency of many modern inventions – in particular the film, the radio and aeroplane – is to weaken his consciousness, dull his curiosity, and, in general, drive him nearer to the animals.' And one might recall that in his darkest book of all, *Nineteen Eighty-Four*, one of the recurring sights that most cheered Winston before Big Brother's minions got him for ever was a vast, red-armed woman hanging out her washing on a line below, singing and singing away at some treacly ballad. Those grotesques in Donald McGill and Orwell's life-long affection for popular songs – anything from 'You can't do that there 'ere' to 'Come where the booze is cheaper' – join together here in a sentimental but heartfelt paean to the sheer doggedness of man against all the odds: culture both as panacea and protest.

T.R. Fyvel
THE YEARS AT *TRIBUNE*

THE special relationship between Orwell and *Tribune*, which lasted roughly
from 1943 to 1949, was clearly of profit to both sides. To *Tribune*, Orwell
gave the cachet of his highly individual outlook. Conversely, the pressure
of weekly journalism must have drawn from him many penetrating shorter
pieces which otherwise would have remained unwritten. Orwell and I had seen a
good deal of each other in the early days of the war and then been separated.
When we met again it was in the spring of 1945, in his final weeks as literary
editor of *Tribune*; I myself had just returned from two years in what was then
called the 'Mediterranean Theatre' and found London at the end of the war a
battered, grey and tired-looking place, at first sight hard to readjust to. On my
arrival, my publisher Fred Warburg had given me the typescript of *Animal Farm*
to read, adding that certain people in London, like Victor Gollancz, actually
opposed its publication for fear that it might harm the Anglo-Soviet alliance.
Back from the wars (if at several removes) I shook my head at this self-centred
literary notion of the level at which Stalin operated. Reading George's strangely
moving fable, I was impressed how enormously he had gained in literary
technique – but also how pessimistic he had become since the heyday of the
optimistic socialist beliefs which we had shared in 1940–1.

George himself, tall, gaunt, with lines of suffering etched more deeply in his
face, also seemed to me tired, and looking more than just two years older, when I
called on him in the little literary office of *Tribune* where he sat sadly eyeing a
pile of new books for review like a set of enemies. He asked whether I would be
interested in taking over his job. I said that I would rather like it, but could
only do so in the autumn. He declared that he would soon leave in any case – he
was desperate to be free. I was sure he had performed the job of literary editor
meticulously because he could simply not tackle a job of work in any other way;
but he had sat in this little office since November 1943, the war was now nearing
its weary end and he felt tired and constrained.

A word about *Tribune*. Like many a successful left-wing journal, it was a fluke
that came off. As a small Socialist weekly, it was started (and owned) in 1937 by
Sir Stafford Cripps – a wealthy and briefly violently left-wing Labour Party
leader – to support his ideas for a popular 'United Front' of the British Labour,
Liberal and Communist Parties. These ideas of a 'United Front' with Communists
proved short-lived (Labour stalwarts like Ernest Bevin soon saw to that!), and
when in 1940 Churchill, as War Premier, appointed Cripps British Ambassador
to Moscow, Cripps wanted to close *Tribune* down. But at the last minute it was
taken over by Victor Gollancz, London's famous and enthusiastic left-wing
publisher. This arrangement also proved temporary as under the impact of war,
Gollancz's enthusiasms shifted from politics towards Christianity; and so he was

pleased when in 1943, in a second last-minute rescue, *Tribune* and its financial burden were taken over jointly by George Strauss, a well-to-do Labour MP, and Israel Sieff, a noted intellectual Jewish businessman and philanthropist, mainly to provide a platform for their friend Aneurin Bevan – that rising, fiery Labour Party star from the Welsh mining valleys.

Now, like Bevan's political career, *Tribune* in the latter part of the war suddenly came to life. Bevan stood on the Labour left less because his views were extreme than because his Socialism was vibrant and confident. Under his direction *Tribune* was pro-Russian but at the same time libertarian and anti-Communist, calling persistently for a Socialist government to take over from Churchill after the war. Indeed, with both Labour and Conservative ministers included in Churchill's Coalition Government, *Tribune* was often the only Fleet Street voice which dared directly to attack Churchill's war policies. As his editor, Bevan had brought in Jon Kimche, a prominent wartime journalist; to serve as literary editor, Kimche chose his old friend George Orwell – they had known each other as far back as 1934 when they had both been employed in a bookshop in Hampstead where Kimche, as he recalls, sold books with enjoyment in the mornings while Orwell did the same in moody anger during the afternoons.

I had come across a few copies of the magazine while in Italy. Flipping the pages, I had wondered how Nye Bevan with his Welsh rhetoric and his itch for office and his wish to reform British health, housing and (as he had told me in an interview) the popular press, got on with Orwell, who, amidst the euphoria of a world war being won, held fast to his incorruptible pessimism about the future. Evelyn Anderson, then assistant-editor, told me that there was really no conflict: in their casts of mind Bevan and Orwell moved on parallel lines which would never meet. In Jon Kimche's recollection, the weekly editorial meetings were rather like a stage play by Pinter: the participants spoke only in monologues. For instance, Nye Bevan might give a fervent lecture on national-izing the coal industry, his editorial for the week. After this, George ('dressed like a typical left-wing intellectual which he was not') would observe how depressing it was getting rid of Hitler only to be left with a world dominated by Stalin, American millionaires and some tinpot dictator like de Gaulle – this would be *his* theme for his weekly 'As I Please' column. Yet the result of this non-dialogue was an exciting wartime weekly journal.

While Orwell tried hard to be a reasonable literary editor, dealing with other people's work was not his strong side. But his 'As I Please' column gave the same distinction to the paper's literary end that Aneurin Bevan's Socialist line gave to the front half. It was written in that style of personal reportage which had produced some of the most vivid literature of the period, the style of a writer turned reporter who has participated in the events he describes and so gives them an extra dimension – Hemingway at Caporetto and in the Caribbean, Orwell in Burma and Barcelona, Isherwood in Berlin, Koestler in jail, Vincent Sheean in various places. This literary style, special to its age, can probably not be repeated (Norman Mailer describing a march on the Pentagon is, by comparison, writing a deliberately mannered account about a 'Happening') and Orwell's 'As I Please' stands out as perhaps the only example of its being used for sustained routine journalism.

What surprised me when we met again in 1945 was how he had turned himself from a rather agonized writer who claimed he re-wrote each page four or five times into an efficient and indeed prolific journalist. In addition to his *Tribune* job, and while completing *Animal Farm*, he had, for two years, managed to write regular book reviews for the *Manchester Evening News* and the *Observer* and a regular London Letter for *Partisan Review*, a surprising output amidst the endless time-wasting of war. But by the spring of 1945 he had reached exhaustion point as wartime journalist. I found that his personal life was also in tragic dislocation. His wife Eileen had died under a minor operation, leaving him with a baby son whom they had just adopted. Above all he wanted to shed the pressures of being *Tribune*'s literary editor. He felt he was not suited to an office job.

There he was right. During his own solitary years of writing he had lost the editorial toughness to shape and cut other people's work. The book reviews in *Tribune* were very ordinary. Perhaps one forgets how hard it was to function as literary editor during the war, with so many writers away, with barren publishers' lists, postal uncertainty and, of course, the flying bombs. At any rate, it seems Orwell rarely *sent* books out for review. Instead, news of a possible soft touch soon got round and there was a steady stream of callers to George's little office in the Strand, eager to get a book for review or leave an article or poem. As I noted when I succeeded him, apart from personal friends of George's like Stevie Smith, Alex Comfort and Julian Symons, the literary standard of these *Tribune* regulars was not very high.

But what could he do? To Evelyn Anderson, who worked on the political section in the next room, he seemed constantly burdened by the dilemma of what should have priority – his own high standards of English language and style or the desire to help a struggling, impecunious fellow-writer for whom *Tribune*'s fee of a guinea for a review plus the sale of the book might mean the difference, as George saw it, between eating or not eating. He was also worried over misprints in *Tribune*, inevitable under the sketchy wartime proof-reading. Mrs Anderson remembers him being upset for days because she herself, through fatigue, had allowed 'verbiosity' to appear in one of his own paragraphs. Yet his basic problem, however fiercely he might flay intellectuals in general, was that he had not the heart to tell a would-be contributor that the piece on which he had slaved was fit only for rejection. At the same time he would not print anything that was downright bad. In face of this dilemma, Orwell's famous honesty sometimes deserted him: he failed to answer letters, or he pretended he had not yet got round to reading the thing; and so the drawers of his desk became gradually filled with a whole mass of unrejected literary rejects which I found when I took over, and which he was only too glad to hand on.

In 1945 I was given twice as many literary pages on *Tribune* as George had had and young contributors returning from the forces – Roy Fuller, Alan Ross, Richard Hoggart, Richard Findlater, Emanuel Litvinoff and others – struck a fresh postwar note.

To Orwell as journalist, even after he had left his office, *Tribune* was still his first love. He remained a close friend of Evelyn Anderson and Michael Foot who now edited the paper. He would often drop into the office and ask one of the secretaries to share a sandwich and glass of beer at the next-door pub. The arrangement when I started as literary editor was that he would write occasional non-political pieces, but the first one he proposed almost started us off on the wrong foot. In his first contribution as an outsider, he intended to say that the new Labour Government must make it its first Socialist task to abolish all titles, the House of Lords and the Public Schools and that Aneurin Bevan with such purely bureaucratic reforms as the National Health Service and council house estates was quite on the wrong track. I protested that I could not start off my job with such a direct attack on Nye Bevan and laughed George out of the idea. This essay was never written. Rather a pity, I now think.

Against this, I was able several times to tempt him to write essays by pushing special themes his way. One of the best originated when we discovered how, as children, we had both enjoyed that one-time fabulous American bestseller, *Helen's Babies* by John Habberton. From this starting point, he wrote that moving little essay 'Riding Down to Bangor'. Indeed, in 1947, before he departed for the Isle of Jura and before his final illness, he contributed another short series of 'As I Please' pieces which included some of the gayest and wittiest of his essays, classics like 'The Sporting Spirit'. As I knew, Orwell could rewrite even such slight pieces three or four times, paring them of each unnecessary phrase. They represent the lighter, warmer aspect of his mind while he was writing *Nineteen Eighty-Four*: there was always spring, there were flowers and the common toad, children's books and nonsense rhymes, there was his own, prejudiced self to laugh at. It is worth noting, in fact, how *Tribune* journalism continued to bring out this other side of Orwell's nature.

Edward Crankshaw
ORWELL
AND COMMUNISM

To READ, or re-read, everything Orwell wrote about Communism is to make some surprising discoveries. By Communism I mean what Orwell meant by that word: the Moscow rule-book. And I suppose it would be generally agreed that he did more to bring home to a wide public the essential nature of the Communist fraud than any Western writer, including Koestler. He was one of the first to illuminate the brutality and perfidy of Communist methods and to expose Stalin's betrayal of revolutionary idealism in the interests of the Soviet Union. In 1938, without seeking to hedge in any way, he condemned by ridicule the notorious treason trials, which, by the sheer size and effrontery of the lies embodied in them, had undermined the scepticism of many who were by no means sold on Stalin, persuading them that there must be substance of some kind behind the 'confessions' and those monstrous and lunatic accusations which Vyshinsky threw about with the air of a man dispensing platitudes. He gave his name to the concept of a nightmare society more closely approached in the Soviet Union than anywhere else in the world. He produced memorable words and phrases fixing indelibly the nastiness of Communist practices and institutions. He did all this, as a would-be Socialist, in the teeth of outraged opposition from the main body of fellow left-wing intellectuals then trying desperately to knock together some sort of a shelter for themselves with rotten planks and broken timbers salvaged from the wreck of the great Soviet experiment – and he accepted no help from the Right, which he abhorred even while he valued certain human qualities found more often on the Right than on the Left.

It was an extraordinary achievement, and the first surprise, looking back, is the economy of the means employed to pull it off. What Orwell had to say directly about the matter added up to no more than a very small fraction of his output; certain parts of *Homage to Catalonia*, a few book reviews, a couple of dozen articles in small-circulation periodicals, a short and lambent allegory, his masterpiece, *Animal Farm*. Indeed, as far as the general public was concerned, it was *Animal Farm* that did the trick: until it appeared in 1945 Orwell was known only to the few. *Nineteen Eighty-Four* was also read as an essay in anti-Communism. It is the fashion nowadays to say that it was nothing of the kind. Certainly Orwell was here stalking bigger game than Stalin. But the fact remains that *Nineteen Eighty-Four* took its colour from his views about Communism, seen as a prime example of totalitarian fantasy. Many of the ideas it contains had already been floated in his occasional writings about Communism. And if 'Newspeak', 'Doublethink' and the rest may be applied to what are now called consensus attitudes of all kinds, well, so may Snowball's jolly slogan 'Four legs good, two legs bad!' now tediously echoed by the cheer-leaders of the whole spectrum of orthodoxies of all shades of Right and Left in every country in the world, not least our own.

Economy of means is not at all the most striking attribute of Orwell's writing seen as a whole. He was too apt to labour a subject, making heavy weather: sometimes it was only the vividness of his imagery and the sharpness of his eye for the particular that redeemed him from bumbling. Think of the long-drawn-out, repetitive, self-contradictory argument for Socialism in the second half of *The Road to Wigan Pier*, which was later pursued, more or less inconclusively, in countless articles and essays. Contrast this with the sharpness and spareness of the first major assault on Communism, the two-part article, 'Spilling the Spanish Beans'. Then compare the pellucid simplicity of *Animal Farm* with the more or less tentative groping of all the preceding books. From this exercise something should emerge, and I think something does. It was, for me, the second surprise.

What emerges is that Orwell, who did more than anybody else to show up Communism, was not himself seriously engaged with it. Endlessly argumentative, he never argued against Communism. It was not worth arguing about. He dismissed it. It was beyond the pale. His argument was not with Communism, which was self-evidently a disaster, but with the left-wing intellectuals who rushed to be deceived by it, rolling over on their backs, all four paws in the air, begging to be tickled by Uncle Joe. Communism was no more of a problem for him than incest was a problem. He was concerned with it only because it was a problem for others, and the existence of that problem obscured for many of those others a large part of Orwell's own nature. I think it still does.

To re-read Orwell for what he had to say about Communism was for me to be lured irresistibly into reading his entire published output – the more so, perhaps because for one reason and another, I missed the chance of meeting him. It may be that those who enjoyed this privilege have for long known what only recently became clear to me: namely that he did not write at all about a number of things about which he thought and felt deeply. To a greater or less degree this must be true of every writer, inevitably. But in the case of Orwell, whose peculiar value lay in his capacity to sustain a public inquest into the development of his thinking and feeling – and was obviously driven and himself sustained by the need to do this – his silences may be positively misleading. Until suddenly and without warning he will throw out a casual observation like a small bomb, indicating that he has given thought to some matter which had appeared to be outside his range of interest. Thus, for example, he will matter-of-factly remark that the real trouble with the world is the death of religion. Again, having written a good deal about Communism and the Soviet Union without suggesting that he has given a shadow of a thought to the historical background of Stalinism he offers, almost as an aside, the view that things would have been much the same in Russia if Lenin had lived or if Trotsky had won the fight with Stalin.

He had evidently thought a good deal about Communism before he first publicly assailed it in 1937, when he was thirty-four. In 1947 in a letter to Victor Gollancz he wrote of the Soviet Union: 'For quite fifteen years I have regarded that regime with plain horror.' There is no reason to doubt the truth of this. By 1932 there was enough evidence of the irredeemable squalor of the Soviet regime to sicken anyone who did not refuse to see it for what it was (the ubiquity of the GPU, the introduction of large-scale forced labour, the sabotage trials, the murderous circumstances of the collectivization and the consequent famine, the suppression of the best spirits among the Soviet writers, the cynicism of blatantly lying propaganda, etc.). I myself, six years younger than Orwell, had by then decided that no good could come of it. I did not write about it because there seemed nothing much to say. The Soviet Union was horrible, but it was so far away and in such a mess that at that time it seemed irrelevant. I was also, because of personal circumstances, already obsessed by Hitler, who was close at hand and very relevant indeed. I imagine that Orwell had much the same feeling about the irrelevance of Soviet Russia. But his own obsession, what mattered most to him, was his groping progress towards a genuinely revolutionary Socialism and his struggle with the pretensions, the evasions, the intellectual dishonesty of all those liberals and socialists who should, it seemed to him, have been his allies. It was in this context that his writings about Communism were conceived and produced.

What started him off, of course, was Spain. He was driven by his own integrity, his absolute honesty (which is not to say that he was immune from self-deception), his passion for social injustice in general and the weak, exploited and oppressed in particular. It was not until 1937 that he called himself a Socialist, but he had proved his commitment to the under-dog by identifying himself with the lower depths as few professing Socialists had ever done – indeed, by stripping himself of all he had and going to live among the very poor. He had thrown up his police job in Burma, lived as a down-and-out in Paris and London, made his pilgrimage to Wigan Pier. He had gone to Spain ostensibly to report the war, stayed to fight and been badly wounded. Invariably, to borrow Henry James's words about Conrad, he chose 'the way to do a thing that shall make it undergo most doing'. Of himself he wrote in *The Road to Wigan Pier*: 'I had carried my hatred of oppression to extraordinary lengths:

At that time failure seemed to me the only virtue. Every suspicion of self-advancement, even to "succeed" in life to the extent of making a few hundreds a year, seemed to me spiritually ugly, a species of bullying.' A year or so later, in a review of Borkenau's *The Communist International*, he touched on his dream of 'a movement which is genuinely revolutionary, i.e. willing to make drastic changes and use violence if necessary, but which does not lose touch, as Communism and Fascism have done, with the essential values of democracy'. For a moment in Catalonia, fighting in the line with the POUM militia, this high romantic, who disguised himself as a utilitarian, had believed that he had found such a movement and rejoiced in submerging himself in it. All too soon he had to stand by and watch its destruction, not by Franco but by the professed champions of revolution, the Communist Party, commanded and financed by Moscow, operating in unholy alliance with a bourgeois government. The experience shocked him deeply. What made it infinitely more painful was the spectacle of the British left-wing establishment joining in the witch-hunt against his revolutionary heroes, following the Russian line and calling them Fascists, worse still, refusing to publish his own eye-witness account of what was happening in Barcelona – i.e. deliberately suppressing the truth – for fear of giving comfort to Franco.

The article which Kingsley Martin refused to print came out in two parts in the *New English Weekly* in July and September 1937, under the title 'Spilling the Spanish Beans':

For some time past a reign of terror – forcible suppression of political parties, a stifling censorship of the press, ceaseless espionage and mass imprisonment without trial – has been in progress. When I left Barcelona in late June the jails were bulging . . . But the point to notice is that the people who are in prison now are not Fascists but revolutionaries; they are there not because their opinions are too much to the Right, but because they are too much to the Left. And the people responsible for putting them there are those dreadful revolutionaries at whose very name Garvin quakes in his galoshes – the Communists.

This was a declaration of war, not against Communism as such but against its dupes and apologists in England (card-carrying Party members, too, of course), and those who were for ever prepared to give murderers and psychopaths the benefit of the doubt under the unexpressed slogan, 'the Red Flag – Right or Wrong!' He was to go on like that. What had happened was that Communism and Russia had suddenly become relevant: they had swung across his own pre-ordained course. And there was a collision.

Also in that July Orwell wrote in *Time and Tide* a review of Borkenau's *Spanish Cockpit*: 'The most important fact that has emerged from the whole business is that the Communist Party is now (presumably for the sake of Russian foreign policy) an anti-revolutionary force.' He wrote elaborating this thesis to a number of friends, returning to the attack in a letter to *Time and Tide* in February 1938. In April *Homage to Catalonia* appeared, with its remarkably cool and fair assessment of the Communist action which had killed and imprisoned so many of his comrades and all but finished him. In July 1938, in a review of Eugene Lyons' *Assignment in Utopia*, he wrote about the Moscow treason trials with a directness and decision not to be found at that time in anybody who did not possess a built-in gyro-compass guaranteed to take him straight to the heart of a lie:

To get the full sense of our ignorance as to what is really happening in the USSR it is worth trying to translate the most sensational Russian event of the past two years, the Trotskyite trials, into English terms. Make the necessary adjustments, let Left be Right and Right be Left, and you get something like this:

'Mr Winston Churchill, now in exile in Portugal, is plotting to overthrow the British Empire and establish Communism in England. By the use of unlimited Russian money he has succeeded in building up a huge Churchillite organization which includes members of Parliament, factory managers, Roman Catholic bishops and practically the whole of the Primrose League. Almost every day some dastardly act of sabotage is laid bare – sometimes a plot to blow up the House of Lords, sometimes an outbreak of foot and mouth disease in the Royal racing-stables. Eighty per cent of the Beefeaters at the Tower are discovered to be agents of the Comintern. A high official of the Post Office admits brazenly to having embezzled postal orders to the tune of £500,000 and also to having committed *lèse majesté* by drawing moustaches on postage stamps. Lord Nuffield, after a 7-hour interrogation by Mr Norman Birkett, confesses that ever since 1920 he has been fomenting strikes in his own factories. Casual half inch paras in every issue of the newspapers announce that fifty more Churchillite sheep-stealers have been shot in Westmorland or that the proprietress of a village shop in the Cotswolds has been transported to Australia for sucking bulls-eyes and putting them back in the bottle . . .'

I quote that at length because it is the best short comment on the Moscow trials ever written, because it is irresistible, because it is pleasant to be reminded of how funny and high-spirited Orwell could be when he let himself go – and because of its absolute dismissiveness. It was written only a year after Orwell's first, and only, glimpse of Communism in action and at a time when Western intellectuals of a leftish inclination were tying themselves up in knots as they tried to 'explain' the purges and the trials – two years, indeed, before Koestler himself in *Darkness at Noon* produced his own explanation of those trials, laying far too much stress on the psychological pressures which caused the accused to confess to ludicrous crimes and far too little on the physical – i.e. torture.

Orwell never seems to have had the least doubt that the confessions were obtained by torture of the cruelest kind. We know so much about this now, and from the mouth of Khrushchev himself, that it is hard to realize that in 1938, and for long after, it was by no means taken for granted. Orwell never gave his reasons for this certainty nor, except obliquely in *Nineteen Eighty-Four* did he indicate how he thought the victims were first broken, then rehearsed and made word perfect, then fattened up for show. No doubt he could have done so had he been asked. It did not seem worth his while. It had no bearing on his main preoccupation: this with one half of his mind was to define his own attitude to society and propose a political system in which he could believe, and, with the other, to castigate and ridicule intellectual traitors and buffoons. The first task he found immensely, indeed impossibly, difficult, because, with all his marvellous insights and perceptions, he lacked the sort of logical mind which could either knit such perceptions into a coherent (if illusory) system, or else show him conclusively that he must allow equal weight to those observed facts which lent support to his humane instincts and those which seemed to contradict them. But that is another story.

He went on writing intermittently about Communism and Russia, always stating, never arguing. His position is made quite clear later in the review quoted above:

The question arises, could anything like this happen in England? Obviously it could not. From our point of view the whole thing is not merely incredible as a genuine conspiracy, it is next door to incredible as a frame-up. It is simply a dark mystery, of which the only seizable fact – sinister enough in its way – is that Communists over here regard it as a good advertisement for Communism.

But he was still not easy in his mind. He couldn't quite leave it at that: 'Meanwhile the truth about Stalin's regime, if only we could get hold of it, is of the first importance. Is it Socialism, or is it a particularly vicious form of state capitalism?' In fact, he has already got at the truth about Stalin's regime for all immediately practical purposes. That last question could only have been asked by a man worrying away about Socialism and not happy about his own answers. The underlying truth about Stalin's regime had to do with Russian history in particular and human obliquity in general. Orwell knew this very well. He never paused to ask the important questions here because they were not relevant to his immediate purpose. Had he done so and found some sort of an answer he would still have written *Animal Farm*, but I don't think he would have written *Nineteen Eighty-Four* as he did in fact write it. So perhaps it is just as well that he did not ask those questions. *Nineteen Eighty-Four* had to be written; but it could only have been carried through by a man who was either partly blind to the tragic poetry of human aspiration – *or* who, for his own purposes, was excluding it from his consciousness. It has been said often enough that Orwell was in fact blind in this way. I do not think he was. There are so many flashes in which the human reality breaks through. I think Orwell's obsession with his own development, and with the here and now that must here and now be changed, encouraged him to exclude from his thinking, more or less deliberately, large areas of consciousness for fear of going soft and losing the cutting flame of his indignation. The man who could write of a doomed, anonymous Italian revolutionary

> No bomb that ever burst
> Shatters the crystal spirit

was a poet at heart and knew all about the tragic sense of life. *Animal Farm* is poetry all the way through. But it seems to me that for most of his too short life Orwell believed that times were too bleak for poetry.

They were also too bleak for sitting back and speculating about Lenin, who was dead, or the historical background to Fascism and Communism, which had to be exposed simply for what they were and for what they were doing to the human mind. By September 1938 he had finally got his ideas about Communism into order. It was Borkenau again who acted as the catalyst. Reviewing *The Communist International* in the *New English Weekly*, Orwell produced the best short summary of Stalinism in foreign policy offered by anyone for years to come. He ran through the development of the Comintern, starting as an international revolutionary movement; degenerating by swift stages into an instrument for controlling foreign Communist parties in the interest of Russian power; for destroying not only foreign social democratic movements but also foreign Communists who showed independence of judgment or, worse, might be considered to owe allegiance to an ideal; for collaborating with Hitler in the ruin of German democracy, then howling for a Popular Front against the bogey Stalin himself had helped to raise. Orwell gets his story slightly wrong in detail, but right in essence – astonishingly right for that time. He knew very little about the Russianness of the Bolsheviks. He did not appreciate that when Lenin formed the Cominterm, the Third International, in 1920, he was already in retreat from the ideal of world revolution and thinking in terms of the consolidation of Soviet power. He was never quite able to see Stalin for what he was, attributing to his treacheries (in Spain for example) subtler motives than the single-minded desire to root out and destroy any movement anywhere which might serve as a nucleus for an independent reformist or revolutionary force. But he saw much clearer than most.

He continued to see and to write when the occasion called for it. His first task had been to delouse the left-wing establishment. His next task was even more ungrateful: while profoundly moved and stirred by the endurance and the heroism of the Soviet people in defence of their homeland (and, with it, their rulers), he still had to speak out not only against the manifest evil of the Soviet regime and the Doublethink of English Communists, but also against the un-restrained adulation of so many Englishmen for all things Russian and the betrayal of decency by those who, for example, blackguarded the Warsaw Poles for their desperate and heroic rising, or assisted in the handing over in droves, to be shot by Stalin, those unfortunate Soviet citizens, military and civilian, who sought sanctuary in the West.

At the same time, in his writings on a broader scale about the nature of totalitarianism and the meaning of liberty, about the British Empire, the British social system and domestic politics, he was still fighting towards the light, still seeking to achieve those elusive certainties he had pursued for so long and now seemed farther away than ever as the shared ordeal of a nation in peril made it harder for him to maintain his highly personal rigidities. In his later war-time writings he showed quite frequently a realization that, at least as far as England was concerned, he had attributed too much that he detested to deliberate, cal-culated predation and too little to the more or less greedy, more or less generous, more or less kindly, more or less unimaginative, more or less lazy, more or less frightened, almost wholly muddled behaviour of the ordinary human being, rich or poor – though, of course, the rich had the harder task, quite properly, in getting past his fierce-eyed guardianship of the needle's eye. 'I do not believe', he had once written, 'that a man with £5000 a year and a man with 15/- a week either can, or will cooperate.' (This was à propos of Borkenau's alternative to Fascism or Communism: 'orderly reconstruction through the cooperation of all classes'.) 'The nature of their relationship is, quite simply, that the one is robbing the other, and there is no reason to think that the robber will turn over a new leaf.' The very rich, then, some of them, rob the very poor . . . The less rich? The slightly less poor? Towards the end of the war Orwell was beginning to see wickedness in terms of individuals as distinct from classes.

It is against this background that the miracle of *Animal Farm* is best con-sidered. In a surpassingly silly book called *The Making of George Orwell* Mr Keith Aldritt avers that *Animal Farm* has been greatly over-rated, the whole concept being 'only a clever form for expressing a set of opinions that have been held so long that they no longer admit the complexity of the experience they claim to explain'. Leaving aside the fact that in *Animal Farm* there is no claim to explain anything at all, the central fact about it is that it is the only book which shows what Orwell could do when he had made up his mind about a subject all the way through. What Mr Aldritt calls 'Orwell's long-nurtured cynicism about Communism' (an unhappy phrase to characterize the blazing anger, contempt and pity of a man made vulnerable by his lack of even the thinnest shield of cynicism) was the outcome of an immediate, direct and passionate rejection of a combination of disgusting qualities in which he could find no redeeming feature. When he is writing about the poor and oppressed, about the mental contortions of the Left, about the selfishness of the rich, about many other things, his attack, while shattering in detail and deeply penetrating, is, in the long run, uncertain – blunted here, exaggerated there – precisely because he was always at the back of his mind aware of features which could and did redeem. This man who was for ever insisting on arrangements in sharp black and white, had great trouble in reaching a firm and settled attitude towards a complex problem. About a few things he knew just where he stood: about, for example, hanging, about colonial rule. And it was because of this, and his consequent ability to distance himself from the subject, that his two essays, 'Shooting an Elephant' and 'A Hanging' are so nearly perfect. He was also sure about Communism, as I have tried to show. For eight years he had struggled, as occasion arose, to shame and ridicule others into sharing his view. It had not been enough. In *Animal Farm* he made a supreme effort, echoing Conrad: 'It is, before all, to make you *see*.' He succeeded at last and there was no more to be done.

The astonishing thing is that this writer, whose especial value had lain in an unending, brooding, irritable dialogue with himself, a questioning, a doubting and a self-doubting, should have found himself able to take up a subject which was crystal clear in his mind and transmute it into a finished, wholly self-sufficient work of art, standing back and sublimating his indignation through an exercise in compassion which showed what he might have done had he been given health and time to discover his true position in face of other problems, subtler and more complex, which crowded in on him.

Michael Meyer
MEMORIES OF GEORGE ORWELL

I FIRST met George Orwell in April 1943 through that odd character Tambi-muttu, the Singhalese editor of *Poetry, London*. I had expressed admiration of Orwell's work, and Tambimuttu said: 'Would you like to meet him? I'll tell him you'll be writing to him.' Even more than most of Tambi's promises, this seemed unlikely to bear fruit, but when a few days later I did write timidly to Orwell asking if he would lunch with me I received a courteous letter of acceptance, on BBC notepaper (he was in the midst of what he was later to describe as his 'two wasted years' in that organization).

We met, as so often later, at the Hungarian Czarda in Dean Street. I remember being surprised by his great height and thinness, his staring pale-blue eyes and his high-pitched drawl with its markedly Old Etonian accent, so out of keeping with most (not all) of what he wrote. I recall little of our conversation at that first meeting except that he asked: 'Isn't that an Old Wellingtonian tie?' (what on earth could have made me choose to wear that for a meeting with Orwell?), and talked of the single term he had spent at that formidable military establish-ment in 1917 before moving on to Eton. He had found Wellington terrifyingly Spartan, as indeed it was when I went there seventeen years later, and the only pleasant memory he retained was of skating on the lake. I see from the School Register that he was a contemporary there of Tyrone Guthrie.

When we parted he invited me to come and have supper with him, and a week or so later I visited him in his small flat in Mortimer Crescent, off the junction of Maida Vale and Kilburn High Street. His wife Eileen, a pretty brown-haired girl, cooked an imaginative meal. Somehow the conversation got on to H. G. Wells, and George told me the sad story of the end of their friend-ship, which I don't think has been related elsewhere. Some time earlier Wells had offered them the use of a flat above the garage of his house in Regent's Park. They had been very happy there until one day Wells got it into his head, as he so often did about people, that George had been saying unkind things about him behind his back, and ordered him to leave immediately; nor could George persuade him that his suspicions were unfounded, so they had to go. A few months later the Orwells thought they would try to patch things up, so they wrote to Wells inviting him to dinner. Wells replied at once with a warm accept-ance and expressed wonder at their having left the flat he had lent them so suddenly and without explanation. He turned up full of amiability and began by warning them that he had stomach trouble and could not eat anything rich. 'Oh dear,' said Eileen. 'I've cooked a curry.' 'I mustn't touch that', said Wells. 'Just give me a very little.' He ate two huge helpings, as well as drinking plenti-fully, and chatted away in excellent form. After dinner William Plomer (or was it William Empson?) arrived. It transpired that he had not eaten, and the curry, thanks to Wells's greed, was finished, so Eileen said: 'All I can offer you is some plum cake.' 'Plum cake?' said Wells, overhearing this. 'I don't think I could manage that.' 'I'm not offering it to you, it's for Bill', said Eileen, but when it appeared Wells observed that it looked uncommonly good and took two slices. Around midnight they put him into a taxi, in the best of spirits, and as he drove off he cried: 'Don't lose touch with me for so long again!' They congratulated themselves on having repaired the friendship, but a week later they got a furious letter from Wells saying: 'You knew I was ill and on a diet, you deliberately plied me with food and drink,' etc., and declaring that he never wanted to see either of them again. (This must be the letter referred to in Orwell's diary for 27 March 1942 in which Wells 'addresses me as "you shit" among other things'.) Apparently Wells had been taken violently ill in the taxi and had had to be rushed to hospital; obviously, they had conspired against him in revenge for (he now remembered) the trouble over the flat. I believe they never did see each other again.

Once when I visited him around the end of that year he outlined the plot of a short book he was writing, a 'kind of parable' to remind people of the realities of Stalinist Communism, which he felt people were in danger of forgetting because of their sympathy for Russian resistance to the Germans. Like so many writers, he was hopeless at telling the story of any of his books. His summary went something like: 'There's a farm, and the animals get fed up with the way the farmer runs it, so they chuck him out and try to run it themselves. But they run it just as badly as the farmer and become tyrants like him, and in the end they invite the humans back and gang up with them to bully the other animals.' 'Yes?', I said encouragingly, and George said: 'It's a kind of parable, you see.' It really sounded desperately unpromising, and I was hardly surprised when on my next visit George said: 'That damn fool Victor Gollancz has turned my book down. He doesn't want to publish anything anti-Russian.' Each time I visited him I heard of some new publisher who had rejected it, Cape and Faber on political grounds, Collins because although they approved of it they thought there would be no market for a novel of only thirty thousand words. George felt so strongly about the book that at one time he was considering publishing it at his own expense as a pamphlet. I remember my astonishment at its brilliance when it finally appeared from Secker and Warburg. Never can a book have been so much better than its author's account of it.

In June 1944 the Orwells were bombed out of Mortimer Crescent, and that autumn they moved to a flat in Canonbury Square, then by no means the fashionable quarter it has since become. I visited them often there, for tea or dinner; the tea was always very black and strong, with large leaves floating on top, poured by George from a huge metal pot with two handles which must have held the best part of a gallon. He was very proud of his skill at carpentry, which in fact was minimal. There was a dreadful chair he had made himself and in which one had to sit; it was impossible to be comfortable in it in any position. One day he told my father, who was a timber merchant, that he wanted to make some bookshelves but couldn't get hold of the wood because of wartime rationing. My father took the hint and procured him several lengths of the most beautiful cherry-wood. George was delighted and grateful, and a few weeks later asked me along to see the finished product. It was awful beyond belief. He had whitewashed it, a criminal way to treat cherry-wood, and had not put in sufficient supports, so that the shelves curved like hammocks. I am glad my father never saw them.

George spoke much about his early life. His literary earnings up to the war, he once told me, had averaged a pound a week. He talked about an unpleasant school where he had briefly taught for some pathetic salary (I think, though I am not sure, that he got £80 a year plus his keep *during term-time*). The headmaster had been a monster, and some years after leaving George had been pleased to read in the *News of the World* that the man had been jailed for messing about with the boys. The judge, in passing sentence, had observed that a particularly bad feature of the case had been that the headmaster had also been the school scoutmaster and had put the boys on their honour as scouts to say nothing about it. Homosexuality was something for which George always felt a particular revulsion, curious in one so liberal; he mentioned with distaste various attempts that had been made on him at one time and another. Speaking of the novelists he admired, he surprised me by naming Somerset Maugham and praising the unadorned simplicity of his style.

Late in 1944 the Olivier-Richardson season opened at the New Theatre, and when they introduced the two parts of *Henry IV* into the repertory George remarked that one ought to take the opportunity to see both parts on the same day. I discovered a day when *Part 1* was being performed in the afternoon and *Part 2* in the evening and booked a couple of tickets. We lunched at a Cypriot restaurant in Percy Street called the Akropolis (it is now a night-club under the same ownership); we finished rather late, and I walked him fast the half-mile or so to the New Theatre, where we arrived after curtain up. I remember the dreadful whistling heaviness of his breathing for five or ten minutes after we had taken our seats, and my shame at having forgotten the state of his lungs. At the end of *Part 2* we had a Chinese dinner at the Hong Kong restaurant in Shaftesbury Avenue; we were both so exhausted by the seven hours of Shakespeare we had seen that we ate, for once, in virtual silence.

Early in 1945 I met Graham Greene. I found that he had never met George, and thought it would be fun to bring them together, so I told George that Graham admired him (which was true), and Graham that George admired him (which was only partly true), and invited them both to lunch on my birthday at the Czarda. They got on extremely well, as one might have expected with two such modest and likeable men, though I was disappointed that for most of the time they talked politics rather than literature. I felt very small beside them, physically as well as intellectually, as they both measured well over six feet. George happened to mention his fondness for the Edwardian novelist Leonard Merrick, and Graham asked him if he would like to write an introduction to one of Merrick's works for a series of forgotten classics called the Century Library which Graham was editing for Eyre and Spottiswoode. George said: 'I'd jump at it' and suggested *The Position of Peggy Harper*; but although he wrote the introduction later that year, for some reason the book did not appear.*
They conversed so eagerly that when the restaurant closed we continued in a pub across the road called the Crown and Two Chairmen, and when that shut George suggested that we should both lunch with him the following week at a restaurant named the Elysée. This was in Percy Street exactly opposite the Akropolis, which George had ceased to patronize because of a quarrel with the proprietor, who had asked him to replace his jacket when George had removed it on a particularly hot day. George had deliberately chosen the Elysée as his new haunt so that the proprietor of the Akropolis, who had the habit of standing in his doorway, could see him going in and out. A week or two later Graham stood us both a lunch at Rule's in Maiden Lane, where the claret arrived the temperature of warm bath-water.

After the first of these meetings George borrowed *The Power and the Glory* (which he had never read) from me; but he did not like it, any more than he did Graham's other religious novels – though he allowed it some merit, which was more than he did to *The Heart of the Matter*, of which he wrote a very hostile and oddly insensitive review for the *New Yorker* three years later. But George had a blind spot where religion was concerned; he thought it an evasion of the world's problems, and he disliked Eliot's *Four Quartets* for the same reason. He was interested in the leftness of Greene's politics.

'You refer to him as an extreme Conservative, the usual Catholic reactionary type,' [he wrote to T. R. Fyvel in 1949]. 'This isn't so at all, either in his books or privately. Of course he is a Catholic and in some issues has to take sides politically with the church, but in outlook he is just a mild Left with faint CP leanings. I have even thought that he

* Graham Greene tells me that he left Eyre and Spottiswoode that year, whereupon Douglas Jerrold, the firm's chairman, discontinued the series.

might become our first Catholic fellow-traveller, a thing that doesn't exist in France but does in England.'

Another of George's blind spots was philosophy; like so many distinguished creative writers (Ibsen for one) he had little patience with abstract thought.

When the war ended I went back to Oxford. In May 1946 George moved into the house he had rented on Jura in the Hebrides and asked me to get him some black powder and percussion caps for his gun; but the shop in St Aldate's told me I would have to show a gun licence to buy the powder, and when I asked George to post me his he replied that he didn't have one, as there was no policeman on the island. He invited me to stay. 'It's not such an impossible journey', he explained, adding discouragingly that it was about forty-eight hours from London and that if the weather was bad the local taxi would not go beyond a certain point and I would have to walk the last five or six miles with my bag. I couldn't get up that year (or was I waiting until travelling got easier?). In 1947 I took up a job in Sweden; when I returned on vacation in the summer of 1948 I wanted to visit him, but unfortunately the time I suggested proved impossible for him ('at the moment we have 4 adults and 3 children in a house with 5 bedrooms, and prospectively 8 adults and 3 children, as some people are coming to help with the harvest'). 'Come next year if you can', he added, but that winter he was removed to the sanatorium at Cranham.

> I began to relapse last September [he wrote to me on 12 March 1949], and should have gone for treatment earlier, but I had to finish that beastly book which I had been struggling with for so long [*Nineteen Eighty-Four*]. It is a great bore, my health breaking up like this. I cannot resign myself to leading a sedentary life, which I suppose I shall have to from now on. I shall at any rate have to spend the winters in some get-atable place near a doctor, perhaps in somewhere like Brighton.

I did not see him when I came to England that summer; I was hoping to do so when I returned for Christmas, but one afternoon in January I opened the *Evening News* and read that he was dead.

I remember him as, not merely the most courteous, kindly and lovable man I have known, but as the one of all my friends with whom, if I could today, I would choose to spend an evening. I have heard people describe him as taciturn; one brilliant talker of my acquaintance once referred to him as 'gloomy George'. I never found him gloomy. He had a weak voice and could not raise it to make himself heard above a loud adversary or a general conversation. Once he took me to one of the weekly lunches which he, Anthony Powell and Malcolm Muggeridge used to hold (at the Bourgogne Restaurant in Gerrard Street), and I remember him trying several times to say something and abandoning the attempt half-way because of the noise. Another time I took him to supper with a politician who was later to become a cabinet minister, a delightful man but inclined to hold forth in a powerful voice. I had much looked forward to listening to them debate; but after a few unsuccessful efforts to get a word in, George quietly and with perfect courtesy became a silent auditor like the rest of us.

He was a shy man; but if one prompted him and listened, he was a most rewarding conversationalist. Above all, he was the best informed and most illuminating talker about politics whom I have ever met. His conversation was like his writing, unaffected, lucid, witty and humane; and he was, even to those of us who were young and brash, the kindest and most encouraging of listeners. Apart from the odd paranoiac like Wells, I wonder if he died with a single enemy.

Last years

69 Fatherhood.

70 Barnhill, Orwell's home on the Isle of Jura from May 1946 to January 1949.

71 The handyman, 1946.

Friends
and
contemporaries

75 (*Left*) Sir Richard Rees
(1900–1970), painter, author and
Editor, one of Orwell's closest
friends from around 1930. He
did a great deal to help and
encourage him over the years.
76 (*Below left*) Cyril Connolly
(b. 1903) a lifelong friend.
77 (*Below right*) The novelist
Anthony Powell (b. 1905), a
close friend in the 1940s.

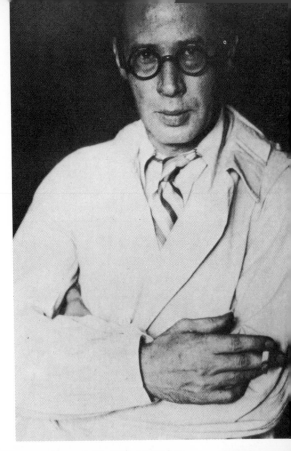

78 Henry Miller (b. 1891) whom Orwell discusses in 'Inside the Whale'.

79 Kingsley Martin (1897–1969), Editor of the *New Statesman*, leading spokesman of the intellectual Left, here taking part in 'the Brains Trust'.

80 (*Above left*) Julian Symons (b. 1912) writer and friend of Orwell's during his later years.

81 (*Above right*) Fredric Warburg (b. 1897) publisher of *Homage to Catalonia*, *Animal Farm*, *Nineteen Eighty-Four* and other books by Orwell.

82 Malcolm Muggeridge (b. 1903) a close friend in the 1940s.

83 Victor Gollancz (1893–1967),
Orwell's first English publisher.

Matthew Hodgart
FROM
ANIMAL FARM
TO
NINETEEN EIGHTY-FOUR

*O*LDTHINKERS *unbellyfeel Ingsoc*, in the classic Newspeak phrase. The shortest translation of this typical sentence from a *Times* leading article, Orwell tells us, would be: 'those whose ideas were formed before the Revolution cannot have a full emotional understanding of the principles of English Socialism'; though 'only a person thoroughly grounded in Ingsoc could appreciate the full force of the world *bellyfeel*, which implied a blind, enthusiastic acceptance difficult to imagine today; or of the word *oldthink*, which was inextricably mixed up with the ideas of wickedness and decadence'. Orwell, very English and an oldthinking socialist, unbellyfelt (no, *unbellyfeeled*) Stalin-ism. The driving force behind his two satires is an intense revulsion against totalitarianism, combined with an even stronger revulsion against its defend-ers among left-wing intellectuals. From about 1935 he was convinced that Russia had taken the wrong path and had become a tyranny: it was therefore important for the cause of world socialism to show up the Stalin myth. In the nineteen-thirties and forties, especially after Russia had come into the war, a large proportion of the younger British intellectuals had become Com-munist Party members or fellow-travellers, and were in Orwell's opinion com-pounding with the lies put out by the Stalinist propaganda *apparat*, at the expense of truth, freedom and ultimately of literature.

In his essay 'The Prevention of Literature' Orwell describes a meeting of the PEN Club held late in the Second World War:

> There were four speakers on the platform. One of them delivered a speech which did deal with the freedom of the press, but only in relation to India; another said hesitantly, and in very general terms, that liberty was a good thing; a third delivered an attack on the laws relating to obscenity in literature. The fourth devoted most of his speech to a defence of the Russian purges. Of the speeches from the body of the hall, some reverted to the question of obscenity and the laws that dealt with it, others were simply eulogies of Soviet Russia. Moral liberty – the liberty to discuss sex questions frankly in print – seemed to be generally approved, but political liberty was not mentioned.

Those who were around at the time will recognize this as a true picture of the activist intellectual scene. Elsewhere in this admirable essay he makes it clear that the left-wing attitude to one particular issue, namely the Hitler-Stalin pact of 1939, was what disgusted him most.

> Consider, for example, the various attitudes completely incompatible with one another which an English Communist or 'fellow-traveller' had to adopt towards the war between Britain and Germany. For years before September, 1939, he was expected to be in a continuous stew about 'the horrors of Nazism' and to twist everything he wrote into a denunciation of Hitler: after September, 1939, he had to believe that Germany was

more sinned against than sinning, and the word 'Nazi', at least as far as print went, had to drop right out of his vocabulary. Immediately after hearing the 8 o'clock news bulletin on the morning of 22 June 1941, he had to start believing once again that Nazism was the most hideous evil that the world had ever seen.

This essay spells out what he had already written as parable in *Animal Farm*, and was to elaborate more bitterly in the line-switching episodes of *Nineteen Eighty-Four*. Sudden reversals of the Party line are bad enough in themselves, but they lead to an even greater crime, which is the rewriting of history. The Russians had been guilty of this many times, most notoriously in the *History of the CPSU (B)*, a horrible travesty of the historical record. The instant and continuous falsifying of all history by the Ministry of Truth in *Nineteen Eighty-Four*, including file copies of *The Times*, is only a slight exaggeration. Orwell believed that freedom to tell the truth was at all times the greatest good; that this freedom has usually to be defended against the Right, but sometimes the Left is its chief enemy; and that the greatest sin of the intellectuals was to creep before power, whether that of Fascism or Stalinism. (It would be interesting to know what he would have thought of professors in many countries today creeping before the power of student terrorists.)

The starting-point of any successful satire is a militant, combative attitude to political experience, and in particular to the politics of the satirists' own peers, the writers and intellectuals, who ought to know better. This was the starting-point of the greatest of English satirists, as Orwell pointed out in another memorable essay ('Politics vs. Literature: an Examination of Gulliver's Travels'). He characterized Swift politically as 'one of those people who are driven into a sort of perverse Toryism by the follies of the progressive party of the moment'. To his credit, Orwell did not pervert to Toryism: he remained with the Left of the Labour Party, but his sympathy with Swift is obviously very deep, despite some unfair and even unscholarly comments on Swift's politics. When I read this essay in 1946, I wrote to Orwell to the effect that he had not mentioned the affair of the Drapier's Letters, when Swift personally took on the English Ascendancy in Ireland, at great personal risk (though not a traitor could be found, to sell him for six hundred pound); and for this and other reasons Swift deserved the description of himself in his epitaph as 'strenuous champion of liberty'. Orwell replied politely, but on this point, I thought, evasively: I am sure that if he had thought more about Swift and Ireland he would have been able to justify more adequately the admiration he shows for Swift as a writer. In fact, the intense pessimism of *Nineteen Eighty-Four*, the pity expressed for the proles and contempt poured on the educated, the emphasis on physical disgust and finally on madness, place Orwell very close to Swift.

The second prerequisite of successful satire is the right medium. Satire has to be funny or it remains mere polemic and satiric humour demands travesty, the vision of the world upside-down. The number of ways in which travesty can be presented is evidently limited, and classic satire has usually been confined to a rather small number of traditional *genres*: the traveller's tale, the moral fable, and so on. The satiric *genres* are often travesties of the serious *genres* of literature, and parody is the main technique by which the one is transformed into the other, as epic into mock-heroic. The writer's main pleasure and *élan* will come from the ingenuity demanded by parody and the aggressive mockery that it releases. There is probably a fair amount of luck in the creation of satire. Even if the satirist has found the right subject and worked up a properly belly-feeling approach to it, he still has to find the form: he may never do so, but if he does the satire will practically write itself. This must have been the case with *Animal Farm*, a gay, fluent work, completed in a few months in the midst of Orwell's wartime preoccupations. He chose a very ancient *genre*, based on the animal story found in the folk-tales of all primitive and peasant cultures, and reflecting a familiarity and sympathy with animals which Orwell seems to have shared. The central figure is often the trickster, spider in Africa, fox in Europe and pig in Orwell. The Aesopian fable, perfected by La Fontaine, is a sophisticated version, which carries a moral or political lesson; still more elaborate are the medieval beast-epics of Renart, represented in English by Chaucer's tale of Chaunticlere. Orwell tells us that the idea came to him from the sight of an animal, a huge cart-horse driven by a little boy, who was whipping it whenever it tried to turn. 'It struck me that if only such animals became aware of their strength we should have no power over them, and that men exploit animals in much the same way as the rich exploit the proletariat.' Thus Boxer, representing the long-suffering Russian workers and peasants, is the hero of the tale. Once he had this image in his head, Orwell went on to develop Old Major's (Marx's) theory of revolution as applied to animals. He used the animal-story tradition with great confidence and deftness, and since he wanted to reach the widest possible world public, through translation, he also parodied the style of children's books; but not patronizingly, since Orwell, I think, liked children as much as he liked animals. Although the betrayal of the revolution is a 'sad story' it is told with the straightness that children demand, and with childlike cunning and charm.

Animal Farm also belongs to the *genre* of allegory, since it has a point-to-point correspondence with the events of Russian history from 1917 to 1943: the war of intervention, the New Economic Plan, the First Five-year Plan, the expulsion of Trotsky and the seizing of supreme power by Stalin, the Stakhanovites, the

Hitler-Stalin Pact and the invasion by Germany are all clearly figured.* It is also an apocalypse, like the Book of Daniel or the sixth book of the *Aeneid*, in that it moves imperceptibly from the past through the present (of which the account though fictionalized is basically true) to the future. It therefore ends with prophecy. Though literally the last episode, when the pigs sit down to drink with the farmers, is meant to represent the Teheran Conference, when Stalin met the Allied leaders, it is also a forecast of Russian politics. And to some extent it has come true, in that the Russians have become just as imperialistic, in their handling of subject peoples, as any of the empires of the past.

Prophecy was a subject that Orwell could not leave alone. This can be seen in his collected essays and journalist articles, as for example in his letters to the *Partisan Review*, in which he would keep on trying to forecast and later very honestly analysed where and why he had gone wrong. He wrote a good deal about Utopian fiction, such as Wells's *The Shape of Things to Come* and Huxley's *Brave New World*, both of which he despised as lacking in a sense of political reality. He greatly preferred Jack London's *The Iron Heel* (1907) and E. I. Zamyatin's *We*, written about 1923 and reviewed by Orwell in 1946, which are presumably his closest models for *Nineteen Eighty-Four*, along with James Burnham's treatises on the managerial revolution. It is fashionable for literary critics to say that Utopian and anti-Utopian novels are not meant to be predictions, but are metaphors of the present state of society or of the permanent human situation. But this won't quite do for Orwell, who was almost naïvely interested in guessing what was going to happen; and so was Huxley, for that matter, as his factual comments in *Brave New World Revisited* reveal. Orwell, of course, also intended *Nineteen Eighty-Four* as an awful warning of what *could* happen, even in England (hence 'Ingsoc'), but that doesn't make it any less of a prophecy. A prophet never makes absolute claims, he can only state what will happen under certain conditions (unless you all repent etc.). So Orwell asks us to judge the book, not only on grounds of humanity and wit, but on whether or not the world is going the way it foretells. As we get nearer to the actual date of 1984 this becomes a little easier.

The first sentence of the book contains a false prophecy. 'It was a bright cold day in April, and the clocks were striking thirteen.' I will take a bet that the clocks will never strike thirteen, because of the difficulty of counting above twelve, even though we have the twenty-four hour timetable, decimalization and parts of the metric system (which Orwell in his old-fashioned way disliked). More significant is the first entry in Winston Smith's diary, describing a movie audience laughing at shots of a refugee ship being bombed: the brutalization

* See Howard Fink, *Animal Farm* Notes: Coles, Toronto, 1965.

of audiences, who laugh at the disgusting *M.A.S.H.* and *Catch 22*, is a simple fact of 1971. On a larger scale, the most brilliant predictions are that the world would continue to be in permanent state of non-atomic war, and that two great Communist powers would be at war with each other – the latter has been so nearly true as to make little difference. Russia no longer looks quite as like *Nineteen Eighty-Four* as it did twenty years ago, since Stakhanovite enthusiasm and the equivalents of the Two Minutes Hate seem to have waned; but travel is still as restricted as it was for Winston and Julia, the historical records go on being falsified and the press is just as idiotic. China, however, from some reports, shows more than the lineaments of Orwellian fantasy. The most beautiful anticipation of Chinese style is Winston's fabrication of Comrade Ogilvy, the Maoist ideal.

At the age of three Comrade Ogilvy had refused all toys except a drum, a sub-machine gun, and a model helicopter. At six – a year early, by a special relaxation of the rules – he had joined the Spies; at nine he had been a troop leader. At eleven he had denounced his uncle to the Thought Police ... At twenty-three he had perished in action. Pursued by enemy jet planes while flying over the Indian Ocean with important despatches, he had weighted his body with his machine gun and leapt out of the helicopter into deep water, despatches and all – an end, said Big Brother, which it was impossible to contemplate without feelings of envy ...

Winston Smith sealed his own doom by being as clever as that, and it all came true in 1963, when the Chinese press immortalized the young hero Lei Feng.* This paragon accused the landlord who had caused the death of his mother and saw him executed; worked his way up through the Young Pioneers and the Young Communist League, and wrote in his diary: 'For the sake of the party and people's undertakings, I am even willing to plunge into a sea of fire ...' When he joined the army he 'mended the clothes of the other soldiers and took only one uniform a year instead of the two he was allowed'. When you reread the book, every decade or so, you get many similar surprises, of pure delight.

The book is a better prophecy than London's *The Iron Heel*, which Orwell praised for its content, despite its crude prose. London's book deeply impressed Anatole France, Trotsky and Aneurin Bevan and is still popular in Russia. The actual date, 1984, seems to be taken from London's account of the coming of Fascism in the USA. In fact, I found its content as disappointing as the style, since it doesn't tell one much about the repressive methods of totalitarian governments. What it does give is a lively account of the 'Fighting Groups', the guerrilla resistance, who display, as their author does, just the right mixture

* See Ralph A. Ranald, *George Orwell's '1984'*, Monarch Press, N.Y., quoting the *New York Times* 7 April 1963.

of Boy-Scout-Robin-Hood gaiety and bloodthirsty paranoia. This part, from which Orwell took some details for his counter-revolutionary brotherhood, did come true in the sixties. But what Orwell learned from London is undoubtedly sound: that the Fascist ruling party and the left-wing revolutionaries are both primarily concerned, not with economic or cultural improvement, but with power, just power. If Orwell is rather weak on the technological future (science seems to have bored him), he does show a much finer understanding than any other Utopian novelist of the naked aggression in all politics. It is this insight that makes O'Brien's words so convincing: 'If you want a picture of the future, imagine a boot stamping on a human face – forever.'

Apart from its predictions, *Nineteen Eighty-Four* contains some of the best pages of satire in English fiction since Dickens. It is not a complete work of art: the last of the three sections, with the torture episodes in the Ministry of Love and Room 101, are very weak, as Orwell admitted in one of his last letters. True, his common sense told him the truth about brain-washing, which is that it is produced by torture and the fear of torture, and not by the fancy psychological devices imagined by Koestler. But common sense does not lift the writing above the commonplace. The book does not even have to be considered as a novel: there is no progression or surprise in the plot, and no depth in the characterization. Orwell evidently chose that this should be the case: Winston knows that as soon as he has committed the thoughtcrime of writing a diary he is a dead man and so nothing new can ever happen to him. Nothing can happen to Julia either, who is an uninteresting character (though an accurately portrayed type of the Second World War period). The couple are caught up in the winds of stasis, whirled about outside time like Paolo and Francesca; and indeed the whole book is a comic inferno, a descent into the unchanging underworld. The closest infernal analogues in English are Book III of *Gulliver's Travels* (Laputa) and Pope's *Dunciad*, both of which are immensely funny visions of hell. And in *Nineteen Eighty-Four*, as in the *Dunciad*, the malice is irresistible, and directed at the whole class of the dunces, the intellectuals of England, who ought to know better. There is some pity for them, since their situation is intolerable, literally like the war in 1944–5, with rocket bombs and rationing going on endlessly; while they live in crumbling houses and work in vast and gloomy ministries or the BBC. But in a horribly lively way they accommodate themselves to a monstrous political system, some enthusiastic and boring like Parsons, others like Syme devious but still playing the game. As in all great satire the characters are reduced to automata, endowed with wholly predictable reactions, but showing immense energy while they pursue their imbecile and deadly careers.

The ultimate object of satirical attack is the corruption of the English language. Language was a subject on which Orwell felt as deeply as Swift. He was an amateur philologist of genius, possessed of a skill in manufacturing absurd and memorable slogans unequalled by anyone in the advertising profession. 'Newspeak' is his finest invention, the result of many years of thinking about the connexion between politics and the abuses of language. Some parts of its vocabulary are possibly immortal, like *doublethink* and *thoughtcrime*; less familiar terms like *duckspeaker* (with its plus and minus connotations) are just as beautiful. If he could not finish the book to his own satisfaction, Orwell left at the end an appendix on 'The Principles of Newspeak', ten pages which reach the heights of satire. *Doubleplusgood.*

David Pryce-Jones
ORWELL'S REPUTATION

THE moment he began to write about his experiences of failure, whether in Burma or in Paris or in England, Orwell was bound to draw attention to the stern example he was setting, to the awkward person he was so absorbingly becoming. With one part of his nature he always continued to caricature himself as the shabby writer in his dressing-gown harried through the morning, and in the evening the prey of the verminous little lions and bumsuckers. His literary earnings, he told T. R. Fyvel and others too, averaged only three pounds a week throughout the thirties – hence the work in the Hampstead bookshop or in The Stores in Wallington. He was best able to suit himself, to confuse success and failure as ambiguously as possible, by being both inside and outside the world of literary journalism; in it but not of it.

From 1930 he began to publish articles and reviews in the *Adelphi*, at the time a quarterly run by Middleton Murry and Sir Richard Rees. Eventually *Horizon, Partisan Review* and *Polemic* were to solicit him for contributions, and he was to be literary editor of *Tribune* from 1943 to 45 while writing its 'As I Please' column which he continued to do until 1947. During this time he also wrote frequently for *The Observer*. Before being so established, and after, for that matter, he published in less influential places, in Orage's *New English Weekly*, in Lady Rhondda's *Time and Tide*, in the *Manchester Evening News*.

There was one serious, if notorious, setback when the editor of the *New Statesman*, Kingsley Martin, rejected his articles on the Spanish Civil War. Orwell recounts it:

As soon as I got out of Spain I wired from France asking if they would like an article and of course they said yes, but when they saw my article was on the suppression of the POUM they said they couldn't print it. To sugar the pill they sent me to review a very good book which appeared recently, *The Spanish Cockpit*, which blows the gaff pretty well on what has been happening. But once again when they saw my review they couldn't print it as it was 'against editorial policy'.

Edward Hyams, the author of the *New Statesman*'s official history, writes that Orwell came back to Britain with a blistering series of articles attacking the Spanish Government, and that Kingsley Martin did not disbelieve them. But 'the *New Statesman* had become a "committed" paper while recognizing that, Fascism defeated, we might then have to fight for our principles against the worst elements in Communism'. Deciding that the *New Statesman* had 'the mentality of a whore', Orwell as an alternative published his views on Spain in the *New English Weekly*, where his *Homage to Catalonia* would also receive one of its most perceptive reviews, from Philip Mairet: 'It shows us the heart of innocence that lies in revolution; also the miasma of lying that, far more than the cruelty, takes the heart out of it.'

144

'Much has been made of my refusal to publish a series of articles from George Orwell', comes Kingsley Martin's riposte in *Editor*, a second volume of his autobiography published in 1968. 'I am not surprised that I did not publish the articles ... nearly all the papers were full of attacks on Negrin, the humane and liberal Prime Minister, and I objected to adding my venom for much the same reasons as I should have hesitated about doing propaganda for Goebbels in the war against Germany ... I knew that whatever else was true the war would certainly be lost if its direction fell into the hands of the Anarchists, many of whom were admirable people and abominably treated.' The passage concludes, 'Maybe if I had known more, I should have been revolted by Communist behaviour, but were not Western liberals ready to endorse bombing of civilians in the Second World War?' Hindsight does nothing to help this rhetorical question, nor explain how Goebbels comes into it.

Deep as the *New Statesman* rejection bit into him, Orwell already knew the extent to which he had forfeited left-wing support. As he wrote to Cyril Connolly from Spain, 'It doesn't do me any good to have been mixed up with the POUM – I have already had to change my publisher.' This was a reference to Victor Gollancz who had refused him an advance for a book on Spain for the Left Book Club because of what had just happened over *The Road to Wigan Pier*. According to Philip Toynbee, [*Encounter*, August 1959] *The Road to Wigan Pier* had been received 'with considerable obloquy by Communists and fellow-travellers, but with enthusiasm by many'. Walter Greenwood, author of the best-selling *Love on the Dole*, wrote, 'I cannot remember having been so infuriated for a long time as by some of the things he says here.' (*Tribune*, March 1937). In the *Daily Worker* (which twice had reviewed earlier Orwell books quite favourably) Harry Pollitt discovered in Orwell 'a disillusioned little middle-class boy' who had only to hear what Left Book circles would say about him before resolving never to write again on any subject that he did not understand. From now on, it became standard practice on the far Left to make some play about the Blair/Orwell change of name, and a mention of Eton and the Indian Imperial Police was almost obligatory.

To raise money to go to Spain, Orwell had pawned the family silver spoons and forks and had accepted an advance of £150 from Fredric Warburg, then starting up as a publisher. With the help of Fenner (later Lord) Brockway, Warburg hoped to make a small corner in the works of Independent Labour Party politicians and sympathizers. *Homage to Catalonia*, Warburg writes in his autobiography, 'when it was published in April 1938, caused barely a ripple on the political pond. It was ignored or hectored into failure'. Nine hundred copies were sold out of a printing of fifteen hundred and the advance was not to be earned until a few months after Orwell's death. *The Daily Worker* was polemical about 'books produced by individuals who have splashed their eyes for a few months with Spanish blood ... The value of the book is that it gives an honest picture of the sort of mentality that toys with revolutionary romanticism but shies violently at revolutionary discipline. It should be read as a warning.' The break with the Communists had become clear-cut.

Gollancz, however, was unable to follow their example and make up his mind about Orwell. As his contract permitted, he published *Coming Up for Air* in 1939, and did not finally part company with Orwell until 1944, when he held that the war-time alliance put the Russians beyond criticism and therefore he could not accept *Animal Farm* – much to Orwell's relief. Gollancz had been in a comparable position before, when he had rejected *Burmese Days* for fear of giving offence in India and Burma. That novel had first appeared in New York, where-upon Gollancz changed his view about it and published it. *Down and Out in Paris and London* had also been turned down in its preliminary versions. The first of Orwell's books – 'a trivial little story', as Christopher Hollis recalls him describing it, one which people might find entertaining like a travel diary – it was nevertheless well received. Cecil Day-Lewis took the line that 'the body of active reformers in this country would be inevitably increased by the numbers of readers of this book'. In America, James T. Farrell whose *Studs Lonigan* had caught the wave of social realism, said much the same. W. H. Davies, himself a Super-Tramp, wrote in the *New Statesman*, 'This is the kind of book I like to read, where I get the truth in chapters of real life.' Those who had given Orwell the benefit of their opinion tended to receive his in return, and ten years later Orwell was to review favourably Davies's *Collected Poems*. Henry Miller, pinned down in 'Inside the Whale', went in for rather a backhanded exchange of this kind when he said in a *Paris Review* interview in 1962 that he was crazy about Orwell's first book. 'I think it's a classic. For me it's still his best book. Though he was a wonderful chap in his way, Orwell, in the end I thought him stupid. He was like so many English people, an idealist, and it seemed to me, a foolish idealist.'

Cyril Connolly had liked *Burmese Days* and he also reviewed *Keep the Aspidistra Flying* twice within a month of its publication. Unique witness, Connolly over the years not only recorded what he remembered of Orwell at their prep-school and at Eton, but also reviewed most of his books, beginning his notice of *Animal Farm* with the much-quoted remark that Orwell was a revolutionary in love with 1910. And twice Orwell seems to have made a point of reviewing books by Connolly, *The Rock Pool* in 1936 and *The Unquiet Grave* nine years later. On neither occasion does he make allowances for a friend whose life had touched his own. On the contrary, he austerely avoids the personal note, he takes his distance.

Apart from Connolly, nobody could be counted on to keep a special look-out for Orwell. Compton Mackenzie rather unexpectedly praised him. From L. P. Hartley, V. S. Pritchett, Goronwy Rees, Peter Quennell, at different times and in snippets, Orwell had the late-Bloomsbury privilege of receiving neither more nor less than his due. The luck of the draw produced reviewers who had nothing in common with him and often said so, such as Margery Allingham, James Hilton and A. G. MacDonell, whose book about merrie cricketing has the title *England, Their England*.

Only one essay attempted something of a summary of Orwell's pre-war books, and it was by Mrs Q. D. Leavis in the September 1940 issue of her husband's quarterly journal, *Scrutiny*. Familiar Leavisite preoccupations mark the essay's opening: 'Mr Orwell belongs by birth and education to the "right Left people", the nucleus of the literary world who christian-name each other and are in honour bound to advance each other's literary careers; he figures indeed in Connolly's autobiography as a schoolfellow. This is probably why he has received indulgent treatment in the literary press. He differs from them in having grown up.' Yet Mrs Leavis could admit that there was more to it than that. 'Starting from an inside knowledge of the working class, painfully acquired, he can see through the Marxist theory, and being innately decent (he displays and approves of bourgeois morality) he is disgusted with the callous theorizing inhumanity of the pro-Marxists ... Mr Orwell must have wasted a lot of energy trying to be a novelist – I think I must have read three or four novels by him, and the only impression those dreary books left on me is that nature didn't intend him to be a novelist. Yet his equivalent works in non-fiction are stimulating.' Apart from subsequent special pleadings on behalf of one or other of the early novels, this has come to represent received opinion. The verdict may have affected Orwell who once or twice afterwards says of himself that he was not a real novelist.

With the publication of *Animal Farm*, a new interest in Orwell and his doings became inevitable. In John Lehmann's autobiography it is recalled that Orwell came to *Penguin New Writing* parties 'full of friendliness and stimulating talk', which Mrs Leavis might find evidence of his christian-naming his way round the literary world. But fuller recollections have been left by other acquaintances or colleagues, including Anthony Powell, Richard Rees, Julian Symons, Paul Potts and John Morris. Rayner Heppenstall shared lodgings with him in the thirties and his book, *Four Absentees*, shows how remote Orwell's day-to-day life was from anything suggesting a literary coterie. All these memoirs were written after Orwell had died, when he was already becoming a slightly mythical figure, and most of them depend on that peculiar English love of the pointed anecdote, as if a man's whole personality could be taken on trust through his attitude towards tea, say, or having lunch in a restaurant. These writer-friends are responsible for the composite but broadly agreed picture of Orwell – uncompromising to the point of eccentricity, shy, kind-hearted, contrary: and in the two words which so many of his critics have exhausted on him, honest and decent.

Animal Farm, Orwell later wrote, 'was the first book in which I tried, with full consciousness of what I was doing, to fuse political purpose and artistic purpose into one whole'. Three English and some twenty American publishers followed Gollancz's lead and turned the book down for fear of upsetting a military ally, though some thought that it was too short at 30,000 words to make a book at all. T. S. Eliot, editorial director of Faber and Faber, was among those who rejected it, and for some months Orwell was gloomy about the book's prospects. The publishers who did bring it out sold half a million copies within three years.

A reversal of public opinion manipulated by politicians and apparatchiks for the sake of expediency had always been one of Orwell's subjects. Now he found himself caught in just such a reversal (and indignation about such a thing gives his next book, *Nineteen Eighty-Four*, some of its passion). Just as *Animal Farm* could not be accepted for the satire it was when Soviet friendship was sought, so now that Soviet enmity was open and declared, it still could not be accepted for what it was, though for opposite reasons. Circumstances had changed, and truth had to fall in line with them – books were equal, one might say, but some books were more equal than others. 'It took courage,' writes Anthony Powell, 'in that now largely forgotten, but then rather nauseating, political climate of the immediately postwar period (where the things attacked in the book are concerned) to fire the broadside of *Animal Farm*, especially on the part of a writer of left-wing principles, liable to be smeared in a manner that could do him real professional harm.' Critics on both sides of the Atlantic could soon be divided into two camps: the ayes – led by Edmund Wilson, who thought the book absolutely first-rate – mentioned Swift and Voltaire; the noes yoked Orwell to Koestler in disparagement, the latter having become the bugbear of the Left on account of *Darkness at Noon*. Koestler and Orwell – how many vituperative articles were shot at the pair! One after another, the Party writers went into action on this sector of the literature front.

Nineteen Eighty-Four was published when the Cold War was acute, in June 1949, at a time when the anti-Tito campaign was ushering in a wave of purges and show-trials in the satellite countries of Eastern Europe whose allegiance to Communism was as new as it was shaky. 'Big Brother' and 'Doublethink' were even more apposite to the moment of publication than Orwell could have realized when he had begun to write the book in the summer of 1946. All that the ayes and the noes had already said about *Animal Farm* was now compounded. Rehearsing every ideological grudge, the review which Arthur Calder-Marshall wrote in *Reynolds News*, a mass-circulation Sunday paper belonging to the Cooperative movement, may serve as an example of the sort of smears Anthony Powell mentions (though in 1966 in *The Times* Calder-Marshall was apologizing for it). 'The POUM for Spain was as exclusive as Eton ... [it] could pride itself on being as anti-Russian as Churchill, Hitler or Franco: and at the same time, terrifically Left. To write *Animal Farm*, attacking the Soviet Union at the moment that the defenders of Stalingrad struck one of the decisive blows which won the war for the United Nations was for Blair/Orwell an act of integrity. Only incidentally did it bring him a fortune from reactionaries in this country and the USA.' *Nineteen Eighty-Four*, Calder-Marshall thought, would be Tory election propaganda. 'The hero of this jejune affair is a dreary little man whose christian name is Winston. The sooner Comrade Orwell assumes the pen-name of Eric Blair, the better. Except, of course, that Mr Blair, ex-Etonian, ex-civil servant, has no literary reputation at all.' But scarcely less hysterical than this was the book's success. It was the July selection of the Book-of-the-Month Club and it was condensed into twenty-five pages in the September *Reader's Digest*. *Life* simplified the novel into several pages of illustrated summary. For two years it remained on the best-seller list.

By the time Orwell came to write *Nineteen Eighty-Four*, he was convinced that most intellectuals were tainted by totalitarian attitudes of one kind or another, 'the smelly little orthodoxies which are now contending for our souls'. His critics proved the truth of this for him. The Right wished *Nineteen Eighty-Four* to spread anti-Soviet propaganda: 'Big Brother' belonged to the family whose Uncle Joe was Stalin. And perhaps *Animal Farm* and *Nineteen Eighty-Four*, decried by a writer in the *Marxist Quarterly* [January 1956] as 'a couple of horror comics', did have more influence on Western public opinion than any amount of plain reportage could have done. *Nineteen Eighty-Four* certainly was an attack on whatever totalitarian future might lie ahead. If it had been only a pamphlet, it might have provided a programme, or a call to action. That it was obviously a novel had to be overlooked for the sake of controversy. Some of the ayes and all of the noes decided for themselves that this novel was intended to be the blue-print of the future, a literal description; as though those elements in the present which undoubtedly corresponded to parts of the novel justified blind polemics about the whole. But if a reader turns to a fiction in order to find in it a close and particular critique of the Communist Party, or more wildly still, of the British Labour Party, he reveals only his own limitations, his own preoccupations. Orwell was not acting as guide to immediate politics: he had imagination, and powers of projection, as well as those self-preserving instincts against interference from society which every novelist needs.

The Socialist Left, or those who believed that equality and progress were compatible even under centralized direction, had to find arguments above the level of abuse to refute Orwell's vision. Kingsley Martin had shown the way to do this, in a review of *Animal Farm*, to which he reacted just as he had done to the articles on Spain seven years earlier. He admitted that the story had its truth, and that 'the shafts strike home'. But the logic of Orwell's satire, he believed, is ultimate cynicism, and that could not be permitted. Orwell, he thought, 'has not quite the courage to see that he has lost faith, not in Russia but in mankind'. It was beside the point that Orwell had never had faith in Russia or in mankind, whatever faith in mankind may mean. The argument enabled the Socialist Left to go in for a bit of doublethink: to accept that Orwell was a truthful, admirable and perhaps great writer, but simultaneously to discount him because he was a pessimist. Those who think like this have in the end to say that as a matter of temperament it is unbearable to them to have a work offering neither hope nor solutions: the more gifted the work, the more unbearable; and the more easily exploited by unscrupulous conservatives. The pessimistic tone of *Nineteen Eighty-Four* can also be refined away by saying that Orwell was dying and afraid of the future as he wrote it. Isaac Deutscher put such criticisms into a concise essay, and others, including Raymond Williams, have been content to rehearse them over the years with diminishing skill.

After Orwell's death in January 1950, E. M. Forster and Bertrand Russell were among those who paid him tributes. Arthur Koestler, with whom he had so often been linked, called him 'the only writer of genius among the *littérateurs* of social revolt between the two wars'. In the *New Statesman* V. S. Pritchett wrote, 'George Orwell was the wintry conscience of a generation which in the thirties had heard the call of the rasher assumptions of political faith. He was a kind of saint and, in that character, more likely in politics to chastise his own side than the enemy.' This was one of five articles which V. S. Pritchett had given over to Orwell in the *New Statesman* in slightly more than ten years, with an impartiality and justice which made amends for its past. The idea of Orwell as a kind of saint persists, as when the producer of a recent BBC television documentary about him could say, 'I'm sick to death of these saint artists on television – though Orwell, as it happens, is nearer a saint than most'.

Reprints, or sometimes in America first publication, of his books followed. Second time round, the critics were a great deal more favourable, though some complained that a cult was being created. Two noteworthy, if incoherent, attacks came from men older than Orwell: one from Wyndham Lewis, himself trailing the rags of his pre-war Fascism, but who could write that Orwell might have made a good SS man; and the other from Sean O'Casey whose witches' brew of Communism and Irish nationalism had met with Orwell's disapproval. Although Wyndham Lewis and O'Casey in theory held opposing positions, their voices merged into the single sound of disgruntled ego. O'Casey also revealed that when Gollancz had once asked him for a reader's report on Orwell's novel *A Clergyman's Daughter*, he had recommended its rejection. But now Orwell has been translated into nearly sixty languages. Koestler, defending him in a controversy, was able to point out that the concepts of Doublethink, Newspeak and Big Brother have become international currency all over the civilized world. 'Orwellian' has entered our speech to evoke the nastiness of anything totalitarian.

Animal Farm, translated as *Animal Kolkhoz*, was to have been broadcast twice on the Czech radio. The first occasion, in 1948, was forestalled by the Communists coming to power, and the second, in 1968, by the Russians replacing the Dubcek Government. There is also a Slovene translation, as yet unreleased, while a scholarly journal in Zagreb has taken up some points made by English academics. Otherwise Orwell is an unperson behind the Iron Curtain. A glimpse into the situation is to be found in Czeslaw Milosz's *The Captive Mind*, a book published in 1953 about Polish intellectuals. 'A few have become acquainted with Orwell's *Nineteen Eighty-Four*; because it is both difficult to obtain and dangerous to possess, it is known only to certain members of the Inner Party. Orwell fascinates them through his insight into details they know well and through his use of Swiftian satire. Such a form of writing is forbidden by the New Faith because allegory, by nature manifold in meaning, would trespass beyond the prescriptions of Socialist realism and the demands of the censor. Even those who know Orwell only by hearsay are amazed that a writer who never lived in Russia should have so keen a perception into its life.'

In *Pravda*, I. Anisimov reviewed *Nineteen Eighty-Four* a year after its publication. 'Mr Orwell is in every way similar to Mr Huxley in *Ape and Essence*, especially in his contempt for people, in his aim of slandering man. And while one cries out, "The voice of the proletariat is the voice of the devil", the other, slobbering with spittle, does not lag far behind him. For in describing a monstrous future in store for man, he imputes every evil to the people.'* In 1962

---

* This extract, and the one which follows, are quoted in Dr. David Rankin's unpublished thesis at University College, London, *The critical reception of the art and thought of George Orwell*. The librarian generously gave permission to consult it and its full bibliography.

another article appeared in *Pravda Ukrainy*, by V. Babich. 'Recently the American [*sic*] writer George Orwell wrote a novel depicting America in 1984. He predicted that by that time the private lives of Americans will be investigated by means of secretly installed television screens ... His fantasy does not foretell happenings, but lags behind "the American way of life". The boldest predictions of Orwell for 1984, are, so to speak, fulfilled and overfulfilled in the United States today ... There are millions and tens of millions of innocent people who are victims of the notorious House Un-American Activities Committee.'

Nothing is so surprising as the entirely predictable – but who can say for sure whether such criticism is a sign of Orwell's success or his failure? As for Orwell himself, when overtaken by recognition, he went to Jura, to an island as far away as possible from the centres of limelight. He disliked publicity, he wanted neither interviews nor a biography nor the invasion of privacy which went with those editions of millions, the very idea of which smacks absurdly of Big Brother. Somehow he had to keep alive for himself the illusion, the virtue, as he called it, of failure, although success alone could dispel the ugly forces which he saw pressing on the human race. A contradiction indeed. Others can suffer it too, if they have the courage, like the young Russian who called his book *Will the Soviet Union Survive till 1984?* and went to prison for it – the sort of grim compliment not often paid by one writer to another.

D.A.N. Jones
ARGUMENTS AGAINST ORWELL

A WRITER has only so much time, so much energy, so much 'space' in the papers. George Orwell wasted too much of his quota on crafty self-praise and destructive criticism of fellow-Socialists.

Imagine yourself a middle-class leftist in the thirties. You write some political verse; and Orwell's reaction will be: 'What use are these nancy poets to the miners up north sweating their guts out underground?', or he might himself versify:

> Back to the dear old game of scratch-my-neighbour,
> In sleek reviews financed by coolie labour.

('A Letter to Obadiah Hornbrooke' *Tribune*, June 1943)

A fair point, you think. So you join an anti-imperialist committee, to help the 'coolies' in their struggle for emancipation. But Orwell despises committees – his friend, Paul Potts, reports [*London Magazine*, March 1957] that he was once tempted to join a committee, 'just so that he could resign' – and he jeers at the members: weedy-looking specimens and shiny-bottomed bureaucrats, gutless and lacking in common decency; little better than the purple-faced blimps and pimply Fascists on the Right; middle-class pacifists and feminists, bearded vegetarians in sandals, not a working-man in sight. Besides Orwell has been out there, east of Suez, and it must be honestly admitted that the Burmese are repulsive. There's a lot to be said for the white *Sahibs* who built the railways, and why can't middle-class leftists like E. M. Forster give them their due? (Which Forster did, of course, but Orwell hadn't noticed.)

So you pull up your middle-class roots – which sounds quite easy: the rather fatuous conclusion to *The Road to Wigan Pier* reads: 'We have nothing to lose but our aitches.' Already, though, Orwell has begun to grumble about Socialists who attack the middle class instead of trying to win its members over: and your new contacts with working-class trade unionists will get you nowhere because, Orwell says, no real working man is a Socialist, it's a purely middle-class idea, and middle-class people can't get on with working-class people because, let's be honest, the latter stink – but no one except Orwell and Somerset Maugham has the guts to say so.

It all seems pretty hopeless: better go and fight for the republican Government in Spain, or at any rate write articles supporting the cause. No good: Orwell's been there already and seen through the Loyalists' façade. The Stalinists have taken over and they're just as bad as Franco; anyone who fails to publish Orwell's letters and articles on this theme is either a dupe or a crypto-Stalinist.

So Franco wins, and you try to activate the British public against the growing threat of Franco's allies, Hitler and Mussolini. Now Orwell is rebuking left-wing war-mongers: he blames the Labour Party for 'exploiting anti-fascist stuff' and accuses the *New Statesman* of 'longing for war' (Letter to John Sceats, 1938). As war becomes inevitable, he suggests that Socialists should sabotage the British war effort, expecting that 'idealistic Hitler-fascists more or less represented by Mosley' [Letter to Herbert Read, March 1939] would carry out similar sabotage.

So far, he seems less like the conscience of the Left than a bloody-minded nagger, a Mrs Gummidge. If you took Orwell's advice, you'd end up doing nothing. So many of his rebukes seem trivial, futile. Why shouldn't a Socialist be a 'nancy', like Edward Carpenter and E. M. Forster? Come to that, what's the point of calling the Fascists 'pimpled' and 'weedy-looking'? Some of them look quite tough, unfortunately.

How's the sabotage of the war effort going? He's writing unhelpful articles in an American journal, about whether Jews are unpopular in London, and whether they're taking up too much space in the air-raid shelters, and how many Labour MPs are crypto-Communists, and which pacifists are 'objectively' Fascists. But he's definitely patriotic now. He goes on about the loveliness of the English people and the need to rally round the flag. It's irritating for Labour men to have to support Churchill, and still more irritating for Tories to ally themselves with Stalin; but Orwell gets self-righteously indignant with anyone who expresses such irritations. Clement Attlee and Evelyn Waugh soldier on, glum and taciturn, but enthusiastic Orwell writes: [London Letter to *Partisan Review*, August 1941] 'Good luck to Comrade Stalin' – which is definitely overdoing it.

In 1943, Alex Comfort wrote a Byronic poem in *Tribune*, attacking Churchill, the bombing of German civilians and war-minded jingo writers. Part of Orwell's egotistic reply runs:

> But you don't hoot at Stalin – that's 'not done' –
> Only at Churchill; I've no wish to praise him,
> I'd gladly shoot him when the war is won,
> Or now, if there were someone to replace him.
> But, unlike some, I'll pay him what I owe him ...
> (Letter to Obadiah Hornbrooke, *Tribune*, 1943)

Surely he didn't really want to shoot Churchill (any more than the kids today really want to 'disembowel Enoch Powell') – so why pretend he did? He wanted to maintain his pose as an international revolutionary, even while announcing his enthusiastic support for the Churchill–Stalin alliance.

Comfort had expressed the opinion of a tiny minority of pacifists and conscientious objectors, challenging the general enthusiasm for killing Germans,

and the way in which Churchillian rhetoric glossed over the horror and brutalization. Orwell's reply might be summarized: 'What about the Russians?
Anyway, I'm a communist myself (with a small "c", not a *member* of anything)
and I want to kill Churchill as well as the Germans. But I'm so English and
decent and fair-minded that I'll stick with Churchill for now, all on my own.'
You would think Orwell was in the minority, and Comfort's pacifists a powerful
persecuting force. He goes on, in his hot, cross, plucky-chap way:

> I wrote in 1940 that at need
> I'd fight to keep the Nazis out of Britain;
> And Christ! how shocked the pinks were! Two years later
> I hadn't lived it down; one had the effrontery
> To write three pages calling me a 'traitor',
> So black a crime it is to love one's country.
> Yet where's the pink that would have thought it odd of me
> To write a shelf of books in praise of sodomy?

But surely, almost everyone was ready (and most had been ready before Orwell
was) to resist a Nazi invasion. Orwell has cast himself as lone Horatius, being
badly let down by a defeatist regiment of pink sodomites. He convinced Paul
Potts that he 'loved England, about the only left-wing middle-class intellectual of the time to do so' and that he was 'very English, as English as the grass
that grows along the Thames at Runnymede'. (*London Magazine*, March 1957.)

This self-congratulatory usage, 'very English', has become tiresome. Orwell
wrote, in *Homage to Catalonia*, about an enemy soldier he had seen rushing to
the latrine, holding up his trousers, and about how Orwell did not shoot him
because 'a man caught short like that is not a fascist'. Potts comments smugly:
'I wonder what his political commissar thought of that bit of Englishness' – but
might not a Swede, a Russian or a Welshman have similarly held fire? W. H.
Auden has recently [*Spectator*, 16 January 1971] written of this anecdote that it
shows Orwell to have been Christian – which seems even more far-fetched,
especially as Orwell told Potts that he 'liked the Church of England better than
Our Lord'.

So far you, the thirties leftist, have done nothing right, in Orwell's eyes.
Perhaps now you can win his approval by following his own example and
working for the BBC as a propagandist. Not so: in his anti-Comfort poem, he
calls this job the 'dirty work' of 'the radio hack, the hired pep-talker':

> All propaganda's lying, yours or mine;
> It's lying even when its facts are true.

This doesn't make much sense. Some BBC propaganda was truthful and some was lying. Then there was the tendency to overpraise those who were our allies ('Good luck to Comrade Stalin', in Orwell's words) and the failings of those who were not. Readers and listeners had to make allowance for the publicists' exaggerations. As a child I was sentimentally attracted by the publicity about our Yugoslav ally, General Mihailovic, and was sorry when he was written off, in favour of bespectacled, sensitive-looking Tito. After the war we were told that Tito was a dictator, and the photographs made him look like Goering. Press and BBC favour was extended to Tito again, after his quarrel with Moscow, and only last year a *New Statesman* writer was telling me that Tito's state was the only tolerable regime in Europe; but I had just read an article by a Hungarian *émigré*, in the *Spectator*, about the iniquities of the Yugoslav secret police, and I remembered that *Tribune's* Yugoslav correspondents had been imprisoned by Tito – and, in short, I have never felt like saying, 'Good luck to Comrade Tito'. It is possible to support or cooperate with a statesman without turning him into Big Brother, and possible to oppose him without conducting a Hate Session.

Orwell invented these useful expressions, and might have employed them in self-criticism. He was over-ready to cry 'Hooray' and 'Boo'. When he found that his heroes were flawed and his villains not wholly worthless, he became angry and depressed. Instead of blaming himself, he accused others – especially his own comrades – of being hero-worshippers, hypocrites, and seeing conflicts in crudely black-and-white imagery. He might have taken it for granted that propaganda, even though not deliberately lying, is bound to involve some exaggeration and wishful thinking. But his disgust with BBC propaganda, together with his depression at the shortages and urban squalor of wartime London, became the imaginative basis for the nightmare world of *Nineteen Eighty-Four*. He blackened the picture, imposed the London atmosphere upon an exaggerated version of a Stalinist state – with references to Stalin and Trotsky, rather than Churchill and Hitler – and introduced extra cruelty. His favourite question, 'What about the workers?', had been reduced to a vague feeling that our only hope lies in 'the proles'. More obvious was the question, addressed angrily to all opponents of capitalism: 'What about the Russians?' His mind had got stuck in an anti-Soviet groove. Yet he still honestly thought he was an underdog, a gallant spokesman for an anti-Soviet minority, even while the cash-registers of the western world were ringing his praises.

Nowadays, when a demonstration is mounted against the American war in Vietnam, or an all-white South African cricket team, there is always someone to say: 'What about the Communists? What about the Viet Cong atrocities? Why do you not harass the Red Army choir?' These naggers may also draw cartoons of the demonstrators, especially if they are bearded, sandalled, vegetarian (or macrobiotic), feminist (Women's Lib), pansy (Gay Power) or pacifist. Such critics are among the heirs of George Orwell. They are a distraction and an irrelevance.

What I have written above is purely destructive. It is not my present function to praise Orwell, who has more than enough disciples already. For instance there are such writers as Robert Conquest and Kingsley Amis, who think themselves to be anti-Communists of Orwell's kind, and who keenly support the American war against the Communists in Vietnam. But in a recent TV programme about Orwell ('The Road to the Left', by Melvyn Bragg) two American leftists, Noam Chomsky and Norman Mailer, felt able to cite Orwell in support of their own position as opponents of their government's war policy. It seems that people of almost any political persuasion can find some of their beliefs expressed in Orwell's work, very eloquently.

The reason for this is that he had at least four political personalities, each with its own merits and failings, and these personalities conflict with each other, like characters in a Shakespearian play, neither wholly good nor wholly bad, but always expressive and challenging.

To the first character we will give his real name – Eric, the good-hearted public schoolboy, angry at the social injustices of Britain and the Empire. The working classes are almost as alien to him as the subject races; but he is anxious to understand and support them. He is fighting against English snobbery, his own at least as much as other people's, and he sees conflicts of class and race, anywhere in the world, as aspects of that snobbery. Eric wrote *Burmese Days* and *Keep the Aspidistra Flying* and *The Road to Wigan Pier*. By studying his populism and class-consciousness, we gain in understanding not only of the English Left but also of some radical Conservatives and prewar Fascists.

The second character is a revolutionary international socialist: the poet Blair who wanted to shoot Churchill in 1943. He was hoping for an English revolution which would 'shoot traitors' and 'crush any open revolt promptly and cruelly'. ('The Lion and the Unicorn') Blair's merits are best expressed in *Homage to Catalonia*, but even here we may be alarmed by his enthusiasm for the gutting of churches and his tolerance for mob spontaneity which he, too glibly, labels 'working-class'.

Third comes St George, the super-patriot. Being rather patriotic myself, I feel embarrassed when George wags his flag. He sounds like a Tory. You know the kind who writes, week after week, 'Today is a day Britain can be proud of', or who spouts, untruthfully, 'It may be unfashionable . . .' and '*I'm* not ashamed

Recognition

84 (and 85 *Overleaf*) Scenes from the film of *Nineteen Eighty-Four* with Edmond O'Brien as Winston Smith.

86 (*Opposite above*) Colin Blakely as George Brown in the television version of *Coming Up for Air*, 1965.
87 (*Opposite below*) Scene from the television version of *Keep the Aspidistra Flying* with Alfred Lynch as Gordon Comstock and Anne Stalleybrass as Rosemary, 1965.

88 The French
version of *Down
and out in Paris
and London*, 1935.

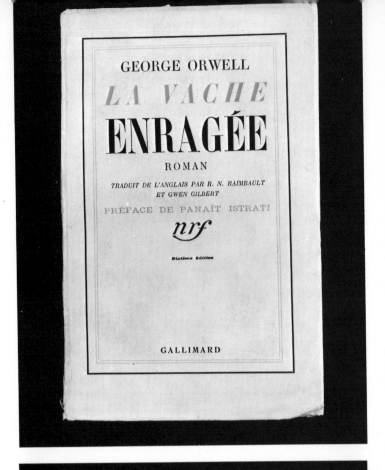

89 A Spanish
edition of *Homage
to Catalonia*
printed in Buenos
Aires in 1963.

90 The Ukrainian translation of *Animal Farm*, printed in Munich in 1947.

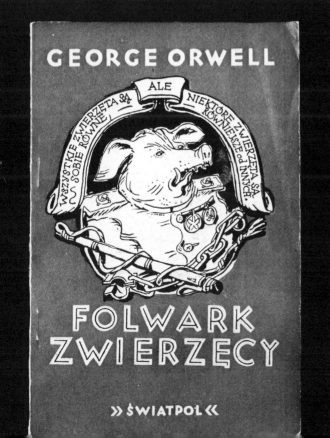

91 *Animal Farm* in Polish, printed in London, 1947.

アニマル.ファーム
動物農場

ジョージ.オーウェル 著
永島啓輔 訳

ANIMAL
FARM

by
GEORGE ORWELL

第一回翻訳許可書

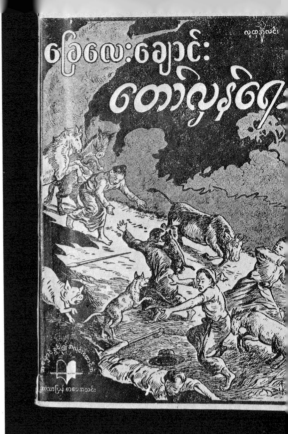

CUỘC
CÁCH
MẠNG
TRONG TRẠI
SÚC-VẬT

TRÍCH TRONG CHUYỆN
THẦN - THOẠI
cúa
GEORGE ORWELL

Георг Орвелл

СКОТСКИЙ

ХУТОР

92 (*Opposite above left*) A Japanese *Animal Farm* published in 1948.
93 (*Opposite above right*) The Burmese edition, printed in Rangoon, 1951.
94 (*Opposite below left*) A translation into Vietnamese printed in Saigon, 1951.
95 (*Opposite below right*) The second edition (1967) of the Russian translation, first printed in Frankfurt-am-Main in 1949.

Shamba la Wanyama

masimulizi ya GEORGE ORWELL

Kimefasiriwa na Kawegere Fortunatus

96 (*Above right*) The Swahili edition of *Animal Farm* printed in Nairobi, 1967.
97 (*Right*) *Nineteen Eighty-Four* in Finnish, published 1967.

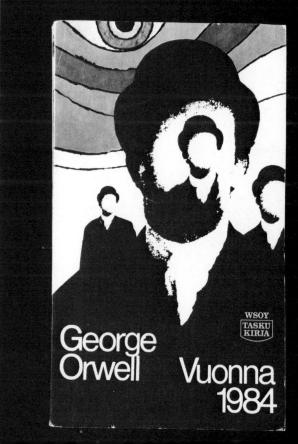

George Orwell Vuonna 1984

WSOY TASKU KIRJA

98 Plaque at the corner of Pond St and South End Rd in Hampstead, unveiled in November 1969.

to be British' (after all, who is?) and 'Patriotism is a dirty word nowadays' and (day after day) 'Just for once, let's blow our own trumpet!' George's gruff incantations about our decency, gentleness and fairness may be more seductive than Enoch Powell's gush;* but there is too much self-congratulation, disparagement of foreigners, eagerness to charge more reticent persons with a lack of patriotism – as if this characteristic were a moral virtue, rather than a natural and involuntary affection. In this mood he resembles Hilaire Belloc (also half-French) and Rudyard Kipling (also brought up in imperial Asia and harsh upper-class boarding schools). He lacked local roots and family loyalty, so he needed to belong to a nation-state. One of George's heirs is Kingsley Amis, who writes in praise of England because he thinks it impossible 'to be patriotic about south-west London'.

Fourth comes the character to whom the word 'Orwellian' most frequently refers. This is Orwell the anti-Soviet propagandist, made famous and posthumously successful by the brilliant *Animal Farm* and the flawed but powerful *Nineteen Eighty-Four*. I used *Animal Farm* to taunt a member of the Young Communist League when I was still at school. Twelve years later, I had to 'teach' it, as a 'set book', to Nigerian schoolchildren. It was difficult to give my pupils background material for this satire on Soviet Communism, since Marxist and Leninist writings were almost unobtainable in Nigeria. Under British rule, they had been made illegal. This might be called the *Nineteen Eighty-Four* aspect of imperialism.

Our school text of *Animal Farm* had a foreword about Orwell's life and hostility to Communism: his involvement in the war against Franco was passed over quickly, on the ground that it would be a pity to reopen old wounds, since the Spanish are a fine people. One of the reasons why *Animal Farm*, rather than *Homage to Catalonia*, is a favourite set book in British and Commonwealth schools is a political one. The book is, for better or worse, a clear-cut expression of the anti-Communist orthodoxy.

On Bragg's TV programme, Orwell's publisher, Fredric Warburg, said that *Nineteen Eighty-Four* was 'the most powerful anti-Soviet Communism tract you will find' – not only an 'awe-inspiring book' but (for the Continent more than for Britain) 'a political action'. It is much quoted by the sort of 'Orwellians' who

---

* 'Speak to us in our own English tongue, the tongue made for telling truth in, tuned already to songs that haunt the hearer like the sadness of spring . . . These are not thoughts for every day, nor words for every company; but on St George's Eve, in the Society of St George, may we not fitly think and speak them, to renew and strengthen in ourselves the resolves and the loyalties which English reserve keeps otherwise and best in silence?' Instead of taking his own advice, Mr Powell reprinted this speech as the climax of *Freedom and Reality* in order that his patriotic emotions might be admired by a larger audience.

have been prepared to work for *Encounter*, the Congress for Cultural Freedom and the Central Intelligence Agency of the USA. Conor Cruise O'Brien's criticisms of Orwell are connected with his justified contempt for those *Encounter* Orwellians whom O'Brien describes as a 'literary Mafia' – 'anti-communists dedicated to the unavowed service of United States policy, and standing in all essentials in the same relation to Washington as the crypto-Communists had stood to Moscow'. (*Listener*, 12 December 1968.) O'Brien suggests that if Orwell were still alive he would attack his Washington-line admirers as vigorously as he did his Moscow-line opponents in the thirties. Perhaps he would.

One of Orwell's more impressive admirers is Michael Foot MP, who presides over *Tribune*, the Socialist journal for which Orwell worked (as I have done). Foot was the first speaker in Bragg's TV programme, and began by quoting Orwell's sayings: 'Big Brother is watching you. Doublethink. Newspeak. All animals are equal but some are more equal than others.' Foot said that Orwell supplied us with a language to talk about 'totalitarian things'.

Other writers admired by Foot include William Hazlitt and John Osborne. He did not compare Orwell's best essays with those of Hazlitt (which would have been a good point) but rather spoke of him as if he were a playwright, like Osborne, whose sayings and play-titles have entered the language. The eloquent phrases of Osborne's characters can be used by Socialist orators and writers to express ideas which are consistent with a coherent political philosophy – and they are vivid expressions which stir up a large public and lend to vague sentiments a sharper definition. But we don't suppose that the playwright has himself a consistent political philosophy; nor need we suppose this of Orwell. His lines are often appropriate to a character in a play: his arguments are often dramatizations of the author's temporary mood. Much of the eloquent dialogue of Jimmy Porter in *Look Back in Anger* was closely adapted from Orwell's essays (notes T. R. Fyvel in *Intellectuals Today*), in his 'Eric' role or mood, expressing anger at the British and imperial social system. Osborne also expresses Orwell's 'St George' patriotism – draught Bass, Edwardian sunset and 'Damn you, England' in *Tribune*.

Foot's reference to 'totalitarian things' may make us uneasy. O'Brien has compared it with 'that blessed word, Mesopotamia'. What does it mean? Though rather old-fashioned now, it is still used in *Encounter* and *Socialist Worker*. But in that useful essay, 'Politics and the English Language', Orwell himself lists it, with 'progressive' and 'reactionary', among the 'meaningless words', all three being expressions, 'used in variable meanings, in most cases more or less dishonestly'. I looked up 'totalitarian' in two anti-Communist word-lists, published in 1966. Maurice Cranston has omitted it (though he includes 'progressive' and 'reactionary') from his *Glossary of Political Terms*. But in Elliott and Summerskill's *Dictionary of Politics*, we are told that 'totalitarian' may be 'correctly applied to the USSR, China, Nazi Germany and Fascist Italy', even though the authors admit that the Nazis and Fascists failed to achieve 'the complete centralization of power and authority that would exist in a truly totalitarian state'.

All four societies are, however, notorious for their almost total control over, at least, the communications media. This is offensive to the controllers of the media in our own, more 'pluralist', society (who have also had to recognize the four 'totalitarian' states as ideological enemies of Western capitalism) and still more offensive to our writers and journalists, many of whom naturally tend to regard state control of the media as one of the worst failings a society can have. I don't agree. The Nazis' domination of the media seems to me almost trivial in comparison with their cruelty; my hostility to the Soviet state's repression of the media is modified by my respect for its achievement in mass education and working-class culture. I hope my necessary brevity here will not seem slick or perverse.

A few smacks at Orwell's best books. Actually *The Road to Wigan Pier* is said to be his *worst* book, by Tom Hopkinson in his chilly British Council pamphlet on Orwell. Surely the first part was very good: though I agree with all the criticisms made by Victor Gollancz in his foreword, and with the trade unionists in Bragg's TV programme who said, sadly 'He didn't understand the working class' and 'He's steeling himself, holding his nose before he plunges down' (a sentence Orwell would have much admired). As for the second half, it is there to be examined, not believed: primarily, it is an autobiographical study, showing how Orwell got so confused about class. Compare *Enemies of Promise* by his friend and schoolmate, Cyril Connolly: the first half is a critique of modern literature and the second half an autobiographical explanation of how the author came by his subjective standards. *Wigan Pier* is the same kind of thing: take it as confessions, rather than gospel, and it is useful.

Of *Homage to Catalonia* an admirer wrote in 1968 [*New Statesman*, 13 September] that it showed Orwell to be 'a revolutionary, an early Che Guevara ... He joined POUM just because a new social order was their first priority ... He attacked the Communist Party from the Left ... The hero of *Animal Farm* (if there is one) is not man but horse.' This correspondent was attacking an article of mine in the *New Statesman*. I was able to answer him by quoting Orwell's own account of his own political ignorance and his belief that he was fighting in Spain for nothing more precise than 'common decency'.

As for the suggestion that *Animal Farm*'s hero is honest Boxer, that is the trouble with the book. The only working-class hero the author could imagine was a nice, loyal, stupid carthorse – easily led astray by smelly, pink intellectuals. Paul Potts [*London Magazine*, March 1943] has compared Boxer with Little Nell, a comparison more damaging than he realizes. As for 'Some are more equal than others' – which nation-state began life with the declaration that 'all men are created equal' and added (to use another Orwell phrase) 'not counting niggers'? Have any of the Communist states contravened the doctrine of racial equality to the extent that the United States has done? *Animal Farm* and *Nineteen Eighty-Four* are unsuitable weapons for the Cold War, since both books are criticisms of cruel people's hypocrisy and humbug: these vices, though attacked exclusively in a Soviet context, are in fact even more apparent in that 'free world' which includes Saudi Arabia and Brazil as well as the more democratic Arkansas and Mississippi.

Doublethink, Newspeak and Big Brother are common to both capitalist and Soviet societies. Even in our own mixed economy, we have to look out for them in two separate areas of life, in the private-enterprise world no less than the government-controlled sector. Admired rather than loved, *Nineteen Eighty-Four* is often said to be too horrible, too pessimistic, the product of a diseased imagination. Let us respect it then as a vision of Hell, rather than of any real society. The ending – 'he loved Big Brother' – could come from a polemic against Almighty God. Many children have been taught to love a Father in Heaven who is capable of giving them hell.

One *Nineteen Eighty-Four* aspect of 1970 is illustrated by the fog surrounding our anti-Communist Kremlinologists. We do not know which of them are CIA agents, which are KGB agents, and which are sincere men whose work is being used by such agencies. This atmosphere is enough to make us think, like Orwell, 'Why, this is Hell, nor am I out of it.' We can at least say, for Orwell, that he obviously meant what he said. So did the furious British Communist who wrote, unfairly, in the *Marxist Quarterly* [J. Walsh, January 1956, cf. Raymond Williams *Culture and Society* chapter 6], that Orwell had 'run shrieking into the arms of the capitalist publishers with a couple of horror comics which brought him fame and fortune'. A. L. Morton, discussing *Nineteen Eighty-Four* in his fine study, *The English Utopia*, puts a Communist case more reasonably:

As an intellectual attack on Marxism, it is beneath contempt. What Orwell does with great skill is to play upon the lowest fears and prejudices engendered by bourgeois society in dissolution. His object is not to argue a case but to induce an irrational conviction in the minds of his readers that any attempt to realize socialism must lead to a world of corruption, torture and insecurity.

It is true that the book can have such an effect, but such was surely not the author's 'object'. Novels and plays do not have to 'argue a case'. Their authors' political beliefs may be less advanced than the opinions which their work stimulates in readers – as Morton would accept in discussing the merits of, say, religious or royalist writers like Blake, More and Shakespeare.

Kingsley Amis, of all people, has written [*What Became of Jane Austen*, 1970]: 'I often feel that I will never pick up a book by Orwell again until I have read a frank discussion of the dishonesty and hysteria that mar some of his best work.' In fact, there have been several such discussions. Mary McCarthy's effort [*The Writing on the Wall*, 1970] seemed to me weak and nagging, and was well answered by Orwell's widow, Sonia. Better is Tom Hopkinson's British Council pamphlet, but perhaps too chilly and harsh. Conor Cruise O'Brien [*Writers and Politics*] is gentler, wittier, concentrating on Orwell as 'a Tory eccentric with a taste for self-immolation', and rebuking not so much Orwell himself as his CIA-sponsored imitators – who thought that by reiterating in the sixties what Orwell said in the thirties and forties, and by saying 'honest, decent, fair' in his hot, cross tone, they would magically acquire Orwell's good qualities. Perhaps the best critic so far is Raymond Williams [*Orwell*, and *Culture and Society*], whose conclusion is roughly that Orwell should not be treated as a master or a prophet but as a confused and divided man, to be carefully examined. 'The only useful thing now is to understand how it happened. The thing to do with his work, his history, is to read it, not imitate it.' Even so, whatever faults we find in Orwell, most of us will have to admit that we've done worse.

Malcolm Muggeridge
A KNIGHT OF THE
WOEFUL COUNTENANCE

I FIRST became aware of the existence of George Orwell in the middle thirties when I read some articles of his on the Spanish Civil War which appeared in the *New English Weekly*, a publication founded by A. R. Orage to expound the principles of Social Credit. They provided the basis for *Homage to Catalonia*, one of his best books. These articles made a great impression on me. I liked their clear, simple style, and the obvious honesty of purpose which informed them. They touched a chord of personal sympathy, too. I saw in Orwell's strong reaction to the villainies of the Communist *apparat* in Spain a comparable experience to my own disgust some years previously with the Soviet regime and its fawning admirers among the intelligentsia of the West as a result of a stint as Moscow correspondent of the *Manchester Guardian*. So I sent Orwell an appreciative note, to which I received a polite reply.

Later, when I got to know Orwell, he told me the story of how the articles had been turned down by Kingsley Martin, then editor of the *New Statesman*. I pointed out that, in the same sort of way, my messages to the *Guardian* from the USSR – for instance, about the famine caused by Stalin's collectivization policy in the Ukraine and the Caucasus, and about the arrest of some British engineers on spurious espionage charges – had been either whittled down or unused when they were more than mildly critical of the Soviet regime. Orwell certainly felt very strongly about this matter. Once when we were lunching together at a Greek restaurant in Percy Street he asked me if I would mind changing places. I readily agreed, but asked him why. He said that he just couldn't bear to look at Kingsley Martin's corrupt face, which, as Kingsley was lunching at an adjoining table, was unavoidable from where he had been sitting before.

Orwell was to have a comparable experience with *Animal Farm*, which was offered first to Gollancz. His loathing of progressive publishers and publications, as a result of these incidents, was even greater than mine. He told me once with great relish that his model for the Ministry of Truth in *Nineteen Eighty-Four* had been the BBC, where he worked without much satisfaction during some of the war years. I was not inclined myself to regard Kingsley Martin, C. P. Scott and the other ostensibly 'enlightened' operators in the communications business as being intrinsically more despicable than the Northcliffes, the Beaverbrooks and the Henry Luces, though of course they brought into what is essentially a competitive, profit- or influence-seeking trade an extra dimension of sanctimoniousness. It gave me no anguish to eat my luncheon with Kingsley Martin in vision. Incidentally, neither Kingsley nor Gollancz retracted from their position *vis-à-vis* the Spanish Civil War articles and *Animal Farm*. In his autobiography Kingsley continues to contend that he was right not to publish the articles, and when I asked Gollancz, in the course of a television interview,

whether he regretted having turned down *Animal Farm*, one of the few un-
doubted masterpieces of our time, he replied that, from the professional publishing point of view, it was undoubtedly a mistake, but he still thought that the
considerations which led him to make it were valid. One of the great weaknesses of the progressive, as distinct from the religious, mind, is that it has no
awareness of truth as such; only of truth in terms of enlightened expediency.
The contrast is well exemplified in two exact contemporaries – Simone Weil
and Simone de Beauvoir; both highly intelligent and earnestly disposed. In all
the fearful moral dilemmas of our time, Simone Weil never once went astray,
whereas Simone de Beauvoir, with I am sure the best of intentions, has found
herself aligned with apologists for some of the most monstrous barbarities and
falsehoods of history.

Orwell himself, of course, would never have accepted this dichotomy; if anything, he would have pronounced himself on the Beauvoir side. He was allergic
to institutional and devotional Christianity, and considered himself – in a way,
justly – as being temperamentally irreligious. Yet there was in him this passionate dedication to truth, and refusal to countenance enlightened expediency
masquerading as it; this unrelenting abhorrence of virtuous attitudes unrelated
to personal conduct such as was to be found in the disparity between Kingsley's
editorial principles and editorial practice. The point is well put in a hitherto
unpublished letter to me from Richard Rees, Orwell's close friend and subsequently mine, dated 8 March 1955, five years after Orwell's death:

I am at the moment engaged in trying to write a longer and better sketch of Eric
(Blair, Orwell's real name) than the one I wrote shortly after his death in which I try
to show that his value consists in his having taken more seriously than most people
the fundamental problem of religion. *Nineteen Eighty-Four*, for example, is more than a
pessimistic political prophesy. The crisis of the book is when the hero, under torture,
says: 'Do it to Julia, don't do it to me.' Eric was appalled, like the saints, by the realization that human nature is fundamentally self-centred; and in *Nineteen Eighty-Four* the
triumph of the totalitarian state is not complete until it has been demonstrated to the
last resister that in the last resort he would sacrifice the person he loves best in order to
save his own skin. Personally, I think the book is morbid, because he was so ill when
he was writing it. But it *does* reveal his true and permanent preoccupation; and that is
why I always think of him as a religious or 'pious atheist'.

The 'longer and better sketch' became Rees's study of Orwell (*George Orwell,
Fugitive from the Camp of Victory*, published in 1961), in my opinion easily the
best there is. Rees was Orwell's closest friend, whom he chose with his widow,
Sonia, to be his joint literary executor, and after whom he named his adopted
son. It was in the *Adelphi*, when Rees was editing it, that Orwell's first published

work appeared (as, indeed, did mine), still signed with his own name, Eric Blair, before he had adopted the pseudonym by which he is now universally known. Only someone who was naturally religious – even if unconsciously so – could possibly have made a friend of Rees, whose own view of life was essentially a mystical one. When, to the great grief of his many friends and admirers, Rees died last year (1970), he had just completed his long arduous, and brilliantly perceptive work on Simone Weil with the publication of her *First and Last Notebooks* – something for which I personally owe him a deep debt of gratitude. I am not saying that Orwell would have shared his admiration for Simone Weil; only that there is support for Rees's view of Orwell as someone concerned with the fundamental problem of religion in the fact that both of them – Orwell and Simone Weil – should have found in Rees their most sensitive interpreter, and Orwell his most intimate friend. Rees came to see me shortly before he died, and we talked about Orwell, as we often did. It struck me then how both of them, in rather different ways, recalled Cervantes's famous Knight of the Woeful Countenance. They were two Don Quixotes who never found a Sancho.

I made Orwell's acquaintance in the flesh through Anthony Powell, with whom for a number of years I was on intimate terms. Now, alas, we are estranged. Powell had spoken to me about Orwell as being an Etonian and a gifted writer, and I mentioned the *New English Weekly* articles. It was arranged that the three of us should lunch together in, I think, a restaurant in Fleet Street, and that was my first sight of Orwell. I had a certain stereotype of an Etonian in my mind, so Orwell's appearance came as a complete surprise. He was dressed in a sort of proletarian fancy dress; an ancient battered sports jacket and corduroy trousers, not actually tied up with string as in old comic drawings, but of the kind that could still be bought in those days in working-class districts and in seaside towns where fishermen live. In this, as in other matters, Orwell was ahead of his time; his costume is now *de rigueur* in public schools and universities, and is more or less the uniform of the middle– and upper-class young. He seemed very tall, the more so because he was so exceedingly thin; his face was decidedly cadaverous, with sad eyes, not particularly bright, and a thin moustache which left a narrow shaved strip between itself and his upper lip. As one can see very clearly in his writings about himself, and in his self-impersonations in his fiction, he was obsessed with the notion that he was physically unattractive. There is, for instance, the ugly birthmark which always shows up with particular vividness on the face of Flory, the hero of *Burmese Days*, in moments of stress and passion. He seems to have seriously believed that the poor smell, as he thought he did himself by comparison with the richer and better favoured boys at his preparatory school and Eton.

This notion of himself as abnormally plain and unalluring was, of course, quite absurd. He was decidedly attractive to both men and women. I personally took to him from the beginning, and grew even fonder of him; not just because of his kindly disposition, true humility and workaday attitude to his writing, and inflexible honesty, but also because there was something charming and winning about him. It was not that he was an amusing talker, or outstandingly original in his ideas. He was original in himself; a card, a dear fellow. If not witty, he was intrinsically funny. For instance, in the extraordinary prejudices he entertained and the naïve confidence with which he propounded them. Thus, he would come out with the proposition: 'All tobacconists are Fascists!', as though this was something so obvious that no one could possibly question his statement. Momentarily, one was swept along. Yes, there was something in it; those little men in their kiosks handing out fags and tobacco all day long – wouldn't they have followed a Hitler or a Mussolini if one had come along? Then the sheer craziness of it took hold of one, and one began to laugh helplessly, until – such was his persuasiveness – one reflected inside one's laughter: after all, they are rather rum birds, those tobacconists. His charming sister, Avril, who kept house for him when he was living in the island of Jura in the Inner Hebrides, gave me another example which greatly pleased me. Talking with a farmer, it seems, he slipped out, as though it was something everyone took for granted, the statement that in the old days ploughmen, following their hand-ploughs, developed an inequality between their shoulder blades, one rising higher than the other, so that special coats had to be made for them taking account of this, some of them even having leather patches for the higher shoulder. The farmer looked incredulous, and subsequent investigation failed to produce any confirmation of Orwell's statement, which he seems to have dreamed up entirely on his own. Even so, I still find myself, if I happen to pass a shop where agricultural clothing is displayed, looking to see whether any of the coats have a single leather shoulder-patch.

I once put the point about Orwell's obsessive sense of being physically unattractive to Cyril Connolly, who was with him at his preparatory school and at Eton. 'He was not a pretty boy', he said laconically, which I took to mean that he was not up to the minimum standard required for participation in the call-boy arrangements prevalent at boarding schools. It is likewise obvious that Orwell did not find relations with the opposite sex easy. (Who, by the way, does?) The subject occasionally cropped up during our subsequent meetings; he and Powell and I got into the habit of lunching regularly, quite often with Julian Symons as well. Orwell characteristically held forth upon the logistic difficulties which dogged the penurious amorist. Where was he to go if he could not afford a hotel room and had no private accommodation at his disposal? He himself, he said, had been forced through poverty to avail himself of public parks and recreation grounds. As he dwelt upon this theme, he began to chuckle – a throaty, rusty, deep-down chuckle very characteristic of him. His laughter had the same rusty quality as did his voice, due, I understood, to a throat wound he received in Spain. It would have been a droll experience, I decided, to come upon Orwell stretched out on a summer's evening with the lady of his choice in Kensington Gardens or Regent's Park.

I never met Orwell's first wife, Eileen, but everyone who knew her speaks well of her. As it happened, I saw something of him in Paris in 1945 when she died. I was stationed there for the last year of the war as liaison officer with the French *Services Spéciaux*, and Orwell turned up as correspondent for the *Observer*. He had tried so hard to get into the army, but his poor state of health disqualified him, and he had to content himself with the Home Guard, in which, as a former belligerent, he was considered a gunnery expert. This, says Fred Warburg who served with him in the same platoon, represented a greater danger than anything they had to fear from the enemy. Now, at last, he was in what passed for being a theatre of war, and wearing battle-dress, though naturally trying to look as much like a private, and as little like an officer, as possible. With his quite extraordinary reticence about everything personal, one had no idea how he felt about his wife's death. I stuttered out a few words of sympathy, as one does, and then we talked of other things. My impression is that he was quite stricken.

Somehow, the memory I have of him in those Paris days is particularly clear and loveable. It was not that we did anything much or said anything much, but in the squalid circumstances of a war ending and an empty victory looming, his presence was reassuring. I always think of him as a hero – a hero of our time in the Lermontov style; and never more so than then, sloping about in his battle-dress, and, presumably, seeking out news stories for the *Observer* – though he never spoke about any such activities, and I never saw any of his messages. I had occasion to go to London from time to time, and he would ask me to bring him back some shag he used for making his deplorable cigarettes. It was difficult to track down in wartime London, and I recalled a remark of Mrs Naidu to Gandhi when he was a guest in her house, and she had been desperately searching round for goat's milk and other of his dietetic specialities: 'You've no idea, Mahatma, how expensive it is providing the wherewithal for you to fast.'

We often talked about India, where, as it happened, I had been – actually, teaching at a Christian college in what was then Travancore and is now Kerala –

when he was serving in the Burma Police. The generally held opinion is that his time in Burma turned him against the British Raj and made an anti-imperialist and Socialist of him; that to, as it were, purge himself of his involvement in the Raj, he subjected himself to the experiences which resulted in *Down and Out in Paris and London*. From our conversations on the subject, and a careful reading of *Burmese Days*, I consider this to be a great over-simplification. In many respects he quite liked his Burma service; Christopher Hollis, a fellow-Etonian, dined with him in Rangoon at the time, and found him a perfectly ordinary and relatively contented officer. There was, remember, a strain of violence in him which came out from time to time. Rayner Heppenstall has described one such occasion, when he was sharing a flat with Orwell and came home drunk, and Orwell beat him up mercilessly. It was a source of great pride to him that he was once arrested in Glasgow for drunken disorder, and spent the night in the cells. The parts of *Burmese Days* that most come alive are when he is describing hunting expeditions, and the general attitude of the book is much more Kipling-esque than Marxist. The 'natives' behave despicably; the *Sahibs* may be boors and bullies, but they dominate the scene in a time of crisis. After all, Orwell came from a family with a strong Anglo-Indian background. In a certain sense, he belonged to the Raj; he once told me that he thought *The Road to Mandalay* the most beautiful poem in the English language. I could sense his disapproval when I described to him how in Travancore I used to wear an Indian *dhoti* made of *kadi*, the homespun cloth which was the uniform of the nationalist movement, and live on Indian food which I ate with my fingers, and travel third-class on the railways, and suffer the tortures of the damned by making myself sit cross-legged on the ground. It was all pretty silly, I am sure, but well meant. To him it signified missionaries, whom he regarded with contempt. What he disapproved of, basic-ally, in the Raj was that we in England, as he was fond of putting it, lived off the backs of under-paid, under-nourished and exploited coolies. This is what he felt he must expiate. Indian independence, when it came, gave him no particular satisfaction, but he saw it as an act of retribution.

Orwell's mania to identify himself with the poor and outcast in England had the same sort of basis. They had been wronged by his class, and he must some-how make it up. So he stayed in workhouses, consorted with down-and-outs, and in *The Road to Wigan Pier* gave what he considered to be an authentic picture of working-class life. Actually, as I occasionally ventured to remark to him, I think his data was derived much more from the *News of the World* and seaside picture postcards – two of his ruling passions – and even from Dickens, than from direct observation. In addition to his proletarian fancy dress, he was always trying to conform to what he considered to be proletarian behaviour.

Hence the shag and the rolled cigarettes; in a public bar he would whisper that a pint of bitter should be ordered in such a way and drunk in such a way. He was concerned lest his voice and bearing should suggest the Etonian. Here, I really believe he need not have worried; but it is true that, however careful he might be about his clothes, his accent and his behaviour, he was always noticeable; not as an Etonian in a public bar, nor, for that matter, as a down-and-out in a saloon bar, but as Orwell, a dear oddity.

Though I should, I suppose, pass for being much more reactionary (whatever that may mean) in my views than Orwell, in our talk it often seemed the other way round. He was always going on about nancy poets and pacifists and sandal-wearing vegetarians with what seemed to me unnecessary and unfair virulence; he was inclined at times to be vaguely anti-Semitic, and he lambasted contemporary literary mandarins in a way that stirred up even in my breast a tepid desire to come to their defence. The truth is he was by temperament deeply conservative. He loved the past, hated the present and dreaded the future. In this he may well have been right, but it somehow went ill with canvassing on behalf of the Bevanites, and being literary editor of *Tribune*. In his own mind, however, he managed to work it all out, and considered himself the most consistent of beings. Part at least of his great popularity, on both sides of the Atlantic, has derived from this conservative undertow in his leftist course. A bourgeoisie like ours on the run is always looking for someone who combines impeccable intelligentsia credentials with a passion, secret or avowed – but better secret – for maintaining the *status quo*. They found it in a T. S. Eliot, in a W. B. Yeats, in an Aldous Huxley, in an Ezra Pound who has at different times expounded racialist views which would make any Afrikaner go pale with horror. They thought they found it, and perhaps to some extent did, in Orwell; though in his case the confection was characteristically weird.

Immediately after the war I saw Orwell occasionally in London, and, of course, rejoiced over the great success of *Animal Farm*. My older children read it with interest, and one of them wrote to him about it, receiving a charming note in reply. Then I went to Washington as a newspaper correspondent, and by the time I returned Orwell had gone to live in Jura. I had a letter from him there asking me to get him a saddle – God knows why, or what particular kind was required. The furthest I got in carrying out the assignment was to look vaguely at a saddle in the window of a shop in St Martin's Lane. I was living practically next door to Powell, and we quite often went for walks round Regent's Park. The subject of Orwell naturally cropped up from time to time. I think I admired him more than Powell did, but he and Powell had more in common; partly, I dare say, because they were both Etonians, and, in the best

sense of the word conservative – something I have never succeeded in being.
When word came that Orwell's health had again collapsed, and that he was in a
sanatorium near Stroud in Gloucestershire, we decided to go and see him.

We walked the last bit of the way. It was a very beautiful day, and I remember
feeling unreasonably cheerful considering the purpose of our journey. Orwell
was in a wooden hut by himself. He looked terribly wasted and thin, and I think
I knew then that he was likely to die. Visiting tuberculosis patients was, for me,
part of the experience of childhood; my father's family was riddled with the
disease, and when I was seven I developed symptoms myself and had to go
away into the country. So I was familar with that particular soft, purring cough;
that almost mystical transparency of the skin – like a thin sheet of fibre-glass
with a furious furnace the other side. Orwell was in good spirits. He had
managed to finish *Nineteen Eighty-Four*, but said little about it. He was as
secretive about his work as about everything else. Incidentally, Avril told me
that this secretiveness was hereditary; their father had been just the same.
Powell and I had been laughing over an incident in a novel by Koestler; the
hero, in seducing one of the female characters, through being circumcised,
reveals that he is a Jew. Orwell was not as amused as we were. Of course it's
not true, he said, that in this country only Jews are circumcised; but it is true
that, generally speaking, the upper classes are and the lower classes aren't. He
cited his own case at Eton, where in the changing-rooms he was very ashamed
at being uncircumcised, and kept himself covered. It was a vintage Orwell
point. On the way back I suggested to Powell that he should tell Evelyn Waugh,
who then lived in the neighbourhood of the sanatorium, that Orwell was there,
so that he might visit him. Whether at Powell's suggestion or someone else's, I
learnt afterwards that Waugh did go and see Orwell several times, and afterwards corresponded with him in a very delightful way. Despite all Waugh's
efforts to appear to be an irascible, deaf old curmudgeon, a sort of innate saintli-
ness kept breaking through. I should have loved to see them together; comple-
mentary figures, his country gentleman's outfit and Orwell's proletarian one
both straight out of back numbers of *Punch*.

Shortly afterwards, Orwell was transferred to University College Hospital,
near to where Powell and I were living. We visited him quite often, but mostly
separately so as to tire him less. He was full of projects for books he was going
to write; on Conrad, on Gissing – a dismal writer for whom he had a great
admiration – on anti-British feeling in the United States. He quoted a remark
in one of Hugh Kingsmill's books to the effect that a writer who has more to
write cannot die. I think that quite often before he would have been glad
enough to die; now he passionately wanted to live. He was going to remarry,

and go to Switzerland; he had become a famous writer, his financial worries were at an end. Sonia Brownell who became his second wife represented everything he had always longed for; she was beautiful, and in a generous, luxuriant way; gifted socially, the familiar of writers and painters. Yet I knew it was all a dream; writers still with things to write *can* die. His mind was turning more than ever on what he had never had and must not look to have – physical strength and beauty. He indignantly showed me an advertisement for sock suspenders that he had cut out of a newspaper; it was based on the notion of Perseus, and showed his gilded winged calves wearing these particular suspenders. How disgusting, he said, to use something so beautiful for so base a purpose! It shocked him more than anything. There seemed rather a lot going on in the world just then to be shocked about, but I let it pass, and agreed that the advertisement was disgraceful.

Sonia and Orwell were married in the hospital. It turned out to be quite an elaborate legal procedure getting permission, the intention being, I suppose, to protect dying millionaires from designing nurses. There was also a long discussion about what Orwell should wear. In the end a mauve velvet smoking-jacket was decided upon, which he wore over his pyjamas. Powell bought it for him at Moss Bros. After the wedding (at which I was not present) he continued to wear the smoking-jacket in bed. I see him now in it, sitting up and holding forth about how, when he and Sonia set up house, all the kitchen fitments were to be in black rubber. At the bottom of the bed he had his fishing-rod, all ready for when they went to Switzerland in a few days time by special charter flight. Lucian Freud was going to accompany them. It never happened, of course. He died the day before they were due to leave. Sonia came to see us the same evening. She cried and cried. I shall always love her for her true tears on that occasion.

It turned out that Orwell had left in his will that he wanted a church funeral and to be buried in a country churchyard. Powell and I had the task of arranging the service. First, we went to an undertaker in Warren Street, and he said he would deal with all that side of things. Then we visited the rector of a nearby Regency church. He had, it was clear, never heard of Orwell, but we were able to persuade him that he was a writer of distinction. When he heard the name of the undertaker he noticeably cheered up; the two of them were, he said, in close touch. We imagined them ringing one another up – 'Anything doing today?' The service went off without a hitch, though it was obvious that a good many of those present were unfamiliar with Anglican liturgy. The thing that held my attention all the time was the enormous length of the coffin. It seemed they had difficulty in procuring one long enough. Arranging for his burial was more difficult. In the end the problem was solved by invoking the help of the Astor influence to find a place for him in a country churchyard. It somehow recalled Bakunin's death in Geneva, where in the public cemetery, along with other data, the profession of the deceased has to be indicated. As being an anarchist is not a profession, the only thing they could put in Bakunin's case was: 'Bakunin – Rentier'.

Another provision in Orwell's will was that no biography of him should be written. This did not prevent the publication of a number of books about him, and in the end Sonia decided that it would be best to announce an authorized biography, with me as the putative author. I made various vague moves in the direction of doing it; such as going through whatever letters and other documents there are, meeting various people who had been connected with him, and trying to sort out my own thoughts on the subject. In the end the project defeated me, partly through my own indolence, and distaste for collecting and absorbing the masses of tape-recorded talk, much of it necessarily intensely boring, which would constitute the bulk of one's material. It seemed to me that Orwell, with a cunning he sometimes displayed in life, had posthumously laid down a great smoke-screen of boredom between himself and any explorer who tried to invade the privacy in which he had lived and died. There was the additional difficulty of the validity to be attached to Orwell's own testimony. Is, for instance, the account of his prep-school days in 'Such, Such Were the Joys' to be taken at its face value? Avril considers that, like Orwell's account of their home life, it is grotesquely distorted. She remembers him as a cheerful, eager schoolboy, and their home as a happy and contented one. Even Connolly suggests in the politest possible way that Orwell laid it on a bit thick. Art is a lie and facts are true; but art is the way to truth, whereas facts lead only down the plastic path of fantasy. Orwell is an artist, and as such lived and wrote his own biography. I think, as he wished, his will prove the definitive work.

Acknowledgments

The publishers gratefully acknowledge permission to reproduce photographs and other material from the following collections:

Roger Beadon 18
Bill Brandt 35
Dr. Maung Htin Aung 18
Fredric Warburg 81

Edward Arnold Ltd. 10
Associated British Picture Corps Ltd. (and National Film Archive) 84, 85
Barnaby's Picture Library 30
BBC 60, 86, 87
Foto Bulloz 78
Wm. Collins Sons & Co. Ltd. 74, 82
D. Constance Ltd 64, 65
Fox Photos 37
Hampstead and Highgate Express 98
Heinemann Publishers 77
Imperial War Museum 57
Labour Party Photographic Library 48, 49
Popperfoto 17, 36, 38, 39, 40, 42, 43, 44a, 46, 47
Punch 62
Radio Times Hulton Picture Library 9, 22, 27, 28, 29, 31, 63, 76, 83
Sunday Times 80
Tribune 68
University College London Library (Orwell Archive) 13, 15, 16, 34, 41, 53, 54, 55, 56, 58, 59, 66, 67, 70, 73, 75, 88, 89, 90, 91, 92, 93, 94, 95, 96, 97
  And Copyright owners:
  Guinever Buddicom 5, 6, 14
  Cyril Connolly 7, 8
  Dennis Collings 32
  Humphrey Dakin 2, 3, 4
  Avril Dunn 1, 33
  Denys King-Farlow 11, 12
  Vernon Richards 20, 69, 71, 72
Roger Viollet 22, 24, 25, 26
Wiener Library 44b, 45
Elizabeth Wrightson 21

Index